TOP
10
OF EVERYTHING
2010

TOP 10

OF EVERYTHING

2010

Russell Ash

hamlyn

Contents

Produced for Hamlyn by
Palazzo Editions Ltd
2 Wood Street, Bath, BA1 2JQ

Publishing director: Colin Webb
Art director: Bernard Higton
Managing editor: Sonya Newland
Picture researcher: Sophie Hartley

An Hachette UK Company
www.hachette.co.uk

First published in Great Britain in 2009 by
Hamlyn, a division of
Octopus Publishing Group Ltd
2–4 Heron Quays, London E14 4JP
www.octopusbookusa.com

Copyright © Octopus Publishing
Group Ltd 2009
Text copyright © Russell Ash 2009

Distributed in the U.S. and Canada
by Sterling Publishing Co., Inc.
387 Park Avenue South
New York, NY 10016-8810

ISBN 978-0-600-62048-8

A CIP catalogue record for this book is
available from the British Library.

Printed and bound in China.

10 9 8 7 6 5 4 3 2 1

Introduction

AGE OF MAJORITY

Twenty-one was once a significant number—the "age of majority" at which one legally became an adult, traditionally and symbolically given the keys of the door and allowed to vote. There were 21 shillings in a guinea, the 21st Amendment to the Constitution repealed Prohibition and leaders are honored by 21-gun salutes. And a decade into the 21st century, this is the 21st annual edition of *Top 10 of Everything*.

BIG NUMBERS

One of the aims of *Top 10 of Everything* is to offer a snapshot of a wide range of topics—some people buy it as a sort of time capsule or memento of what was happening in the year in which a child was born. Work on this latest edition began as the world economic crisis struck and few escaped: the number of billionaires quickly declined, car makers cut output, and airline traffic dwindled. As the world's debt mountain grew to unprecedented heights, figures in billions and trillions, once a feature of certain major Top 10 lists, became part of our everyday language. Its effects will endure for many years and will increasingly be reflected in future editions of *Top 10*. Yet alongside economic shrinkage, many lists demonstrate the opposite: there are still plenty of companies making vast profits, and as the Burj Dubai, the tallest structure ever built, nears completion we see though a series of Top 10 lists how the world's skyscraper skyline has altered over the past 100 years. We also consider the most common first names across the past 100 years, surnames around the world, and the highest-earning films of each decade, with *Mamma Mia!* becoming highest-earning musical film ever. Four films have now earned more than $1 billion worldwide.

SURPRISE, SURPRISE...

While the world's largest countries and richest economies inevitably make a strong showing in many Top 10 lists, not every entry is a foregone conclusion: I continue to be surprised when the facts and figures reveal the unexpected—that Ireland out-eats the USA in fries and out-drinks the UK in tea; that Britain has the largest Sikh population outside India, while the biggest-selling English newspaper is not published in the USA or UK; that Barack Obama is some way off being the youngest president. Alongside such facts as these, you will discover the fattest, the oldest, and the tallest people, the world's strongest man, the country with the most mailboxes, and the leading teams in the extreme sport of elephant polo, the album that stayed longest at No. 1 in the charts, the most venomous reptiles, the worst forest fires, the most corrupt countries, the countries with the fastest-shrinking populations, the most populous city in the USA in both 1910 and 2000, the most northerly capital cities, the largest cities that are not capitals, and the tallest buildings with holes in them.

MORE THAN JUST THE NO. 1

All these lists follow a rule that has been true since the first edition of *Top 10 of Everything*, which is that every list has to be quantifiable—measurable in some way or other: the biggest, smallest, first, last, tallest, deepest, sunniest, dullest, or worst, or chronologically the first or last. All the lists thus offer more than just the No. 1, and provide

a perspective in which to compare the subjects of the list. There are no "bests," other than bestsellers, and "worsts" are of disasters, military losses, and murders, where they are measured by numbers of victims. Unless otherwise stated, movie lists are based on cumulative global earnings, irrespective of production or marketing budgets and—as is standard in the movie industry—inflation is not taken into account, which means that recent releases tend to feature disproportionately prominently. Countries are independent countries, not dependencies or overseas territories. All the lists are all-time and global unless a specific year or territory is noted. If the USA does not figure in a country-based list, it is generally added as an extra entry.

SOURCES

My sources encompass international organizations, commercial companies and research bodies, specialized publications, and a network of experts around the world who have generously shared their knowledge. As always, I happily acknowledge their important contribution (see page 255 for a full list of credits), along with that of everyone who has been involved with the book at all stages of its development on this and the previous 20 annual editions.

OVER TO YOU

I hope you enjoy the book. Your comments, corrections, and suggestions for new lists are always welcome. Please contact me via the publishers or visit the *Top 10 of Everything* website www.top10ofeverything.com or my own www.RussellAsh.com

Russell Ash

THE UNIVERSE
& THE EARTH

Stars

TOP 10 LARGEST STARS

STAR / SOLAR DIAMETER

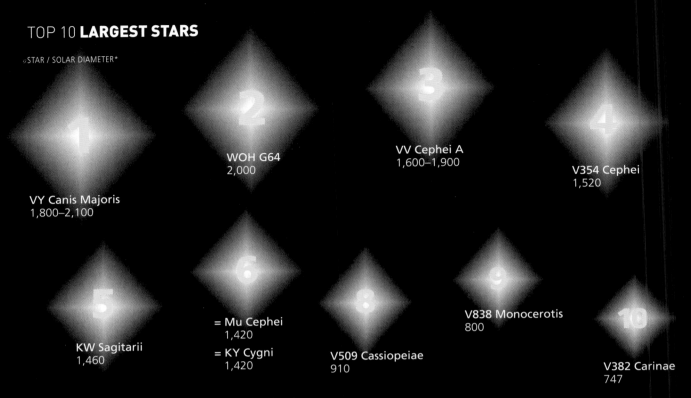

VY Canis Majoris
1,800–2,100

WOH G64
2,000

VV Cephei A
1,600–1,900

V354 Cephei
1,520

KW Sagitarii
1,460

= Mu Cephei
1,420
= KY Cygni
1,420

V509 Cassiopeiae
910

V838 Monocerotis
800

V382 Carinae
747

* Compared with the Sun = 1 (864,950 miles/1,392,000 km)

TOP 10 BRIGHTEST STARS*

	STAR	CONSTELLATION	DISTANCE#	APPARENT MAGNITUDE
1	Sirius	Canis Major	8.61	-1.44
2	Canopus	Carina	312.73	-0.62
3	Arcturus	Boötes	36.39	-0.05†
4	Alpha Centauri A	Centaurus	4.40	-0.01
5	Vega	Lyra	25.31	+0.03
6	Capella	Auriga	42.21	+0.08
7	Rigel	Orion	772.91	+0.18
8	Procyon	Canis Minor	11.42	+0.40
9	Achernar	Eridanus	143.81	+0.45
10	Beta Centauri	Centaurus	525.22	+0.61

* Excluding the Sun
# From the Earth in light years
† Variable

This Top 10 is based on apparent visual magnitude as viewed from Earth—the lower the number, the brighter the star. On this scale, the Sun would be -26.73 and the full Moon -12.6.

TOP 10 STARS NEAREST TO EARTH*

	STAR	LIGHT YEARS	DISTANCE MILES (MILLIONS)	DISTANCE KM (MILLIONS)
1	Proxima Centauri	4.22	24,792,500	39,923,310
2	Alpha Centauri	4.39	25,791,250	41,531,595
3	Barnard's Star	5.94	34,897,500	56,195,370
4	Wolf 359	7.78	45,707,500	73,602,690
5	Lalande 21185	8.31	48,821,250	78,616,755
6	Sirius	8.60	50,525,000	81,360,300
7	Luyten 726-8	8.72	51,230,000	82,495,560
8	Ross 154	9.69	56,928,750	91,672,245
9	Ross 248	10.32	60,630,000	97,632,360
10	Epsilon Eridani	10.49	61,628,750	99,240,645

* Excluding the Sun

Source: Peter Bond, Royal Astronomical Society

Although the nearest stars are just over four light years from Earth, a spaceship traveling at 25,000 mph (40,237 km/h)—faster than any human has yet reached in space—would take more than 113,200 years to reach Earth's closest star, Proxima Centauri.

Starlight
Easily observed from Earth's southern hemisphere, the unusually shaped
lenticular (between elliptical and spiral) Centaurus Galaxy is the fifth brightest.

TOP 10 **BRIGHTEST GALAXIES**

GALAXY/NO.	DISTANCE FROM EARTH (MILLIONS OF LIGHT YEARS)	APPARENT MAGNITUDE
1 Large Magellanic Cloud	0.17	0.91
2 Small Magellanic Cloud	0.21	2.70
3 Andromeda Galaxy/NGC 224 M31	2.6	4.36
4 Triangulum Galaxy/NGC 598 M33	2.8	6.27
5 Centaurus Galaxy/NGC 5128	12.0	7.84
6 Bode's Galaxy/NGC 3031 M81	12.0	7.89
7 Silver Coin Galaxy/NGC 253	8.5	8.04
8 Southern Pinwheel Galaxy/NGC 5236 M83	15.0	8.20
9 Pinwheel Galaxy/NGC 5457 M101	24.0	8.31
10 Cigar Galaxy/NGC 55	4.9	8.42

Messier (M) numbers are named after French astronomer
Charles Messier (1730–1817), who compiled the first catalog
of galaxies, nebulae, and star clusters.

TOP 10 **GALAXIES NEAREST TO EARTH**

GALAXY	DISCOVERED	DIAMETER	APPROX. DISTANCE (1,000 LIGHT YEARS)
1 Sagittarius Dwarf	1994	10	82
2 Large Magellanic Cloud	Prehist.	30	160
3 Small Magellanic Cloud	Prehist.	16	190
4 = Draco Dwarf	1954	3	205
= Ursa Minor Dwarf	1954	2	205
6 Sculptor Dwarf	1937	3	254
7 Sextans Dwarf	1990	4	258
8 Carina Dwarf	1977	2	330
9 Fornax Dwarf	1938	6	450
10 Leo II	1950	3	660

Source: Peter Bond, Royal Astronomical Society

These, and other galaxies, are members of the so-called Local
Group. As the Solar System and Earth are at the outer edge of the
Milky Way, this is excluded. Over the next 100 million years, the
Sagittarius Dwarf Elliptical Galaxy, our nearest neighboring galaxy,
will be progressively absorbed into the Milky Way.

The Solar System

Comet hunter
Caltech's Palomar Observatory, with its 200-inch Hale telescope, a leading member of the Near-Earth Asteroid Tracking program.

TOP 10 LONGEST YEARS IN THE SOLAR SYSTEM

	BODY*	LENGTH OF YEAR# YEARS	DAYS
1	Eris	557	295
2	Makemake	310	33
3	Pluto	247	256
4	Neptune	164	298
5	Uranus	84	4
6	Saturn	29	168
7	Jupiter	11	314
8	Ceres	4	220
9	Mars	1	322
10	Earth	0	365

* Planets and dwarf planets, excluding satellites
\# Period of orbit round the Sun, in Earth years/days

Venus and Mercury are the only planets in the Solar System with years of shorter duration than Earth-years—225 and 88 days respectively.

TOP 10 ASTEROID-DISCOVERY OBSERVATORIES

	OBSERVATORY / PERIOD	ASTEROIDS* DISCOVERED
1	Lincoln Laboratory ETS, New Mexico, USA 1980–2008	96,589
2	Steward Observatory, Kitt Peak-Spacewatch, Arizona, USA 1981–2008	16,594
3	Palomar Mountain/NEAT, California, USA 1988–2007	11,925
4	Lowell Observatory-LONEOS, Arizona, USA 1998–2008	11,721
5	Palomar Mountain, California, USA 1949–2007	6,446
6	European Southern Observatory, La Silla, Chile 1976–2005	5,392
7	Catalina Sky Survey, Arizona, USA 1998–2008	4,859
8	Haleakala-AMOS, Hawaii, USA 1995–2005	4,804
9	Oizumi, Japan 1991–2002	2,422
10	Siding Spring Observatory, New South Wales, Australia 1975–2007	1,714

* Including other Near Earth Objects

TOP 10 LARGEST METEORITES EVER FOUND

	LOCATION / DISCOVERY / PRESENT LOCATION (IF DIFFERENT FROM IMPACT SITE)	ESTIMATED WEIGHT (TONS)
1	Hoba West, Grootfontein, Namibia, 1920	66.14
2	Campo del Cielo ("El Chaco"), Argentina, 1969	40.79
3	Ahnighito ("The Tent"), Cape York, West Greenland, 1894, American Museum of Natural History New York	34.04
4	Armanty, Xinjiang, China, 1895, Xinjiang Geology and Mineral Museum, Urumqi City, Xinjiang	30.86
5	Bacuberito, Sinaloa, Mexico, 1863, Centro de Ciencias, Culiacán, Sinaloa, Mexico	24.25
6	Agpalilik ("The Man"), Cape York, 1963, West Greenland, University of Copenhagen, Denmark	22.16
7	Mbosi, Rungwe, Tanzania, 1930	17.64
8	Campo del Cielo, Argentina, 2005	16.37
9	Williamette, Oregon, USA, 1902, American Museum of Natural History, New York	15.59
10	Chupaderos, Chihuahua, Mexico, 1852, Palacio de Mineria, Mexico City	15.55

This lists only the largest meteorites or parts of meteorites, not the total weight of fragments. The Hoba West was found on a farm of that name in 1920. A 9 x 8 ft (2.73 x 2.43 m) slab, it consists of 82 percent iron and 16 percent nickel.

TOP 10 COMETS COMING CLOSEST TO EARTH

| COMET | DATE* | AU# | DISTANCE | |
			MILES	KM
1 Comet of 1491	Feb 20, 1491	0.0094	873,784	1,406,220
2 Lexell	Jul 1, 1770	0.0151	1,403,633	2,258,928
3 Tempel-Tuttle	Oct 26, 1366	0.0229	2,128,688	3,425,791
4 IRAS-Araki-Alcock	May 11, 1983	0.0313	2,909,516	4,682,413
5 Halley	Apr 10, 837	0.0334	3,104,724	4,996,569
6 Biela	Dec 9, 1805	0.0366	3,402,182	5,475,282
7 Grischow	Feb 8, 1743	0.0390	3,625,276	5,834,317
8 Pons-Winnecke	Jun 26, 1927	0.0394	3,662,458	5,894,156
9 Comet of 1014	Feb 24, 1014	0.0407	3,783,301	6,088,633
10 La Hire	Apr 20, 1702	0.0437	4,062,168	6,537,427

* Of closest approach to Earth
\# Astronomical Units: 1AU = mean distance from the
Earth to the Sun (92,955,793 miles/149,597,870 km)

HALLEY'S COMET

Before British Astronomer Royal Edmond Halley (1656–1742) studied and predicted the return of the famous comet that now bears his name, no one had succeeded in proving that comets travel in predictable orbits. Halley computed the orbits of some 24 comets, but the return in 1759—as he had calculated—of the comet he had observed in 1682 established the science of cometary observation. Because it is a bright "naked-eye" comet, numerous sightings were noted during preceding centuries, and by comparing them with calculations of the comet's orbit, these can now be identified as having been Halley's Comet. There have been about 30 recorded appearances, including that of 1066, believed to presage the victory of William the Conqueror, and the most recent in 1986 when it was examined by the *Giotto* probe.

Above: Halley's Comet on the Bayeux Tapestry, seen as a portent of William's 1066 victory against the Anglo-Saxons.

Right: Westminster Abbey's 1986 memorial plaque to Halley depicts his comet and the Giotto spacecraft.

Europa
The smallest of Jupiter's moons was discovered by Galileo in 1610.

TOP 10 LARGEST PLANETARY MOONS

| MOON / PLANET | DIAMETER | |
	MILES	KM
1 Ganymede Jupiter	3,269.9	5,262.4
2 Titan Saturn	3,200.1	5,150.0
3 Callisto Jupiter	2,994.4	4,820.6
4 Io Jupiter	2,263.4	3,642.6
5 Moon Earth	2,160.0	3,476.2
6 Europa Jupiter	1,939.7	3,121.6
7 Triton Neptune	1,681.9	2,706.8
8 Titania Uranus	980.4	1,577.8
9 Rhea Saturn	947.6	1,528.0
10 Oberon Uranus	946.2	1,522.8

Spaceflight

THE 10 **FIRST MOONWALKERS**

	ASTRONAUT	SPACECRAFT	HRS:MINS	TOTAL EVA* MISSION DATES
1	Neil Armstrong	Apollo 11	2:32	Jul 16–24, 1969
2	Edwin "Buzz" Aldrin	Apollo 11	2:15	Jul 16–24, 1969
3	Charles Conrad, Jr.	Apollo 12	7:45	Nov 14–24, 1969
4	Alan Bean	Apollo 12	7:45	Nov 14–24, 1969
5	Alan Shepard	Apollo 14	9:23	Jan 31–Feb 9, 1971
6	Edgar Mitchell	Apollo 14	9:23	Jan 31–Feb 9, 1971
7	David Scott	Apollo 15	19:08	Jul 26–Aug 7, 1971
8	James Irwin	Apollo 15	18:35	Jul 26–Aug 7, 1971
9	John Young	Apollo 16	20:14	Apr 16–27, 1972
10	Charles Duke, Jr.	Apollo 16	20:14	Apr 16–27, 1972

* Extra Vehicular Activity—time spent out of the lunar module on the Moon's surface

Second step
On July 21, 1969, Edwin "Buzz" Aldrin followed Neil Armstrong to become the second man to set foot on the Moon.

THE 10 **FIRST ANIMALS IN SPACE**

	NAME / ANIMAL / STATUS	COUNTRY	DATE
1	**Laika** (name used by Western press—actually the name of the breed to which the dog named Kudryavka, a female Samoyed husky, belonged) Died in space	USSR	Nov 3, 1957
2 =	**Laska and Benjy** (mice) Re-entered Earth's atmosphere, but not recovered	USA	Dec 13, 1958
4 =	**Able** (female rhesus monkey) **and Baker** (female squirrel monkey) Successfully returned to Earth	USA	May 28, 1959
6 =	**Otvazhnaya** (female Samoyed husky) **and an unnamed rabbit** Recovered	USSR	Jul 2, 1959
8	**Sam** (male rhesus monkey) Recovered	USA	Dec 4, 1959
9	**Miss Sam** (female rhesus monkey) Recovered	USA	Jan 21, 1960
10 =	**Belka and Strelka** (female Samoyed huskies) **plus 40 mice and two rats** First to orbit and return safely	USSR	Aug 19, 1960

Top dog
A stray called Laika was the first animal to orbit the Earth aboard the Soviet Sputnik 2.

TOP 10 **LONGEST SINGLE SPACEFLIGHTS**

	PERSONNEL* / SPACECRAFT / DATES	DURATION DAYS	HRS	MINS
1	**Valeriy V. Polyakov** Soyuz TM-18 / Mir / Soyuz TM-20 Jan 8, 1994–Mar 22, 1995	437	17	58
2	**Sergei V. Avdeyev** Soyuz TM-28 / Mir/ Soyuz TM-29 Aug 13, 1998–Aug 28, 1999	379	14	51
3	**Musa K. Manarov, Vladimir G. Titov** Soyuz TM-4 / Mir / Soyuz TM-6 Dec 21, 1987–Dec 21, 1988	365	22	38
4	**Yuri V. Romanenko** Soyuz TM-2 / Mir / Soyuz TM-3 Feb 5, 1987–Dec 29, 1987	326	11	38
5	**Sergei K. Krikalyov** Soyuz TM-12 / Mir / Soyuz TM-13 May 18, 1991–Mar 25, 1992	311	20	1
6	**Valeriy V. Polyakov** Soyuz TM-6 / Mir / Soyuz TM-7 Aug 29, 1988–Apr 27, 1989	240	22	34
7	**Oleg Y. Atkov, Leonid D. Kizim, Vladimir A. Solovyov** Soyuz T-10 / Salyut 7 / Soyuz T-11 Feb 8–Oct 2, 1984	236	22	49
8	**Michael E. Lopez-Alegria (USA), Mikhail V. Tyurin** Soyuz TMA-9 / ISS / Soyuz TMA-9 Sep 18, 2006–Apr 21, 2007	215	8	22
9	**Anatoli N. Berezovoi, Valentin V. Lebedev** Soyuz T-5 / Salyut / Soyuz T-7 May 13–Dec 10, 1982	211	9	4
10	**Nikolai M. Budarin, Talgat A. Musabayev** Soyuz TM-27 / Mir / Soyuz TM-27 Jan 29–Aug 25, 1998	207	12	51

* All USSR/Russian unless otherwise stated

The longest single spaceflight by a woman was that of Sunita Williams (USA), who traveled to the ISS (International Space Station) on December 10, 2006, returning to Earth on June 22, 2007, a total of 194 days, 18 hours, and 2 minutes.

Time traveler
Her long-duration missions aboard the ISS have placed Peggy Whitson at the top of the US astronauts table and in 20th place worldwide.

TOP 10 **MOST EXPERIENCED US ASTRONAUTS***

	ASTRONAUT	MISSIONS	TOTAL DURATION OF MISSIONS DAYS	HRS	MINS
1	Peggy Whitson	2	376	17	22
2	C. Michael Foale	6	373	18	18
3	Edward M. Fincke	2	365	21	32
4	Michael López-Alegria	4	257	22	46
5	Carl E. Walz	4	230	13	4
6	Leroy Chiao	4	229	8	41
7	Daniel W. Bursch	4	226	22	16
8	William S. McArthur	4	224	22	19
9	Shannon Lucid	5	223	2	50
10	Kenneth Bowersox	5	211	14	12

* To April 8, 2008

The six missions of British-born NASA astronaut Colin Michael Foale, including extended stays on the Mir and International Space Station, established a US duration record, but was overtaken in 2008.

Oceans & Seas

THE 10 DEEPEST OCEANS AND SEAS

| OCEAN/SEA | AVERAGE DEPTH | |
	FT	M
10 Mediterranean Sea	4,688	1,429
9 Gulf of Mexico	4,875	1,486
8 Bering Sea	5,075	1,547
7 Red Sea	5,285	1,611
6 South China Sea	4,150	1,652
5 Caribbean Sea	8,684	2,647
4 Atlantic Ocean	12,999	3,926
3 Indian Ocean	13,002	3,963
2 Pacific Ocean	13,215	4,028
1 Southern Ocean	14,750	4,496
World ocean average	*12,237*	*3,730*

THE 10 DEEPEST DEEP-SEA TRENCHES

| TRENCH* | DEEPEST POINT | |
	FT	M
10 Yap	27,976	8,527
9 Puerto Rico	28,232	8,605
8 Izu	32,087	9,780
7 New Britain	32,612	9,940
6 Bonin	32,789	9,994
5 Kermadec	32,963	10,047
4 Philippine	34,580	10,540
3 Kuril-Kamchatka	34,587	10,542
2 Tonga	35,702	10,882
1 Marianas	35,798	10,911

* With the exception of the Puerto Rico (Atlantic), all the trenches are in the Pacific

Each of the eight deepest ocean trenches would be deep enough to submerge Mount Everest.

TOP 10 **HIGHEST TIDES**

| LOCATION | AVERAGE* | |
	FT	M
1 Burncoat Head (Bay of Fundy), Nova Scotia, Canada#	47.5	14.5
2 La Rance Estuary, France	44.3	13.5
3 Avonmouth, Bristol Channel, UK	40.4	12.3
4 Anchorage, Alaska, USA	29.6	9.0
5 Liverpool, UK	27.1	8.3
6 St. John, New Brunswick, Canada	23.6	7.2
7 Dover, UK	18.6	5.7
8 Cherbourg, France	18.0	5.5
9 Antwerp, Belgium	17.8	5.4
10 Yangôn, Myanmar	17.0	5.2

1 man = approx. 6 ft (1.8 m)

* Average spring tidal range is the average difference between high and low waters during spring tides
# 53.38 ft (16.27 m) maximum

Endangered environment
Among the richest of the world's ecosystems, coral reefs are vulnerable to overfishing, pollution, and the consequences of global warming.

THE 10 **SMALLEST SEAS**

SEA* / OCEAN	APPROX. AREA SQ MILES	SQ KM
1 Gulf of California, Pacific Ocean	59,100	153,070
2 Persian Gulf, Indian Ocean	88,800	230,000
3 Yellow Sea, Pacific Ocean	113,500	293,960
4 Baltic Sea, Atlantic Ocean	147,500	382,000
5 North Sea, Atlantic Ocean	164,900	427,090
6 Red Sea, Indian Ocean	174,900	452,990
7 Black Sea, Atlantic Ocean	196,100	507,900
8 Andaman Sea, Indian Ocean	218,100	564,880
9 East China Sea, Pacific Ocean	256,600	664,590
10 Hudson Bay, Atlantic Ocean	281,900	730,120

* Excludes landlocked seas

The two smallest seas are both gulfs—long bays extending far inland. The Gulf of California stretches southeast from the mouth of the Colorado River, separating the Baja California Peninsula from the Mexican mainland. The Persian Gulf is an arm of the Arabian Sea between Iran and Saudi Arabia.

TOP 10 **COUNTRIES WITH THE LARGEST AREAS OF CORAL REEF**

COUNTRY	REEF AREA (SQ MILES)	% OF WORLD TOTAL
1 Indonesia	19,699	17.95
2 Australia	18,904	17.22
3 The Philippines	9,676	8.81
4 France—overseas territories (Clipperton, French Polynesia, Guadeloupe, Martinique, Mayotte, New Caledonia, Réunion, Wallis, and Futuna islands)	5,514	5.02
5 Papua New Guinea	5,344	4.87
6 Fiji	3,939	3.52
7 Maldives	3,444	3.14
8 Saudi Arabia	2,571	2.34
9 Marshall Islands	2,359	2.15
10 India	2,236	2.04
World total (including those not in Top 10)	*109,769*	*100.00*

Source: UNEP World Conservation Monitoring Centre, *World Atlas of Coral Reefs*

Waterways

TOP 10 **LONGEST RIVERS**

RIVER / LOCATION	APPROX. LENGTH MILES	KM
1 Nile Burundi, Dem. Rep. of Congo, Egypt, Eritrea, Ethiopia, Kenya, Rwanda, Sudan, Tanzania, Uganda	4,132	6,650
2 Amazon Bolivia, Brazil, Colombia, Ecuador, Peru, Venezuela	3,976	6,400
3 Yangtze (Chang Jiang) China	3,915	6,300
4 Mississippi-Missouri USA	3,899	6,275
5 Yenisei-Angara-Selenga Mongolia, Russia	3,441	5,539
6 Yellow (Huang He) China	3,395	5,464
7 Ob-Irtysh China, Kazakhstan, Russia	3,362	5,410
8 Congo-Chambeshi Angola, Burundi Cameroon, Dem. Rep. of Congo, Rep. of Congo, Central African Republic, Rwanda, Tanzania, Zambia	2,920	4,700
9 Amur-Argun China, Mongolia, Russia	2,761	4,444
10 Lena Russia	2,734	4,400

The source of the Nile was discovered in 1858, when British explorer John Hanning Speke reached lake Victoria Nyanza. By following the Amazon from its source up the Rio Pará, it is possible to sail for some 4,195 miles (6,750 km)—longer than the Nile—but because this entire route is not regarded as part of the Amazon basin, the Nile is still considered the world's longest river.

Major river
The Nile and its tributaries flow though nine countries in East Africa.

TOP 10 **LONGEST RIVERS IN THE USA**

RIVER	LENGTH MILES	KM
1 Missouri-Red Rock	2,540	4,088
2 Mississippi	2,348	3,779
3 Missouri	2,315	3,726
4 Yukon	1,979	3,185
5 Rio Grande	1,760	2,832
6 Arkansas	1,459	2,348
7 Colorado	1,450	2,334
8 Ohio-Allegheny	1,306	2,102
9 Red	1,290	2,076
10 Columbia	1,243	2,000

TOP 10 **HIGHEST WATERFALLS**

WATERFALL / RIVER	LOCATION	TOTAL DROP FT	M
1 Angel Carrao	Venezuela	3,212	979*
2 Tugela Tugela	South Africa	3,110	948
3 Ramnefjellsfossen Jostedal Glacier	Nesdale, Norway	2,625	800
4 Mongefossen Monge	Mongebekk, Norway	2,540	774
5 Gocta Cataracta Cocahuayco	Peru	2,531	771
6 Mutarazi Mutarazi River	Zimbabwe	2,499	762
7 Yosemite Yosemite Creek	California, USA	2,425	739
8 Østre Mardøla Foss Mardals	Eikisdal, Norway	2,152	656
9 Tyssestrengane Tysso	Hardanger, Norway	2,120	646
10 Cuquenán Arabopo	Venezuela	2,000	610

* Longest single drop 2,648 ft (807 m)

Angel Falls
American adventurer James Angel (1899–1956) first sighted the world's tallest falls from his aircraft in 1933. When his discovery was confirmed, they were named Salto Angel, or Angel Falls, in his honor.

TOP 10 **GREATEST* RIVER SYSTEMS**

RIVER SYSTEM	CONTINENT	AVERAGE DISCHARGE AT MOUTH CU FT/SEC	CU M/SEC
1 Amazon	South America	7,733,912	219,000
2 Congo (Zaïre)	Africa	1,476,153	41,800
3 Yangtze (Chang Jiang)	Asia	1,126,538	31,900
4 Orinoco	South America	1,059,440	30,000
5 Paraná	South America	907,587	25,700
6 Yenisei-Angara	Asia	692,168	19,600
7 Brahmaputra (Tsangpo)	Asia	678,042	19,200
8 Lena	Asia	603,881	17,100
9 Madeira-Mamoré	South America	600,349	17,000
10 Mississippi-Missouri	North America	572,098	16,200

* Based on rate of discharge at mouth

Lakes

THE 10 DEEPEST LAKES

	LAKE / LOCATION	GREATEST DEPTH FT	M
10	**Buenos Aires/General Carrera** Argentina/Chile	1,923	586
9	**Matano** Sulawesi, Indonesia	1,936	590
8	**Crater** Oregon, USA	1,949	594
7	**Great Slave** Canada	2,015	614
6	**Issyk-kul** Kyrgyzstan	2,191	668
5	**Malawi** Malawi/Mozambique/Tanzania	2,316	706
4	**O'Higgins/San Martín** Chile/Argentina	2,743	836
3	**Caspian Sea** Azerbaijan/Iran Kazakhstan/Russia/Turkmenistan	3,363	1,025
2	**Tanganyika** Burundi/Tanzania/ Dem. Rep. of Congo/Zambia	4,8256	1,471
1	**Baikal** Russia	5,712	1,741

In 1990, Russian explorer Anatoly Sagalevitch set the record for the deepest freshwater dive (5,371 ft/1,637 m) in Lake Baikal in a *Pisces* submersible. On July 29, 2008, *MIR I*, a Russian minisubmarine, claimed it had set a new record in Baikal, but subsequently reported that it had attained only 5,223 ft (1,592 m). Lake Vostok, Antarctica, may be up to 3,281 ft (1,000 m) deep in parts, but it lies beneath the ice.

TOP 10 LARGEST LAKES

	LAKE / LOCATION	APPROX. AREA SQ MILES	SQ KM
1	**Caspian Sea** Azerbaijan/Iran/Kazakhstan/ Russia/Turkmenistan	143,244	371,000
2	**Michigan/Huron*** Canada/USA	45,342	117,436
3	**Superior** Canada/USA	31,700	82,103
4	**Victoria** Kenya/Tanzania/Uganda	26,828	69,485
5	**Tanganyika** Burundi/Tanzania/ Dem. Rep. of Congo/Zambia	12,700	32,893
6	**Baikal** Russia	12,160	31,494
7	**Great Bear** Canada	12,028	31,153
8	**Malawi (Nyasa)** Tanzania/ Malawi/Mozambique	11,429	29,600
9	**Great Slave** Canada	11,030	28,568
10	**Erie** Canada/USA	9,940	25,745

* Now considered two lobes of the same lake

TOP 10 LARGEST FRESHWATER LAKES IN THE USA*

	LAKE	LOCATION	AREA SQ MILES	SQ KM
1	**Michigan#**	Illinois/Indiana/ Michigan/Wisconsin	22,300	57,700
2	**Iliamna**	Alaska	1,000	2,590
3	**Okeechobee**	Florida	700	1,813
4	**Becharof**	Alaska	458	1,186
5	**Red**	Minnesota	451	1,168
6	**Teshepuk**	Alaska	315	816
7	**Naknek**	Alaska	242	627
8	**Winnebago**	Wisconsin	215	557
9	**Mille Lacs**	Minnesota	207	536
10	**Flathead**	Montana	197	510

* Excluding those partly in Canada
# One lobe of Lake Michigan/Huron

TOP 10 **LAKES WITH THE GREATEST VOLUME OF WATER**

LAKE / LOCATION / VOLUME (CU MILES/CU KM)

Caspian Sea
Azerbaijan/Iran/Kazakhstan/
Russia/Turkmenistan
18,760 / 78,200

Baikal
Russia
5,517 / 22,995

Tanganyika
Burundi/Tanzania/
Dem. Rep. of
Congo/Zambia
4,270 / 17,800

Superior
Canada/USA
2,903 / 12,100

Malawi (Nyasa)
Malawi/
Mozambique/
Tanzania
2,015 / 8,400

Michigan/Huron
USA/Canada
1,982 / 8,260

Victoria
Kenya/Tanzania/
Uganda
597 / 2,750

The Caspian Sea is the world's largest inland sea or lake. It contains some 40 percent of all the planet's surface water and receives more water than any other landlocked body of water—an average of 82 cu miles (340 cu km) per annum, which is causing a steady rise in sea level.

Great Bear
Canada
536 / 2,236

Great Slave
Canada
501 / 2,090

Issyk-Kul
Kyrgyzstan
417 / 1,738

TOP 10 **LARGEST RESERVOIRS IN THE USA**

RESERVOIR / DAM / LOCATION	VOLUME	
	CU MILES	CU KM
1 Lake Mead, Hoover, NV	8.36	34.86
2 Lake Powell, Glen Canyon, AZ	7.99	33.31
3 Lake Oahe, Oahe, SD	5.71	23.81
4 Lake Sakakawea, Garrison, ND	5.47	22.82
5 Fort Peck Lake, Fort Peck, MT	4.56	19.00
6 F.D. Roosevelt Reservoir, Grand Coulee, WA	2.83	11.80
7 Lake Koocanusa, Libby, MT	1.72	7.17
8 Shasta Lake, Shasta, CA	1.35	5.62
9 Toledo Bend Reservoir, Toledo Bend, LA	1.32	5.52
10 Lake Francis Case, Fort Randall, SD	1.13	4.69

Great lake
Hydrologically regarded as one entity, Lakes Michigan and Huron are together one of the largest by volume, and the largest freshwater lake by surface area.

Islands

TOP 10 **LARGEST LAKE ISLANDS**

	ISLAND	LAKE / LOCATION	AREA SQ MILES	SQ KM
1	Manitoulin	Huron, Ontario, Canada	1,068	2,766
2	René-Lavasseur	Manicouagan Reservoir, Quebec, Canada	780	2,020
3	Sääminginsalo	Saimaa, Finland	413	1,069
4	Olkhon	Baikal, Russia	282	730
5	Samosir	Toba, Sumatra, Indonesia	243	630
6	Isle Royale	Superior, Michigan, USA	207	535
7	Ukerewe	Victoria, Tanzania	205	530
8	St. Joseph	Huron, Ontario, Canada	141	365
9	Drummond	Huron, Michigan, USA	134	347
10	Idjwi	Kivu, Dem. Rep. of Congo	110	285

Not all islands are surrounded by sea: many sizeable islands are situated in lakes. Vozrozhdeniya Island, Uzbekistan, previously second in this list with an area of approximately 900 sq miles (2,300 sq km), has grown as the Aral Sea contracts, and has now linked up with the surrounding land to become a peninsula. There are even larger islands in freshwater river outlets, including Marajó, in the mouth of the Amazon, Brazil (18,533 sq miles/48,000 sq km), and Bananal, in the River Araguaia, Brazil (7,722 sq miles/20,000 sq km).

Largest Island in a Lake on an Island
Measuring 243 sq miles (630 sq km), Samosir, or Pulau Samosir, an uninhabited volcanic island in Lake Toba on Sumatra (the world's sixth largest island) is the third largest lake island in the world, but the largest island in a lake on an island. The largest island on an island on an island is an unnamed 0.006 sq mile (0.016 sq km) outcrop on Victoria Island, Canada.

Island nation
Honshu is the main island of Japan, the fourth largest island country.

TOP 10 **LARGEST ISLAND COUNTRIES**

	COUNTRY	AREA SQ MILES	SQ KM
1	Indonesia	735,358	1,904,569
2	Madagascar	226,917	587,713
3	Papua New Guinea	178,703	462,840
4	Japan	145,897	377,873
5	Malaysia	127,354	329,847
6	Philippines	115,830	300,000
7	New Zealand	104,453	270,534
8	Cuba	42,803	110,861
9	Iceland	39,768	103,000
10	Sri Lanka	25,332	65,610

All the countries on this list are self-contained island countries.

THE 10 **SMALLEST ISLAND COUNTRIES**

COUNTRY / LOCATION / AREA (SQ MILES/SQ KM)

 1 Nauru
Pacific Ocean
8.2 / 21.2

 2 Tuvalu
Pacific Ocean
10.0 / 26.0

 3 Marshall Islands
Pacific Ocean
70.0 / 181.3

 **4** St. Kitts and Nevis
Caribbean Sea
100.8 / 261.0

 **5** Maldives
Indian Ocean
115.1 / 298.0

TOP 10 **LARGEST ISLANDS**

ISLAND / LOCATION	AREA*	
	SQ MILES	SQ KM
1 Greenland (Kalaatdlit Nunaat)	840,004	2,175,600
2 New Guinea, Papua New Guinea/ Indonesia	303,381	785,753
3 Borneo, Indonesia/Malaysia/Brunei	288,869	748,168
4 Madagascar	226,917	587,713
5 Baffin Island, Canada	194,574	503,944
6 Sumatra, Indonesia	171,068	443,065
7 Honshu, Japan	87,805	227,413
8 Great Britain	84,200	218,077
9 Victoria Island, Canada	83,897	217,292
10 Ellesmere Island, Canada	75,767	196,236

* Mainlands, including areas of inland water, but excluding offshore islands

TOP 10 **LARGEST ISLANDS IN THE USA**

ISLAND / LOCATION	AREA	
	SQ MILES	SQ KM
1 Hawaii, Hawaii	4,028	10,433
2 Kodiak, Alaska	3,588	9,293
3 Prince of Wales, Alaska	2,577	6,675
4 Chicagof, Alaska	2,080	5,388
5 Saint Lawrence, Alaska	1,983	5,135
6 Admiralty, Alaska	1,684	4,362
7 Nunivak, Alaska	1,625	4,209
8 Unimak, Alaska	1,590	4,119
9 Baranof, Alaska	1,569	4,065
10 Long Island, New York	1,401	3,629

6 Malta
Mediterranean Sea
122.0 / 316.0

7 Grenada
Caribbean Sea
132.8 / 344.0

8 St Vincent and the Grenadines
Caribbean Sea
150.2 / 389.0

9 Barbados
Caribbean Sea
166.4 / 431.0

10 Antigua and Barbuda
Caribbean Sea
170.9 / 442.6

Mountains

TOP 10 **HIGHEST MOUNTAINS IN EUROPE**

	MOUNTAIN	COUNTRY	HEIGHT* FT	HEIGHT* M
1	Mont Blanc	France/Italy	15,771	4,807
2	Monte Rosa	Switzerland	15,203	4,634
3	Zumsteinspitze	Italy/Switzerland	14,970	4,564
4	Signalkuppe	Italy/Switzerland	14,941	4,555
5	Dom	Switzerland	14,911	4,545
6	Liskamm	Italy/Switzerland	14,853	4,527
7	Weisshorn	Switzerland	14,780	4,505
8	Täschorn	Switzerland	14,733	4,491
9	Matterhorn	Italy/Switzerland	14,688	4,477
10	Mont Maudit	France/Italy	14,649	4,466

* Height of principal peak; lower peaks of the same mountain are excluded

All 10 of Europe's highest mountains are in the Alps; there are, however, at least 15 mountains in the Caucasus (the mountain range that straddles Europe and Asia) that are taller than Mont Blanc. The highest of them, the west peak of Mount Elbrus, measures 18,510 ft (5,642 m).

Height of Luxury
Europe's highest mountain, Mont Blanc, also has Europe's highest toilets: in 2007 two WCs were carried by helicopter to a height of 13,976 ft (4,260 m). During peak climbing season they are regularly emptied—also by helicopter.

TOP 10 **LONGEST MOUNTAIN RANGES**

	RANGE / LOCATION	LENGTH MILES	LENGTH KM
1	Andes, South America	4,500	7,242
2	Rocky Mountains, North America	3,750	6,035
3	Himalayas/Karakoram/ Hundu Kush, Asia	2,400	3,862
4	Great Dividing Range, Australia	2,250	3,621
5	Trans-Antarctic Mountains, Antarctica	2,200	3,541
6	Brazilian East Coast Range, Brazil	1,900	3,058
7	Sumatran/Javan Range, Sumatra, Java	1,800	2,897
8	Tien Shan, China	1,400	2,253
9	Eastern Ghats, India	1,300	2,092
10 =	Altai, Asia	1,250	2,012
=	Central New Guinean Range, Papua New Guinea	1,250	2,012
=	Urals, Russia	1,250	2,012

This Top 10 includes only ranges that are continuous. The Aleutian Range extends for 1,650 miles (2,655 km), but is fragmented across numerous islands of the northwest Pacific.

TOP 10 **HIGHEST MOUNTAINS**

	MOUNTAIN / LOCATION	FIRST ASCENT	TEAM NATIONALITY	HEIGHT* FT	HEIGHT* M
1	Everest, Nepal/China	May 29, 1953	British/ New Zealand	29,035	8,850
2	K2 (Chogori), Pakistan/China	Jul 31, 1954	Italian	28,251	8,611
3	Kangchenjunga, Nepal/India	May 25, 1955	British	28,169	8,586
4	Lhotse, Nepal/China	May 18, 1956	Swiss	27,940	8,516
5	Makalu I, Nepal/China	May 15, 1955	French	27,838	8,485
6	Cho Oyu, Nepal/China	Oct 19, 1954	Austrian	26,864	8,188
7	Dhaulagiri I, Nepal	May 13, 1960	Swiss/Austrian	26,795	8,167
8	Manaslu I (Kutang I), Nepal	May 9, 1956	Japanese	26,781	8,163
9	Nanga Parbat (Diamir), Pakistan	Jul 3, 1953	German/ Austrian	26,657	8,125
10	Anapurna I, Nepal	Jun 3, 1950	French	26,545	8,091

* Height of principal peak; lower peaks of the same mountain are excluded

TOP 10 **HIGHEST MOUNTAINS IN AUSTRALIA**

	MOUNTAIN	HEIGHT* FT	HEIGHT* M
1	Mount Kosciuszko	7,309	2,228
2	Mount Townsend	7,249	2,209
3	Mount Twynham	7,203	2,195
4	Rams Head	7,185	2,190
5	Unnamed peak, Etheridge Ridge	7,152	2,180
6	Rams Head North	7,142	2,177
7	Alice Rawson Peak	7,086	2,160
8	Unnamed peak, southwest of Abbott Peak	7,083	2,159
9 =	Abbott Peak	7,039	2,145
=	Carruthers Peak	7,039	2,145

* Height of principal peak; lower peaks of the same mountain are excluded

TOP 10 **HIGHEST MOUNTAINS IN NORTH AMERICA**

MOUNTAIN	COUNTRY	HEIGHT* FT	HEIGHT* M
1 McKinley	Alaska, USA	20,320	6,194
2 Logan	Canada	19,545	5,959
3 Citlaltépetl (Orizaba)	Mexico	18,409	5,611
4 St. Elias	Alaska, USA/ Canada	18,008	5,489
5 Popocatépetl	Mexico	17,887	5,452
6 Foraker	Alaska, USA	17,400	5,304
7 Ixtaccihuatl	Mexico	17,343	5,286
8 Lucania	Canada	17,147	5,226
9 King	Canada	16,971	5,173
10 Steele	Canada	16,644	5,073

* Height of principal peak; lower peaks of the same mountain are excluded

Mount McKinley was spotted in 1794 by Captain James Vancouver and in 1896 named after the then-US president. It was first climbed on June 7, 1913 by a party of four led by London-born Reverend Hudson Stuck, archdeacon of the Yukon.

Far-ranging
The Cordillera del Paine, Chile, is part of the Andes, the world's longest mountain range.

TOP 10 **HIGHEST MOUNTAINS IN SOUTH AMERICA**

MOUNTAIN	COUNTRY	HEIGHT* FT	HEIGHT* M
1 Cerro Aconcagua	Argentina	22,841	6,959
2 Ojos del Salado	Argentina/Chile	22,615	6,893
3 Monte Pissis	Argentina/Chile	22,244	6,795
4 Cerro Bonete	Argentina	22,175	6,759
5 Huascarán	Peru	22,133	6,746
6 Llullaillaco	Argentina/Chile	22,109	6,739
7 = Cerro Mercadario	Argentina/Chile	22,047	6,720
= El Libertador	Argentina	22,047	6,720
9 Tres Cruces	Argentina/Chile	21,748	6,629
10 Incahuasi	Argentina/Chile	21,722	6,621

* Height of principal peak; lower peaks of the same mountain are excluded

Land Features

TOP 10 **LARGEST DESERTS**

DESERT / LOCATION	APPROX. AREA SQ MILES	SQ KM
1 Sahara, northern Africa	3,513,530	9,100,000
2 Arabian, southwest Asia	899,618	2,330,000
3 Gobi, central Asia	500,002	1,295,000
4 Patagonian, Argentina/Chile	259,847	673,000
5 Great Basin, USA	189,962	492,000
6 Great Victoria, Australia	163,707	424,000
7 Chihuahuan, Mexico/USA	140,000	362,600
8 Great Sandy, Australia	138,997	360,000
9 Karakum, Turkmenistan	135,136	350,000
10 Sonoran, Mexico/USA	120,078	311,000

This Top 10 presents the approximate areas and ranking of the world's great deserts, which are often either broken down into smaller desert regions or merged. The world deserts cover some 13,615,508 sq miles (35,264,000 sq km), or about one-quarter of the total land area.

Just desert
The Sahara, the world's largest desert, extends into 10 countries in North Africa, its southern border demarcated by the semi-arid Sahel.

TOP 10 **LARGEST METEORITE CRATERS**

CRATER / LOCATION	DIAMETER MILES	KM
1 Vredefort, South Africa	186	300
2 Sudbury, Ontario, Canada	155	250
3 Chicxulub, Yucatan, Mexico	107	170
4 = Manicougan, Quebec, Canada	62	100
= Popigai, Russia	62	100
6 = Acraman, Australia	56	90
= Chesapeake Bay, Virginia, USA	56	90
8 Puchezh-Katunki, Russia	50	80
9 Morokweng, South Africa	43	70
10 Kara, Russia	40	65

Source: Earth Impact Database, Planetary and Space Science Center, University of New Brunswick

Unlike on the Solar System's other planets and moons, many astroblemes (collision sites) on Earth have been weathered over time and obscured, and one of the ongoing debates in geology is whether or not certain crater-like structures are of meteoric origin or the remnants of long-extinct volcanoes.

Maldives
Most of the Maldives has an average elevation of 5 ft (1.5 m) above sea level. Risk of sea-level rises may compel the entire population to move.

THE 10 **COUNTRIES WITH THE LOWEST ELEVATIONS**

COUNTRY*	HIGHEST POINT	ELEVATION FT	M
1 Maldives	Unnamed on Wilingili island in the Addu Atoll	7.8	2.4
2 Tuvalu	Unnamed	16.4	5.0
3 Marshall Islands	Unnamed on Likiep	32.8	10.0
4 The Gambia	Unnamed	173.9	53.0
5 Nauru	Unnamed on plateau rim	200.1	61.0
6 The Bahamas	Mount Alvernia on Cat Island	206.7	63.0
7 Vatican City	Unnamed	246.1	75.0
8 Kiribati	Unnamed on Banaba	265.7	81.0
9 Qatar	Qurayn Abu al Bawl	337.9	103.0
10 Singapore	Bukit Timah	544.6	166.0

* Excludes overseas possessions, territories, and dependencies

Source: CIA, *The World Factbook 2008*

These 10 countries are definitely off the agenda if you are planning a climbing holiday, none of them possessing a single elevation taller than a medium-sized skyscraper. Compared with these, even The Netherlands' 1,050-ft (321-m) Vaalserberg hill makes the country's appellation as one of the "Low Countries" sound somewhat unfair.

THE 10 **DEEPEST CAVES**

CAVE SYSTEM / LOCATION / DEPTH (FT/M)

1 Krubera (Voronja), Georgia
7,188 / 2,191

2 Sniezhnaja-Mezhonnogo (Snezhaya), Georgia
5,751 / 1,753

3 Lamprechtsofen Vogelschacht Weg Schacht, Austria
5,354 / 1,632

4 Gouffre Mirolda, France
5,335 / 1,626

5 Réseau Jean Bernard, France
5,256 / 1,602

6 Torca del Cerro del Cuevon/Torca de las Saxifragas, Spain
5,213 / 1,589

7 Sarma, Georgia
5,062 / 1,543

8 Shakta Vjacheslav Pantjukhina, Georgia
4,948 / 1,508

9 Sima de la Conisa/Torca Magali, Spain
4,944 / 1,507

10 Cehi 2, Slovenia
4,928 / 1,502

Deeper and Deeper
Discovered in 1960, subsequent exploration has progressively extended the known depth of the Voronja Cave, with 6,562 ft (2,000 m) first exceeded by an international expedition in 2004.

World Weather

TOP 10 **SUNNIEST PLACES***

LOCATION# / % OF MAX. POSSIBLE / AVERAGE ANNUAL HOURS SUNSHINE

 Yuma, Arizona, USA 91 / 4,127

 Phoenix, Arizona, USA 90 / 4,041

 Wadi Halfa, Sudan 89 / 3,964

 Bordj Omar Driss, Algeria 88 / 3,899

 Keetmanshoop, Namibia 88 / 3,876

 Aoulef, Algeria 86 / 3,784

 Upington, South Africa 86 / 3,766

 Atbara, Sudan 85 / 3,739

 Mariental, Namibia 84 / 3,707

 Bilma, Niger 84 / 3,699

* Highest yearly sunshine total, averaged over a long period of years
# Maximum of two places per country listed

Source: Philip Eden

TOP 10 **CLOUDIEST PLACES***

LOCATION# / % OF MAX. POSSIBLE / AVERAGE ANNUAL HOURS SUNSHINE

 Ben Nevis, Scotland 16 / 736

 Hoyvik, Faeroes, Denmark 19 / 902

 Maam, Ireland 19 / 929

 Prince Rupert, British Columbia, Canada 20 / 955

 Riksgransen, Sweden 20 / 965

 Akureyri, Iceland 20 / 973

 Raufarhöfn, Iceland 21 / 995

 Nanortalik, Greenland 22 / 1,000

 Dalwhinnie, Scotland 22 / 1,032

 Karasjok, Norway 23 / 1,090

* Lowest yearly sunshine total, averaged over a long period of years
# Maximum of two places per country listed

Source: Philip Eden

TOP 10 **WETTEST INHABITED PLACES**

LOCATION / HIGHEST TOTAL ANNUAL RAINFALL (IN/MM)

 **Lloro,** Colombia 523.6 / 13,299.4

 Mawsynram, India 467.4 / 11,872.0

 Mt. Waialeale, Kauai, Hawaii 460.0 / 11,684.0

 Cherrapuni, India 425.0 / 10,795.0

 Debundscha, Cameroon 405.0 / 10,287.0

 Quibdo, Colombia 354.0 / 8,991.6

 Bellenden Ker, Queensland, Australia 340.0 / 8,636.0

 Andagoya, Colombia 281.0 / 7,137.4

 Henderson Lake, British Colombia, Canada 256.0 / 6,502.4

 Crkvica, Bosnia-Herzegovina 183.0 / 4,648.2

TOP 10 **HOTTEST PLACES**

	LOCATION*	HIGHEST TEMPERATURE °F	°C
1	Al'Azīzīyah, Libya	136.4	58.0
2	Greenland Ranch, Death Valley, USA	134.0	56.7
3 =	Ghudamis, Libya	131.0	55.0
=	Kebili, Tunisia	131.0	55.0
5	Tombouctou, Mali	130.1	54.5
6 =	Araouane, Mali	130.0	54.4
=	Mammoth Tank#, California, USA	130.0	54.4
8	Tirat Tavi, Israel	129.0	54.0
9	Ahwāz, Iran	128.3	53.5
10	Agha Jārī, Iran	128.0	53.3

* Maximum of two places per country listed
# Former weather station

Source: Philip Eden/Roland Bert

Polar opposites
Earth's climatic range, from arid desert to arctic waste, is represented in miniature by some locations that experience remarkable temperature extremes, their hot summers contrasting with sub-zero winters.

TOP 10 **PLACES WITH THE MOST CONTRASTING SEASONS***

	LOCATION#	WINTER °F	°C	SUMMER °F	°C	DIFFERENCE °F	°C
1	Verkhoyansk, Russia	-58.5	-50.3	56.5	13.6	115.0	63.9
2	Yakutsk, Russia	-49.0	-45.0	63.5	17.5	112.5	62.5
3	Manzhouli, China	-15.0	-26.1	69.0	20.6	84.0	46.7
4	Fort Yukon, Alaska, USA	-20.2	-29.0	61.4	16.3	81.6	45.3
5	Fort Good Hope, North West Territory, Canada	-21.8	-29.9	59.5	15.3	81.3	45.2
6	Brochet, Manitoba, Canada	-20.5	-29.2	59.7	15.4	80.2	44.6
7	Tunka, Mongolia	-16.0	-26.7	61.0	16.1	77.0	42.8
8	Fairbanks, Alaska, USA	-11.2	-24.0	60.1	15.6	71.3	39.6
9	Semipalatinsk, Kazakhstan	0.5	-17.7	69.0	20.6	68.5	38.3
10	Jorgen Bronlund Fjørd, Greenland	-23.6	-30.9	43.5	6.4	67.1	37.3

* Biggest differences between mean monthly temperatures in summer and winter
# Maximum of two places per country listed

Source: Philip Eden

TOP 10 **PLACES WITH THE LEAST CONTRASTING SEASONS***

	LOCATION#	COOLEST °F	°C	WARMEST °F	°C	DIFFERENCE °F	°C
1 =	Lorengau, New Guinea	80.0	26.7	81.0	27.2	1.0	0.5
=	Malacca, Malaysia	80.0	26.7	81.0	27.2	1.0	0.5
=	Malden Island, Kiribati	82.0	27.8	83.0	28.3	1.0	0.5
=	Ocean Island, Kiribati	82.0	27.8	83.0	28.3	1.0	0.5
5 =	Kavieng, New Guinea	81.0	27.2	82.0	27.8	1.0	0.6
=	Quito, Ecuador	58.0	14.4	59.0	15.0	1.0	0.6
7 =	Andagoya, Colombia	81.0	27.2	82.4	28.0	1.4	0.8
=	Labuhan, Indonesia	81.0	27.2	82.4	28.0	1.4	0.8
=	Mwanza, Tanzania	72.7	22.6	74.1	23.4	1.4	0.8
10	Belém, Brazil	79.0	26.1	80.5	26.9	1.5	0.8

* Smallest differences between mean monthly temperatures between warmest and coolest months
# Maximum of two places per country listed

Source: Philip Eden

Natural Disasters

THE 10 WORST EARTHQUAKES

LOCATION / DATE / ESTIMATED NO. KILLED

 1 Near East/Mediterranean
May 20, 1202
1,100,000

 2 Shenshi, China
Feb 2, 1556
820,000

 3 Calcutta, India
Oct 11, 1737
300,000

 4 Antioch, Syria
May 20, AD 526
250,000

 5 Tangshan, China
Jul 18, 1976
242,419

 6 Nanshan, China
May 22, 1927
200,000

 7 Yeddo, Japan
Dec 30, 1703
190,000

 8 Kansu, China
Dec 16, 1920
180,000

9 Messina, Italy
Dec 28, 1908
160,000

 10 Tokyo/Yokohama, Japan
Sep 1, 1923
142,807

There are some discrepancies between the "official" death tolls in many of the world's worst earthquakes and the estimates of other authorities: a figure as high as 750,000 is sometimes quoted for the Tangshan earthquake of 1976.

THE 10 WORST EPIDEMICS

EPIDEMIC / LOCATION / DATE / ESTIMATED NO. KILLED

 1 Black Death, Europe/Asia
1347–80s
75,000,000

 2 Influenza, Worldwide
1918–20
20–40,000,000

 3 AIDS, Worldwide
1981–
>25,000,000

 4 Plague of Justinian
Europe/Asia
AD 541–90
<25,000,000

 5 Bubonic plague, India
1896–1948
12,000,000

 6 = Antonine Plague
(probably smallpox)
Roman Empire
AD 165–180
5,000,000

= Plague, India
1896–1907
5,000,000

 8 Typhus, Eastern Europe
1918–22
3,000,000

 9 = Smallpox, Mexico
1530–45
>1,000,000

= Cholera, Russia
1852–60
>1,000,000

Precise figures for deaths during the disruptions of epidemics are inevitably unreliable, but the Black Death, or bubonic plague, is believed to have killed over half the inhabitants of London, some 25 million in Europe, and 50 million in Asia.

THE 10 WORST FLOODS

LOCATION / DATE / ESTIMATED NO. KILLED

 1 Yellow River (Huang He), China
Aug 1931
3,700,000

 2 Yellow River, China
Spring 1887
1,500,000

 3 Holland
Nov 1, 1530
400,000

 4 Kaifeng, China
1642
300,000

 5 Henan, China
Sep–Nov 1939
>200,000

 6 Bengal, India
1876
200,000

 7 Yangtze River (Chang Jiang), China
Aug–Sep 1931
140,000

 8 Holland
1646
110,000

 9 North Vietnam
Aug 30, 1971
>100,000

 10 = Friesland, Holland
1228
100,000

= Dort, Holland
Apr 16, 1421
100,000

= Canton, China
Jun 12, 1915
100,000

= Yangtze River, China
Sep 1911
100,000

THE 10 WORST TSUNAMIS

LOCATIONS AFFECTED / DATE / ESTIMATED NO. KILLED

 Southeast Asia
Dec 26, 2004
>186,983

 Krakatoa, Sumatra/Java*
Aug 27, 1883
36,380

 Sanriku, Japan
Jun 15, 1896
28,000

 Agadir, Morocco#
Feb 29, 1960
12,000

 Lisbon, Portugal
Nov 1, 1755
10,000

 Papua New Guinea
Jul 18, 1998
8,000

 Chile/Pacific islands/Japan
May 22, 1960
5,700

 Philippines
Aug 17, 1976
5,000

 Hyuga to Izu, Japan
Oct 28, 1707
4,900

 Sanriku, Japan
Mar 3, 1933
3,000

* Combined effect of volcanic eruption
and tsunamis
Combined effect of earthquake and tsunamis

Often mistakenly called tidal waves,
tsunamis (from the Japanese *tsu*, "port"
and *nami*, "wave"), are powerful waves
caused by undersea disturbances.

THE 10 WORST HURRICANES, TYPHOONS AND CYCLONES

LOCATION / DATE / ESTIMATED NO. KILLED

 Ganges Delta, Bangladesh
13 Nov 13, 1970
500,000–1,000,000

 Bengal, India
Oct 7, 1737
>300,000

 = **Coringa**, India
Nov 25, 1839
300,000

= **Haiphong**, Vietnam
Oct 8, 1881
300,000

 Bengal, India
Oct 31, 1876
200,000

 Ganges Delta, Bangladesh
Apr 29, 1991
138,000

 Bombay, India
Jun 6, 1882
>100,000

 Southern Japan
Aug 23, 1281
68,000

 North-east China
Aug 2–3, 1922
60,000

 **Calcutta**, India
Oct 5, 1864
50,000–70,000

The cyclone of 1970 hit the Bay of Bengal
with winds of over 120 mph (190 km/h).
Loss of life was worst in the Bhola region,
as a result of which it is often known as
the Bhola Cyclone.

THE 10 WORST FOREST FIRES

INCIDENT / LOCATION / OUTBREAK / ESTIMATED NO. KILLED

 Peshtigo, Wisconsin, USA
Oct 8, 1871
1,500

 Cloquet, Minnesota, USA
Oct 12, 1918
551

 Hinckley, Minnesota, USA
Sep 1, 1894
418

 Thumb, Michigan, USA
Sep 5, 1881
282

 Sumatra,
Kalimantan, Indonesia
Aug 1997
240

 Landes, France
Aug 1949
230

 Matheson,
Ontario, Canada
Jul 29, 1916
223

 Greater Hinggan,
Heilongjiang, China
May 6, 1987
213

 Victoria,
Australia
Feb 7–March 14, 2009
210

 **Miramichi**,
New Brunswick, Canada
Oct 7, 1825
160

Background: Devastation at Aceh
Aceh, Sumatra, was at the epicenter of the
2004 Indian Ocean tsunami that left an
estimated 186,983 dead and 42,883 missing.

2

LIFE ON
EARTH

Extinct & Endangered

Scaled down

Not all dinosaurs were earthshaking monsters: Saltopus, discovered in 1910 and known only from fragmentary remains, is believed to have been the size of a domestic cat.

THE 10 **SMALLEST DINOSAURS**

	DINOSAUR	MAX. SIZE IN	CM
1	Micropachycephalosaurus	20	50
2 =	Saltopus	23	60
=	Yandangornis	23	60
4	Microraptor	30	77
5 =	Lesothosaurus	35	90
=	Nanosaurus	35	90
7 =	Bambiraptor	36	91
=	Sinosauropteryx	36	91
9	Wannanosaurus	39	99
10	Procompsognathus	47	120

Discovered in Argentina, Mussaurus ("mouse lizard") is, at just 7–15 in (18–37 cm), the smallest dinosaur skeleton found, but all known specimens are those of infants.

TOP 10 **CHIMPANZEE COUNTRIES**

	COUNTRY	ESTIMATED CHIMPANZEE POPULATION*
1	Dem. Rep. of Congo	70,000–110,000
2	Gabon	27,000–64,000
3	Cameroon	34,000–44,000
4	Guinea	8,100–29,000
5	Côte d'Ivoire	8,000–12,000
6	Congo	10,000
7	Uganda	4,000–5,700
8	Mali	1,600–5,200
9	Liberia	1,000–5,000
10	Nigeria	2,000–3,000

* Ranked on estimated maximum

Source: Julian Caldecott and Lera Miles, World Atlas of Great Apes and Their Conservation, University of California Press, 2005

All chimpanzees of both species, *Pan troglodytes* and *Pan paniscus* are found in 20 African countries. Estimates of their total population range from 172,200 to 299,200.

THE 10 **FIRST DINOSAURS TO BE NAMED**

	NAME	MEANING	NAMED BY	YEAR
1	Megalosaurus	Great lizard	William Buckland	1824
2	Iguanodon	Iguana tooth	Gideon Mantell	1825
3	Hylaeosaurus	Woodland lizard	Gideon Mantell	1833
4	Macrodontophion	Long tooth snake	A. Zborzewski	1834
5	Palaeosaurus	Ancient lizard	Samuel Stutchbury and Henry Riley	1836
6	Thecodontosaurus	Socket-toothed lizard	Henry Riley and Samuel Stutchbury	1836
7	Plateosaurus	Flat lizard	Hermann von Meyer	1837
8	Poekilopleuron	Varying side	Jacques Armand Eudes-Deslongchamps	1838
9	Cetiosaurus	Whale lizard	Richard Owen	1841
10	Cladeiodon	Branch tooth	Richard Owen	1841

The name Megalosaurus, the first to be given to a dinosaur, was proposed by William Buckland (1784–1856), the Dean of Westminster, an English eccentric who out of scientific curiosity ate the mummified heart of the French King Louis XIV.

TOP 10 **COUNTRIES WITH THE LARGEST PROTECTED AREAS**

	COUNTRY	% OF TOTAL AREA	DESIGNATED AREA SQ MILES	SQ KM
1	USA	24.9	902,091	2,336,406
2	Australia	13.4	395,911	1,025,405
3	Greenland	45.2	379,345	982,500
4	Canada	9.3	357,231	925,226
5	Saudi Arabia	34.4	318,811	825,717
6	China	7.1	263,480	682,410
7	Venezuela	61.7	217,397	563,056
8	Brazil	6.6	215,312	557,656
9	Russia	3.1	204,273	529,067
10	Indonesia	18.6	138,002	357,425

Protected areas encompass national parks, nature reserves, natural monuments, and other sites. There are over 100,000 such designated areas around the world, covering more than 10 percent of the total land area. In the case of some islands, such as Easter Island, almost 100 percent is designated a protected area.

Monkey Business

In 2001, Cheeta, a chimpanzee said to have appeared in *Tarzan* films, was declared to be the world's oldest at 69. In 2008, the *Washington Post* published evidence that suggested that the claim fraudulent.

Reaching the limit
Elephants are found in 22 percent of the African continent, an estimated total of fewer than 500,000.

THE 10 **COUNTRIES WITH THE MOST AFRICAN ELEPHANTS**

	COUNTRY	ELEPHANTS*
1	Botswana	133,829
2	Tanzania	108,816
3	Zimbabwe	84,416
4	Kenya	23,353
5	South Africa	17,847
6	Zambia	16,562
7	Mozambique	14,079
8	Namibia	12,531
9	Burkina Faso	4,154
10	Chad	3,885

* Definite population

Source: International Union for the Conservation of Nature, *African Elephant Status Report 2007*

Amazing Animals

Above: Sumo seals
Elephant seals can weigh as much as three tons and include penguins and sharks in their diets.

Left: Lion king
Although tigers are typically longer, lions are often heavier, at up to 690 lb (313 kg).

TOP 10 **BIGGEST BIG CATS**

	SPECIES / SCIENTIFIC NAME	MAX. LENGTH FT	M
1	Tiger (*Panthera tigris*)	10.8	3.30
2	Lion (*Panthera leo*)	9.2	2.80
3	Cougar (*Puma concolor*)	6.6	2.00
4	Leopard (*Panthera pardus*)	6.2	1.90
5	Jaguar (*Panthera onca*)	5.9	1.80
6	Cheetah (*Acinonyx jubatus*)	4.9	1.50
7 =	Lynx (*Lynx lynx*, etc.)	4.3	1.30
=	Snow leopard (*Uncia uncia*)	4.3	1.30
9	Asian golden cat (*Pardofelis temminckii*)	3.6	1.10
10 =	Bobcat (*Lynx rufus*)	3.3	1.00
=	Clouded leopard (*Neofelis nebulosa*)	3.3	1.00
=	Ocelot (*Leopardus pardalis*)	3.3	1.00
=	Serval (*Leptailurus serval*)	3.3	1.00

TOP 10 **LARGEST CARNIVORES**

	CARNIVORE	LENGTH FT	IN	M	WEIGHT LB	KG
1	Southern elephant seal	21	4	6.5	7,716	3,500
2	Walrus	12	6	3.8	2,646	1,200
3	Steller sea lion	9	8	3	2,425	1,100
4	Grizzly bear	9	8	3	1,720	780
5	Polar bear	8	6	2.6	1,323	600
6	Siberian tiger	10	7	3.3	793	360
7	Lion	6	3	1.9	551	250
8	American black bear	6	0	1.8	500	227
9	Giant panda	5	0	1.5	353	160
10	Spectacled bear	6	0	1.8	309	140

Of more than 260 mammal species in the order *Carnivora*, or meateaters, many are in fact omnivorous, with some 40 specializing in eating fish or insects, including seals and bears—the order's largest terrestrial representatives

TOP 10 HEAVIEST TERRESTRIAL MAMMALS

MAMMAL* / SCIENTIFIC NAME / LENGTH (FT/M)	WEIGHT LB	KG
African elephant (*Loxodonta africana*) 24.6 / 7.5	16,534	7,500
Hippopotamus (*Hippopotamus amphibius*) 16.4 / 5.0	9,920	4,500
White rhinoceros (*Ceratotherium simum*) 13.7 / 4.2	7,937	3,600
Giraffe (*Giraffa camelopardalis*) 15.4 / 4.7	4,255	1,930
American buffalo (*Bison bison*) 11.4 / 3.5	2,205	1,000
Moose (*Alces alces*) 10.1 / 3.1	1,820	825
Grizzly bear (*Ursus arctos*) 9.8 / 3.0	1,720	780
Arabian camel (dromedary) (*Camelus dromedarius*) 11.3 / 3.45	1,521	690
Siberian tiger (*Panthera tigris altaica*) 10.8 / 3.3	793	360
Gorilla (*Gorilla gorilla gorilla*) 6.5 / 2.0	606	275

* Heaviest species per genus; exclusively terrestrial, excluding seals, etc.

The list excludes domesticated cattle and horses, and highlights the extreme heavyweights within distinctive large mammal groups such as bears, deer, big cats, primates, and bovines (ox-like mammals).

Prime primate
The largest of all primates, gorillas can attain weights that exceed those of even the heaviest humans.

TOP 10 HEAVIEST PRIMATES

PRIMATE* / SCIENTIFIC NAME	AVERAGE WEIGHT RANGE# LB	KG
1 Gorilla (*Gorilla gorilla gorilla*)	297–606	135–275
2 Man (*Homo sapiens*)	100–200	45–91
3 Orangutan (*Pongo pygmaeus*)	66–198	30–90
4 Chimpanzee (*Pan troglodytes*)	90–110	40–50
5 Hamadryas baboon (*Papio hamadryas*)	44–99	20–45
6 Japanese (snow) monkey (*Macaca fuscata*)	22–66	10–30
7 Mandrill (*Mandrillus sphinx*)	24–55	11–25
8 Proboscis monkey (*Nasalis lavatus*)	17–50	8–23
9 Gelada baboon (*Theropithecus gelada*)	26–46	12–21
10 Hanuman langur (*Semnopithecus entellus*)	20–44	9–20

* Heaviest species per genus
\# Average weights range across male and female, ranked by maximum

Aquatic Creatures

THE 10 PLACES WHERE MOST PEOPLE ARE ATTACKED BY SHARKS

LOCATION	FATAL ATTACKS	LAST FATAL ATTACK	TOTAL ATTACKS*
1 USA (excluding Hawaii)	38	2005	881
2 Australia	135	2006	345
3 South Africa	42	2004	214
4 Hawaii	23	2004	113
5 Brazil	21	2006	89
6 Papua New Guinea	25	2000	49
7 New Zealand	9	1968	47
8 Mexico	20	1997	37
9 The Bahamas	1	1968	26
10 Iran	8	1985	23

1 fin = 10 attacks

Red fin = 10 fatal attacks

* Confirmed unprovoked attacks, including non-fatal, 1580–2007

Source: International Shark Attack File/ American Elasmobranch Society/ Florida Museum of Natural History

The International Shark Attack File monitors worldwide incidents, a total of 1,969 of which have been recorded since the sixteenth century. The 1990s had the highest attack total (514) of any decade, while 71 unprovoked attacks were recorded in 2007 alone.

TOP 10 HEAVIEST SHARKS

SHARK / SCIENTIFIC NAME	MAX. WEIGHT LB	KG
1 Whale shark (*Rhincodon typus*)	67,240	30,500
2 Basking shark (*Cetorhinus maximus*)	20,410	9,258
3 Great white shark (*Carcharodon carcharias*)	7,731	3,507
4 Megamouth shark (*Megachasma pelagios*)	2,679	1,215
5 Greenland shark (*Somniosus microcephalus*)	2,224	1,009
6 Tiger shark (*Galeocerdo cuvieri*)	2,043	927
7 Great hammerhead shark (*Sphyrna mokarran*)	1,889	857
8 Six-gill shark (*Hexanchus griseus*)	1,327	602
9 Grey nurse shark (*Carcharias taurus*)	1,243	564
10 Mako shark (*Isurus oxyrinchus*)	1,221	554

Source: Lucy T. Verma

Freshwater Record

The heaviest freshwater fish ever caught was a 9-ft (2.7-m) white sturgeon weighing 468 lb (212.28 kg), landed after a seven-hour battle by Joey Pallotta III at Benicia, California, USA, on July 9, 1983.

White sturgeon
A fisherman's prize catch, but a relative tiddler compared with the record-holder.

Green sea turtle
Once hunted as food and for their shells, the large green sea turtle is now protected as an endangered species.

TOP 10 **HEAVIEST TURTLES**

TURTLE / SCIENTIFIC NAME	MAX. WEIGHT LB	KG
1 Pacific leatherback turtle (*Dermochelys coriacea*)*	1,552	704.4
2 Atlantic leatherback turtle (*Dermochelys coriacea*)*	1,018	463.0
3 Green sea turtle (*Chelonia mydas*)	871	391.5
4 Loggerhead turtle (*Caretta caretta*)	568	257.8
5 Alligator snapping turtle (*Macroclemys temmincki*)#	220	100.0
6 Flatback (sea) turtle (*Natator depressus*)	171	78.2
7 Hawksbill (sea) turtle (*Eretmochelys imbricata*)	138	62.7
8 Kemps Ridley turtle (*Lepidochelys kempi*)	133	60.5
9 Olive Ridley turtle (*Lepidochelys olivacea*)	110	49.9
10 Common snapping turtle (*Chelydra serpentina*)#	85	38.5

* One species, differing in size according to where they live
# Freshwater species

Source: Lucy T. Verma

The largest of the 265 species of *Chelonia* (turtles and tortoises) are marine turtles, with the Aldabra giant tortoises the largest of the land-dwellers.

TOP 10 **HEAVIEST MARINE MAMMALS**

MAMMAL / SCIENTIFIC NAME	LENGTH FT	M	WEIGHT (TONS)
1 Blue whale (*Balaenoptera musculus*)	110.0	33.5	151.0
2 Bowhead whale (Greenland right) (*Balaena mysticetus*)	65.0	20.0	94.7
3 Northern right whale (black right) (*Balaena glacialis*)	60.0	18.6	85.6
4 Fin whale (common rorqual) (*Balaenoptera physalus*)	82.0	25.0	69.9
5 Sperm whale (*Physeter catodon*)	59.0	18.0	48.2
6 Grey whale (*Eschrichtius robustus*)	46.0	14.0	38.5
7 Humpback whale (*Megaptera novaeangliae*)	49.2	15.0	38.1
8 Sei whale (*Balaenoptera borealis*)	60.0	18.5	32.4
9 Bryde's whale (*Balaenoptera edeni*)	47.9	14.6	22.0
10 Baird's whale (*Berardius bairdii*)	18.0	5.5	13.3

Source: Lucy T. Verma

Probably the largest animal that ever lived, the blue whale dwarfs even the other whales listed here, all but one of which far outweigh the biggest land animal, the elephant. The elephant seal, with a weight of 3.9 tons, is the largest marine mammal that is not a whale.

Airlife

TOP 10 HEAVIEST FLIGHTLESS BIRDS

BIRD / SCIENTIFIC NAME*	HEIGHT IN	HEIGHT CM	WEIGHT LB	WEIGHT OZ	WEIGHT KG
1 Ostrich (male) (Struthio camelus)	100.4	255.0	343	9	156.0
2 Northern cassowary (Casuarius unappendiculatus)	59.1	150.0	127	9	58.0
3 Emu (female) (Dromaius novaehollandiae)	61.0	155.0	121	6	55.0
4 Emperor penguin (female) (Aptenodytes forsteri)	45.3	115.0	101	4	46.0
5 Greater rhea (Rhea americana)	55.1	140.0	55	2	25.0
6 Flightless steamer# (duck) (Tachyeres brachypterus)	33.1	84.0	13	7	6.2
7 Flightless cormorant (Nannopterum harrisi)	39.4	100.0	9	15	4.5
8 Kiwi (female) (Apteryx haastii)	25.6	65.0	8	4	3.8
9 Takahe (rail) (Porphyrio mantelli)	19.7	50.0	7	2	3.2
10 Kakapo (parrot) (Strigops habroptilus)	25.2	64.0	7	1	3.2

* By species
\# The flightless steamer is 33 in (84 cm) long, but does not stand upright

Source: Chris Mead

The flightless great auk, extinct since 1844, weighed about 17 lb 6 oz (8 kg) and stood about 35.4 in (90 cm) high. Other flightless birds were much bigger. The two heaviest, at almost 1,102 lb 5 oz (500 kg) were the elephant bird (Aepyornis maximus) that became extinct from Madagascar 350 years ago, and the emu-like Dromornis stirtoni from Australia. The tallest, but more lightly built, was the biggest of the moas of New Zealand, Dinornis maximus, that became extinct when the Maoris colonized the country, but prior to European settlement; there is thus no account of any living moa, and all evidence is based on discoveries of bones.

March of the penguins
The emperor penguin, the tallest and heaviest penguin species, is noted for the mass land trek of entire colonies during the breeding season.

TOP 10 LONGEST BIRD MIGRATIONS

SPECIES / SCIENTIFIC NAME	APPROX. DISTANCE MILES	APPROX. DISTANCE KM
1 Pectoral sandpiper (Calidris melanotos)	11,806	19,000*
2 Wheatear (Oenanthe oenanthe)	11,184	18,000
3 Slender-billed shearwater (Puffinus tenuirostris)	10,874	17,500*
4 Ruff (Philomachus pugnax)	10,314	16,600
5 Willow warbler (Phylloscopus trochilus)	10,128	16,300
6 Arctic tern (Sterna paradisaea)	10,066	16,200
7 Parasitic Jaeger (Stercorarius parasiticus)	9,693	15,600
8 Swainson's hawk (Buteo swainsoni)	9,445	15,200
9 Knot (Calidris canutus)	9,320	15,000
10 Barn swallow (Hirundo rustica)	9,258	14,900

* Thought to be only half of the path taken during a whole year

Source: Chris Mead

This list is of the likely extremes for a normal migrant, not one that has become lost and wandered into new territory. Many species fly all year, except when they come to land to breed or, in the case of seabirds, to rest on the sea; such species include some types of swift and house martin, the albatross, petrel, and tern.

TOP 10 COUNTRIES WITH THE MOST BIRD SPECIES

COUNTRY / BIRD SPECIES

1 Colombia 1,897
2 Peru 1,881
3 Brazil 1,772
4 Ecuador 1,670
5 Indonesia 1,632
USA 1,058

6 Bolivia 1,449
7 Venezuela 1,417
8 China 1,319
9 India 1,302
10 Dem. Rep. of Congo 1,174

Source: Avibase

Andean condor
The Andean condor is the largest flighted bird in the western hemisphere.

Above right: Great horned owl
Found across the Americas, the great horned is one of the largest owls.

TOP 10 **LARGEST BIRDS OF PREY***

BIRD / SCIENTIFIC NAME	MAX. LENGTH IN	CM
1 Himalayan Griffon vulture (*Gyps himalayensis*)	59	150
2 Californian condor (*Gymnogyps californianus*)	53	134
3 Andean condor (*Vultur gryphus*)	51	130
4 = Lammergeier (*Gypaetus barbatus*)	45	115
= Lappet-faced vulture (*Torgos tracheliotus*)	45	115
6 Eurasian Griffon vulture (*Gyps fulvus*)	43	110
7 European black vulture (*Aegypus monachus*)	42	107
8 Harpy eagle (*Harpia harpyja*)	41	105
9 Wedge-tailed eagle (*Aquila audax*)	41	104
10 Ruppell's griffon (*Gyps rueppellii*)	40	101

* By length, diurnal only—hence excluding owls

TOP 10 **LARGEST OWLS**

OWL / SCIENTIFIC NAME*	WINGSPAN IN	CM	WEIGHT LB	OZ	KG
1 Eurasian eagle-owl (*Bubo bubo*)	29	75	9	4	4.20
2 Verraux's eagle-owl (*Bubo lacteus*)	26	65	6	14	3.11
3 Snowy owl (*Bubo scandiacus*)	28	70	6	8	2.95
4 Great horned owl (*Bubo virginianus*)	24	60	5	8	2.50
5 Pel's fishing-owl (*Scotopelia peli*)	25	63	5	2	2.32
6 Pharaoh eagle-owl (*Bubo ascalaphus*)	20	50	5	1	2.30
7 Cape eagle-owl (*Bubo capensis*)	23	58	3	15	1.80
8 Great grey owl (*Strix nebulosa*)	27	69	3	12	1.70
9 Powerful owl (*Ninox strenua*)	24	60	3	5	1.50
10 Ural owl (*Strix uralensis*)	24	62	2	14	1.30

* Some owls closely related to these species may be of similar size; most measurements are from female owls as they are usually larger

Source: Chris Mead

Pets

TOP 10 PET DOG POPULATIONS

COUNTRY	ESTIMATED PET DOG POPULATION (2005)
1 USA	63,010,000
2 Brazil	31,408,300
3 China	26,153,600
4 Mexico	16,581,800
5 Japan	12,780,000
6 Russia	11,200,000
7 France	8,495,000
8 Philippines	7,690,000
9 South Africa	7,300,000
10 Thailand	7,440,000

Source: Euromonitor

TOP 10 PET CAT POPULATIONS

COUNTRY	ESTIMATED PET CAT POPULATION (2005)
1 USA	81,420,000
2 China	58,180,100
3 Russia	17,100,000
4 Brazil	12,234,000
5 Japan	11,500,000
6 France	9,960,000
7 UK	9,200,000
8 Germany	7,600,000
9 Ukraine	7,470,000
10 Italy	7,430,000

Source: Euromonitor

TOP 10 TYPES OF PET IN THE USA

PET / ESTIMATED NUMBER

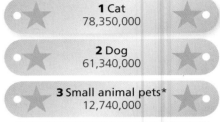

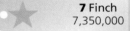

- **1** Cat 78,350,000
- **2** Dog 61,340,000
- **3** Small animal pets* 12,740,000
- **4** Parakeet 11,000,000
- **5** Freshwater fish 10,800,000"
- **6** Reptile 7,540,000
- **7** Finch 7,350,000
- **8** Cockatiel 6,320,000
- **9** Canary 2,580,000
- **10** Parrot 1,550,000

* Includes small rodents—rabbits, ferrets, hamsters, guinea pigs, and gerbils
\# Number of households owning, rather than individual specimens

TOP 10 PET BIRD POPULATIONS

COUNTRY / ESTIMATED PET BIRD POPULATION (2005)

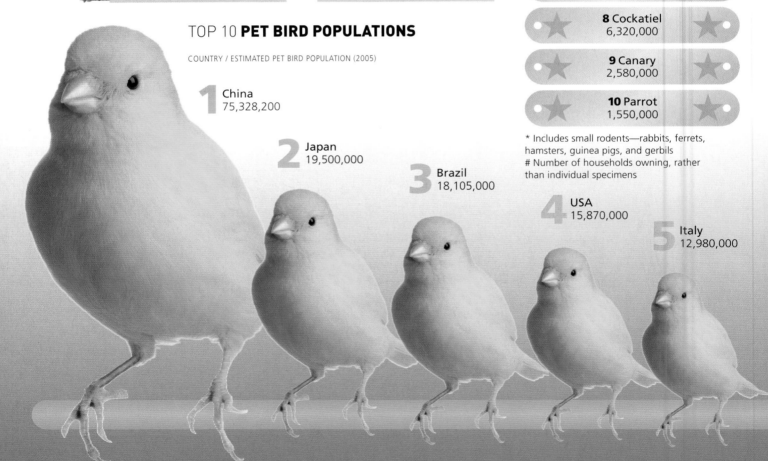

1 China 75,328,200

2 Japan 19,500,000

3 Brazil 18,105,000

4 USA 15,870,000

5 Italy 12,980,000

TOP 10 **PET FISH POPULATIONS**

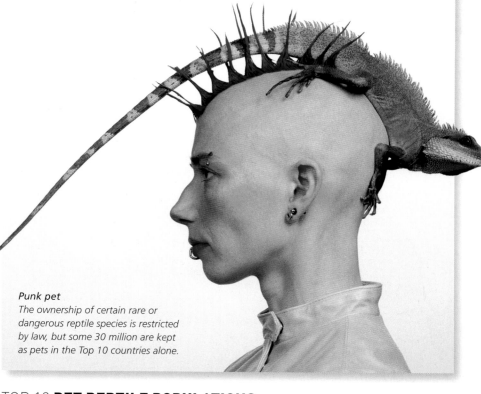

Punk pet
The ownership of certain rare or dangerous reptile species is restricted by law, but some 30 million are kept as pets in the Top 10 countries alone.

	COUNTRY	ESTIMATED PET FISH POPULATION (2005)
1	USA	147,290,000
2	China	140,778,200
3	Germany	53,500,000
4	France	35,910,000
5	Japan	34,550,000
6	Italy	29,400,000
7	UK	21,800,000
8	Russia	20,600,000
9	Philippines	19,552,300
10	Australia	13,600,000

Source: Euromonitor

TOP 10 **PET REPTILE POPULATIONS**

	COUNTRY	ESTIMATED PET REPTILE POPULATION (2005)			
1	USA	18,371,000	6	Russia	600,000
2	China	4,682,100	7	Spain	234,000
3	UK	2,010,000	8	Australia	215,000
4	France	1,500,000	9	Canada	196,000
5	Italy	1,400,000	10	Thailand	195,000

Source: Euromonitor

6 Turkey 10,437,000   **7 Spain** 7,900,000   **8 Australia** 7,850,000   **9 France** 6,590,000   **10 Germany** 4,100,000

Source: Euromonitor

Snakes & Reptiles

TOP 10 **LARGEST REPTILE FAMILIES**

	FAMILY	KNOWN SPECIES
1	Colubridae (snakes)	1,827
2	Scincidae (skinks)	1,305
3	Gekkonidae (geckos)	1,076
4	Polychrotidae (anole lizards)	393
5	Agamidae (lizards)	381
6	Tropiduridae (lizards)	309
7	Lacertidae (true lizards)	279
8	Viperidae (viperid snakes)	259
9	Typhlopidae (blind snakes)	233
10	Gymnophthalmidae (spectacled lizards)	193

The *Colubridae* family encompasses approximately half of all known snake species, from grass snakes to garter snakes, with examples found on every continent except Antarctica.

Tokay gecko
The nocturnal tree-dwelling gecko is found throughout Southeast Asia and is an invasive species in several US states.

TOP 10 **FROGS AND TOADS WITH THE LARGEST CLUTCH SIZES***

	SPECIES / SCIENTIFIC NAME	EGG SIZE (MM)	AVERAGE NO. OF EGGS IN CLUTCH
1	River frog (*Rana fuscigula*)	1.50	15,000
2	Crawfish frog (*Rana areolata*)	1.84	6,000
3	Gulf Coast toad (*Bufo valliceps*)	1.23	4,100
4	Bahia Forest frog (*Macrogenioglottus alipioi*)	1.50	3,650
5	Giant African bullfrog (*Pyxicephalus adspersus*)	2.00	3,500
6	Marbled or veined tree frog (*Phrynohyas venulosa*)	1.60	2,920
7	Mangrove or crab-eating frog (*Rana cancrivora*)	1.25	2,527
8	Cape sand frog (*Tomopterna delalandii*)	1.50	2,500
9	Gladiator frog (*Hyla rosenbergi*)	1.95	2,350
10 =	Wood frog (*Rana sylvatica*)	1.90	1,750
=	Yosemite toad (*Bufo canorus*)	2.00	1,750

* For which data are available; all eggs and larvae aquatic

TOP 10 **LIZARDS WITH THE LARGEST CLUTCH SIZES**

	SPECIES* / SCIENTIFIC NAME	AVERAGE NO. OF EGGS IN CLUTCH
1	Nile monitor (*Varanus niloticus*)	40–60
2	Senegal chameleon (*Chamaeleo senegalensis*)	7–60
3	Flap-necked chameleon (*Chamaeleo dilepis*)	23–50
4	Mexican spiny-tailed iguana (*Ctenosaura pectinata*)	49
5	Green iguana (*Iguana iguana*)	24–45
6	Texas horned lizard (*Phrynosoma cornutum*)	14–37
7	Common tegu (*Tupinambis teguixin*)	6–32
8	Short-horned lizard (*Phrynosoma douglassi*)	5–31
9	Spiny-tailed iguana (*Ctenosaura similis*)	20–30
10	Spiny-tailed or black iguana (*Ctenosaura acanthura*)	17–28

* For which data available, ranked by maxima

Green mamba
The dendrotoxin in the venom of the green mamba is less deadly than that of the black mamba, but still potentially lethal.

TOP 10 **COUNTRIES WITH THE MOST REPTILE SPECIES**

	COUNTRY	REPTILE SPECIES
1	Australia	880
2	Mexico	837
3	Indonesia	749
4	Brazil	651
5	India	521
6	Colombia	518
7	China	424
8	Ecuador	419
9	Malaysia	388
10	Madagascar	383
	USA	*360*

Source: World Conservation Monitoring Centre of the United Nations Environment Programme (UNEP-WCMC)

The world total of reptile species is 8,240. This includes lizards (4,765 species), snakes (2,978), turtles (307), crocodiles (23), and tuataras (2). Although found on every continent except Antarctica, the number of species in each country ranges from the Top 10 down to those with few representatives, such as Ireland, famously having no snakes and just six reptiles.

THE 10 **MOST VENOMOUS REPTILES AND AMPHIBIANS**

CREATURE* / TOXIN / FATAL AMOUNT (MG)#

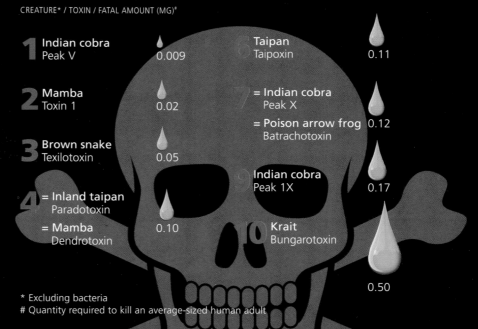

1 Indian cobra
Peak V — 0.009

2 Mamba
Toxin 1 — 0.02

3 Brown snake
Texilotoxin — 0.05

4 = Inland taipan
Paradotoxin

= Mamba
Dendrotoxin — 0.10

6 Taipan
Taipoxin — 0.11

7 = Indian cobra
Peak X

= Poison arrow frog 0.12
Batrachotoxin

Indian cobra
Peak 1X — 0.17

Krait
Bungarotoxin — 0.50

* Excluding bacteria
# Quantity required to kill an average-sized human adult

The venom of these creatures is almost unbelievably powerful: 1 mg (the approximate weight of a banknote) of Mamba Toxin 1 would be sufficient to kill 50 people. Other than reptiles, such creatures as scorpions (0.5 mg) and black widow spiders (1.0 mg) fall just outside the Top 10. Were bacteria included, 12 kg (26 lb) of the deadly Botulinus Toxin A (fatal dose just 0.000002 mg) would easily kill the entire population of the world. Even deadly poisons such as strychnine (35 mg) and cyanide (700 mg) seem relatively innocuous in comparison.

Insects & Spiders

TOP 10 **DEADLIEST SPIDERS**

SPIDER / SCIENTIFIC NAME / RANGE

1 Banana spider (*Phonenutria nigriventer*)
Central and South America

2 Sydney funnelweb (*Atrax robustus*)
Australia

3 Wolf spider (*Lycosa raptoria/erythrognatha*)
Central and South America

4 Black widow (*Latrodectus sp.*)
Widespread

5 Violin spider/Recluse spider (*Loxosceles reclusa*)
Widespread

6 Sac spider (*Cheiracanthium punctorium*)
Central Europe

7 Tarantula (*Eurypelma rubropilosum*)
Neotropics

8 Tarantula (*Acanthoscurria atrox*)
Neotropics

9 Tarantula (*Lasiodora klugi*)
Neotropics

10 Tarantula (*Pamphobeteus sp.*)
Neotropics

This list ranks spiders according to their "lethal potential"—
their venom yield divided by their venom potency.

Sydney funnelweb spider
Australia's deadliest spider can kill in minutes.

TOP 10 **LARGEST SPIDERS**

SPECIES / SCIENTIFIC NAME	LEG SPAN IN	MM
1 Huntsman spider (*Heteropoda maxima*)	11.8	300
2 Brazilian salmon pink (*Lasiodora parahybana*)	10.6	270
3 Brazilian giant tawny red (*Grammostola mollicoma*)	10.2	260
4 = Goliath tarantula or bird-eating spider (*Theraphosa blondi*)	10.0	254
= Wolf spider (*Cupiennius sallei*)	10.0	254
6 = Purple bloom bird-eating (*Xenesthis immanis*)	9.1	230
= Xenesthis monstrosa	9.1	230
8 Hercules baboon (*Hysterocrates hercules*)	8.0	203
9 Hysterocrates sp.	7.0	178
10 Tegenaria parietin	5.5	140

TOP 10 **LARGEST BUTTERFLIES**

BUTTERFLY / SCIENTIFIC NAME	APPROX. WINGSPAN IN	MM
1 Queen Alexandra's birdwing (*Ornithoptera alexandrae*)	11.0	280
2 African giant swallowtail (*Papilio antimachus*)	9.1	230
3 Goliath birdwing (*Ornithoptera goliath*)	8.3	210
4 = Buru opalescent birdwing (*Troides prattorum*)	7.9	200
= Birdwing (*Trogonoptera trojana*)	7.9	200
= Birdwing (*Troides hypolitus*)	7.9	200
7 = Chimaera birdwing (*Ornithoptera chimaera*)	7.5	190
= *Ornithoptera lydius*	7.5	190
= *Troides magellanus*	7.5	190
= *Troides miranda*	7.5	190

TOP 10 **LARGEST MOTHS**

MOTH / SCIENTIFIC NAME	WINGSPAN IN	MM
1 Atlas moth (*Attacus atlas*)	11.8	300
2 Owlet moth (*Thysania agrippina*)*	11.4	290
3 *Haematopis grataria*	10.2	260
4 Hercules emperor moth (*Coscinocera hercules*)	8.3	210
5 Malagasy silk moth (*Argema mitraei*)	7.1	180
6 *Eacles imperialis*	6.9	175
7 = Common emperor moth (*Bunaea alcinoe*)	6.3	160
= Giant peacock moth (*Saturnia pyri*)	6.3	160
9 Gray moth (*Brahmaea wallichii*)	6.1	155
10= Black witch (*Ascalapha odorata*)	5.9	150
= Regal moth (*Citheronia regalis*)	5.9	150
= Polyphemus moth (*Antheraea polyphemus*)	5.9	150

* Exceptional specimen measured at 12.2 in (308 mm)

ACTUAL SIZE

Top: Atlas moth
The Southeast Asian atlas moth is the largest of all members of the Lepidoptera order.

Left: Queen Alexandra's birdwing
The Papua New Guinean Queen Alexandra's birdwing has the greatest wingspan of any butterfly species.

ACTUAL SIZE

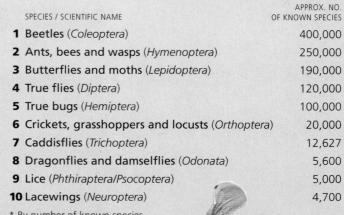

TOP 10 **MOST COMMON INSECTS***

SPECIES / SCIENTIFIC NAME	APPROX. NO. OF KNOWN SPECIES
1 Beetles (*Coleoptera*)	400,000
2 Ants, bees and wasps (*Hymenoptera*)	250,000
3 Butterflies and moths (*Lepidoptera*)	190,000
4 True flies (*Diptera*)	120,000
5 True bugs (*Hemiptera*)	100,000
6 Crickets, grasshoppers and locusts (*Orthoptera*)	20,000
7 Caddisflies (*Trichoptera*)	12,627
8 Dragonflies and damselflies (*Odonata*)	5,600
9 Lice (*Phthiraptera/Psocoptera*)	5,000
10 Lacewings (*Neuroptera*)	4,700

* By number of known species

Farm Animals

TOP 10 SHEEP COUNTRIES

COUNTRY	SHEEP (2007)
1 China	171,961,203
2 Australia	100,000,000
3 India	64,269,000
4 Iran	52,220,000
5 Sudan	49,000,000
6 New Zealand	40,000,000
7 UK	33,582,000
8 Pakistan	26,500,000
9 Turkey	25,400,000
10 South Africa	25,000,000
Top 10 total	*587,932,203*
World total	*1,112,520,621*

Source (all lists): Food and Agriculture
Organization of the United Nations

TOP 10 CATTLE COUNTRIES

COUNTRY	CATTLE (2007)
1 Brazil	207,170,000
2 India	177,840,000
3 China	116,861,393
4 USA	97,003,000
5 Argentina	50,750,000
6 Ethiopia	43,000,000
7 Sudan	39,500,000
8 Pakistan	29,600,000
9 Mexico	29,000,000
10 Australia	28,400,000
Top 10 total	*819,124,393*
World total	*1,389,590,364*

TOP 10 HORSE COUNTRIES

COUNTRY	HORSES (2007)
1 USA	9,500,000
2 China	7,197,465
3 Mexico	6,350,000
4 Brazil	5,800,000
5 Argentina	3,680,000
6 Colombia	2,500,000
7 Mongolia	2,114,800
8 Ethiopia	1,600,000
9 Russia	1,303,837
10 Kazakhstan	1,235,600
Top 10 total	*41,281,702*
World total	*58,408,987*

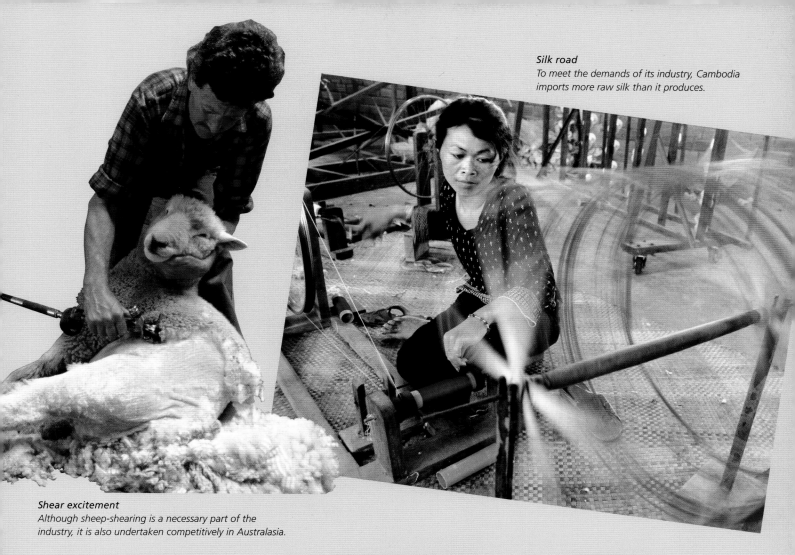

Silk road
To meet the demands of its industry, Cambodia imports more raw silk than it produces.

Shear excitement
Although sheep-shearing is a necessary part of the industry, it is also undertaken competitively in Australasia.

TOP 10 WOOL-PRODUCTION COUNTRIES

	COUNTRY	PRODUCTION 2007 (TONS)
1	Australia	481,710
2	China	435,413
3	New Zealand	240,194
4	Iran	82,673
5	UK	68,343
6	Russia	57,320
7	Uruguay	55,116
8 =	Sudan	50,706
=	Turkey	50,706
10	India	50,155
	USA	19,290
	Top 10 total	1,572,337
	World total	2,242,407

Australia and New Zealand, two relative newcomers to the wool-production industry, today supply one-third of the world market.

TOP 10 BEEHIVE COUNTRIES

	COUNTRY	BEEHIVES (2007)
1	India	9,800,000
2	China	7,407,000
3	Turkey	5,120,000
4	Ethiopia	4,400,000
5	Iran	3,500,000
6	Russia	3,155,007
7	Argentina	2,970,000
8	Tanzania	2,700,000
9 =	Kenya	2,500,000
=	Spain	2,500,000
	USA	2,400,000
	Top 10 total	44,052,007
	World total	72,642,755

In 2007, world honey production stood at 1,182,799 tons—about a third of the total in China—and that of beeswax 67,389 tons.

TOP 10 SILKWORM COUNTRIES

	COUNTRY	PRODUCTION* 2007 (TONS)
1	India	84,878
2	Uzbekistan	19,842
3	Brazil	8,818
4	Iran	6,614
5	Thailand	5,512
6	Vietnam	3,307
7	North Korea	1,543
8 =	Afghanistan	551
=	Japan	551
10	Cambodia	331
	Top 10 total	131,947
	World total	132,967

* Reelable cocoons

Fruit & Nuts

TOP 10 **FRUIT-PRODUCING COUNTRIES**

COUNTRY /
PRODUCTION* 2007
(TONS)

1 China
104,077,588

2 India
56,374,185

3 Brazil
40,585,288

4 USA
27,515,961

5 Italy
19,721,725

6 Spain
16,857,757

7 Mexico
16,580,191

8 Turkey
13,657,669

9 Iran
13,340,502

10 Indonesia
12,803,346

*Top 10 total
321,514,212*

*World total
550,837,472*

* Excluding melons

TOP 10 **ORANGE-PRODUCING COUNTRIES**

COUNTRY / PRODUCTION 2007 (TONS)

1 Brazil
20,149,489

2 USA
8,109,704

3 Mexico
4,585,615

4 India
4,299,014

5 China
3,158,122

6 Spain
2,966,761

7 Indonesia
2,866,009

8 Iran
2,535,316

9 Italy
2,528,114

10 Egypt
1,984,160

Top 10 total 53,182,304
World total 70,444,377

The world's orange crop is equivalent to 12,781 Olympic-sized swimming pools full of juice.

TOP 10 **APPLE-PRODUCING COUNTRIES**

Top 10 total 52,300,336
World total 70,829,586

COUNTRY / PRODUCTION 2007 (TONS)

1 China
30,321,277

2 USA
4,671,298

3 Iran
2,932,148

4 Turkey
2,498,319

5 Russia
2,437,210

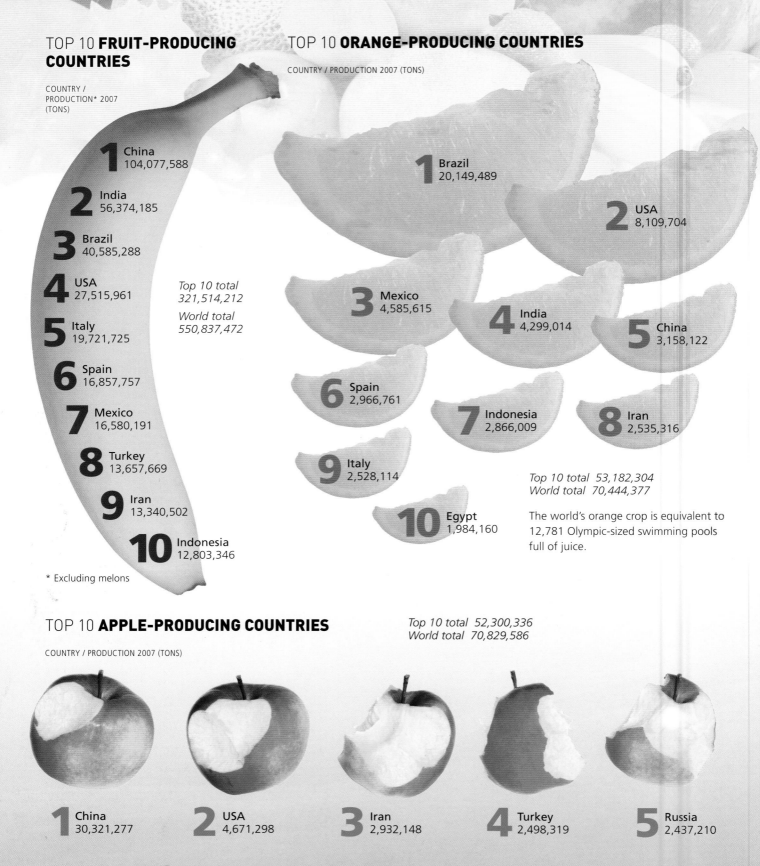

TOP 10 **COCONUT-PRODUCING COUNTRIES**

COUNTRY / PRODUCTION 2007 (TONS)

1 Indonesia
18,739292

2 Philippines
17,174,010

3 India
10,361,726

7
Sri Lanka
1,051,605

6
Vietnam
1,060,423

5
Thailand
1,879,932

4
Brazil
3,054,013

Top 10 total
55,509,091

World total
60,314,555

8 Papua New Guinea
746,265

9 Malaysia
626,113

10 = Myanmar
407,855
= Tanzania
407,855

TOP 10 **NUT-PRODUCING COUNTRIES**

COUNTRY / PRODUCTION 2007 (TONS)

1 USA
130,073

2 Indonesia
114,640

3 Mexico
105,822

4 Ethiopia
82,673

5 China
55,116

6 Australia
41,888

7 Guatemala
29,762

8 Portugal
26,455

9 Thailand
25,353

10 Philippines
15,432

Top 10 total 627,215
World total 799,239

Source (all lists): Food and Agriculture
Organization of the United Nations

6 Italy
2,284,540

7 India
2,206,166

8 France
1,984,160

9 Chile
1,532,212

10 Argentina
1,433,005

Trees & Forests

TOP 10 **COUNTRIES WITH THE LARGEST AREAS OF FOREST**

COUNTRY / SQ MILES/SQ KM / % OF TOTAL

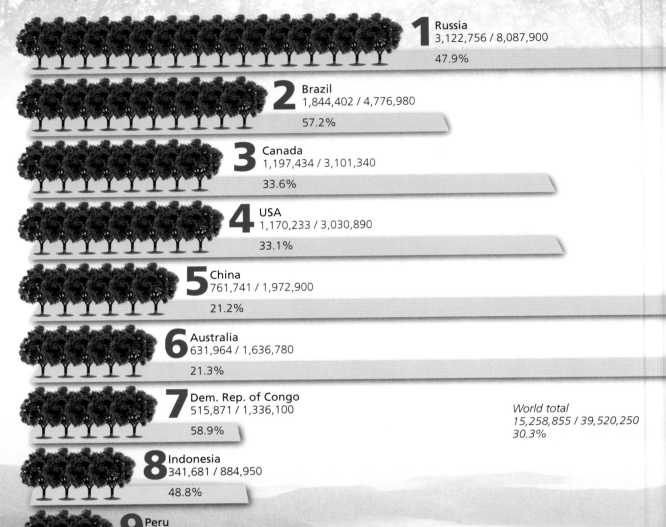

1 Russia
3,122,756 / 8,087,900
47.9%

2 Brazil
1,844,402 / 4,776,980
57.2%

3 Canada
1,197,434 / 3,101,340
33.6%

4 USA
1,170,233 / 3,030,890
33.1%

5 China
761,741 / 1,972,900
21.2%

6 Australia
631,964 / 1,636,780
21.3%

7 Dem. Rep. of Congo
515,871 / 1,336,100
58.9%

8 Indonesia
341,681 / 884,950
48.8%

9 Peru
265,414 / 687,420
53.7%

10 India
261,395 / 677,010
22.8%

World total
15,258,855 / 39,520,250
30.3%

Source: Food and Agriculture Organization of the United Nations, *Global Forest Resources Assessment 2005*

Mangroves
Large areas of the world's mangroves have been cleared for coconut growing, chopped down for fuel or destroyed by shrimp farming.

Tall tree
Species of North American sequoia are the tallest trees in the world.

TOP 10 **COUNTRIES WITH THE LARGEST AREAS OF MANGROVE**

COUNTRY	MANGROVE AREA (HECTARES)
1 Indonesia	3,062,300
2 Australia	1,451,411
3 Brazil	1,012,376
4 Nigeria	997,700
5 Mexico	882,032
6 Malaysia	564,971
7 Cuba	545,805
8 Myanmar	518,646
9 Bangladesh	476,215
10 India	446,100
USA	*197,648*
Top 10 total	*9,957,556*
World total	*15,705,000*

Source: Food and Agriculture Organization of the United Nations, *The World's Mangroves 1980–2005, 2007*

A total of 124 countries have been identified as having mangroves—species of trees and shrubs that are specially adapted to growing in saline coasts of tropical and subtropical regions. A survey conducted in 1980 put the global total mangrove area at 18.8 million hectares, so over three million hectares have been lost in the past 30 years.

TOP 10 **TALLEST TREES IN THE USA**

SPECIES* / LOCATION	HEIGHT FT	M
1 Coast redwood (*Sequoia sempervirens*) Jedediah Smith Redwoods State Park, CA	321	97.8
2 Coast Douglas-fir (*Pseudotsuga menziesii var menziesii*) Jedediah Smith Redwoods State Park, CA	301	91.7
3 Giant sequoia (*Sequoiadendron giganteum*) Sequoia National Park, CA	274	83.5
4 Noble fir (*Abies procera*) Mt. St. Helens National Monument, WA	272	82.9
5 Grand fir (*Abies grandis*) Redwood National Park, CA	257	78.3
6 Port Orford cedar (*Chamaecyparis lawsoniana*) Siskiyou National Forest, OR	242	73.8
7 Ponderosa pine (*Pinus ponderosa var. ponderosa*) Trinity, CA	240	73.2
8 Western hemlock (*Tsuga heterophylla*) Olympic National Park, WA	237	72.2
9 Pacific silver fir (*Abies amabilis*) Olympic National Park, WA	218	66.4
10 California white fir (*Abies concolor var. lowiana*) Yosemite National Park, CA	217	66.1

* Tallest example of each species only

TOP 10 **MOST COMMON TREES IN THE USA**

TREE / SCIENTIFIC NAME
1 Silver maple (*Acer saccharinum*)
2 Black cherry (*Prunus serotina*)
3 Box elder (*Acer negundo*)
4 Eastern cottonwood (*Populus deltoides*)
5 Black willow (*Salix nigra*)
6 Northern red oak (*Quercus rubra*)
7 Flowering dogwood (*Cornus florida*)
8 Black oak (*Quercus kelloggii*)
9 Ponderosa pine (*Pinus ponderosa*)
10 Coast Douglas fir (*Pseudotsuga menziesii*)

Source: American Forests

Hardwood trees native to the eastern and southern states prevail in this list, while the Ponderosa pine and Douglas fir are softwoods most typical of the northwest coast forests.

THE HUMAN WORLD

3

Human Extremes

TOP 10 **TALLEST PEOPLE**

NAME / DATES / COUNTRY	FT	HEIGHT IN	CM
1 Robert Pershing Wadlow (1918–40) USA	8	11.2	274
2 John William Rogan (1868–1905) USA	8	9.8	268
3 John Aasen (1887–1938) USA	8	9.7	267
4 John F. Carroll (1932–69) USA	8	7.6	264
5 Al Tomaini (1918–62) USA	8	4.4	255
6 Trijntje Keever* (1616-33) Netherlands	8	3.3	254
7 Edouard Beaupré (1881–1904) Canada	8	2.5	250
8 = Bernard Coyne (1897–1921) USA	8	1.2	249
= Don Koehler (1925–81) USA	8	1.2	249
10 = Jeng Jinlian* (1964–82) China	8	1.1	248
= Väinö Myllyrinne (1909–63) Finland	8	1.1	248

* Female; all others male

Robert Wadlow
Photographed in 1938, actress Maureen O'Sullivan (5 ft 3 in/1.6 m) is dwarfed by world's tallest man Robert Wadlow.

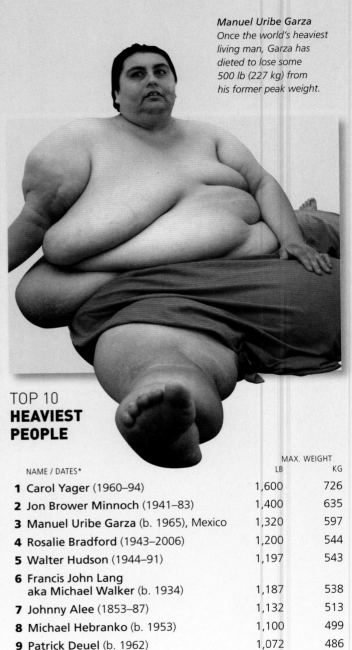

Manuel Uribe Garza
Once the world's heaviest living man, Garza has dieted to lose some 500 lb (227 kg) from his former peak weight.

TOP 10 HEAVIEST PEOPLE

NAME / DATES*	MAX. WEIGHT LB	KG
1 Carol Yager (1960–94)	1,600	726
2 Jon Brower Minnoch (1941–83)	1,400	635
3 Manuel Uribe Garza (b. 1965), Mexico	1,320	597
4 Rosalie Bradford (1943–2006)	1,200	544
5 Walter Hudson (1944–91)	1,197	543
6 Francis John Lang aka Michael Walker (b. 1934)	1,187	538
7 Johnny Alee (1853–87)	1,132	513
8 Michael Hebranko (b. 1953)	1,100	499
9 Patrick Deuel (b. 1962)	1,072	486
10 Robert Earl Hughes (1926–58)	1,069	485

* All USA unless otherwise stated

Precise weights of certain people were exaggerated for commercial reasons or never verified, while some were so huge that they could not be moved, or broke the scales, but these are the main contenders for the list of "world's heaviest," based on records of their peak weights. Some later dieted and reduced their weights—in the case of Rosalie Bradford, down from her 1987 peak to 283 lb (128 kg) in 1994.

Sarah Knauss
The longest-lived American with her great-great-grandson, shortly before her death at the age of 119.

THE 10 **MOST OBESE COUNTRIES—ADULTS**

	COUNTRY	% OF OBESE ADULTS*	
		MEN	WOMEN
1	Tonga	46.6	70.3
2	Samoa	32.9	63.0
3	Nauru	55.7	60.5
4	Qatar	34.6	45.3
5	Saudi Arabia	26.4	44.0
6	Lebanon	36.3	38.3
7	Paraguay	22.9	35.7
8	Albania#	22.8	35.6
9	Mexico	24.4	34.5
10	Seychelles	14.7	34.2
	USA	*31.1*	*33.2*

* Ranked by percentage of obese women (those with a BMI greater than 30) in those countries and latest year for which data available
# Urban population

Source: International Obesity Task Force (IOTF)

THE 10 **OLDEST WOMEN IN THE WORLD***

	NAME / COUNTRY	BORN	DIED	YRS	AGE MTHS	DAYS
1	Jeanne Calment, France	Feb 21, 1875	Aug 4, 1997	122	5	14
2	Sarah Knauss, USA	Sep 24, 1880	Dec 30, 1999	119	3	6
3	Lucy Hannah, USA	Jul 16, 1875	Mar 21, 1993	117	8	5
4	Marie-Louise Meilleur, Canada	Aug 29, 1880	Apr 16, 1998	117	7	19
5	María Capovilla, Ecuador	Sep 14, 1889	Aug 27, 2006	116	11	13
6	Tane Ikai, Japan	Jan 18, 1879	Jul 12, 1995	116	5	24
7	Elizabeth Bolden, USA	Aug 15, 1890	Dec 11, 2006	116	3	26
8	Maggie Barnes, USA	Mar 6, 1882	Jan 19, 1998	115	10	13
9	Charlotte Hughes, UK	Aug 1, 1877	Mar 17, 1993	115	7	16
10	Edna Parker, USA	Apr 20, 1893	Nov 26, 2008	115	7	6

* Includes only women whose birth and death dates are undisputed

THE 10 **OLDEST MEN IN THE WORLD***

	NAME / COUNTRY	BORN	DIED	YRS	AGE MTHS	DAYS
1	Christian Mortensen, Denmark/USA	Aug 16, 1882	Apr 25, 1998	115	8	9
2	Emiliano Mercado Del Toro, Puerto Rico	Aug 21, 1891	Jan 24, 2007	115	5	3
3	Yukichi Chuganji, Japan	Mar 23, 1889	Sep 28, 2003	114	6	5
4	Joan Riudavets, Spain	Dec 15, 1889	Mar 5, 2004	114	2	19
5	Fred H. Hale, USA	Dec 1, 1890	Nov 19, 2004	113	11	18
6	Johnson Parks, USA	Oct 15, 1884	Jul 17, 1998	113	9	2
7	John Ingram McMorran, USA	Jun 19, 1889	Feb 24, 2003	113	8	5
8	Tomoji Tanabe, Japan	Sep 18, 1895	#	113	6	27
9	Frederick L. Frazier, USA	Jan 27, 1880	Jun 14, 1993	113	4	18
10	Walter Richardson, USA	Nov 7, 1885	Dec 25, 1998	113	1	18

* Includes only men whose birth and death dates are undisputed
# Alive as of April 27, 2009

Joan Riudavets
Europe's longest-lived man was a retired cobbler from Minorca, Spain.

Life & Death

TOP 10 COUNTRIES WITH THE HIGHEST LIFE EXPECTANCY

COUNTRY	MALE	LIFE EXPECTANCY AT BIRTH (2010) FEMALE	BOTH
① Andorra	80.30	84.55	82.36
② Japan	78.87	85.66	82.17
③ = San Marino	78.63	81.75	82.06
= Singapore	79.45	84.87	82.06
⑤ Australia	79.33	84.25	81.72
⑥ Canada	78.72	84.00	81.29
⑦ France	77.91	84.44	81.09
⑧ = Sweden	78.69	83.40	80.97
= Switzerland	78.14	83.95	80.97
⑩ Iceland	78.63	83.04	80.79
USA	*75.78*	*80.81*	*78.24*
World average	*64.80*	*69.20*	*66.90*

Source: US Census Bureau, International Data Base

TOP 10 COUNTRIES WITH THE MOST BIRTHS

COUNTRY	ESTIMATED BIRTHS (2010)
① India	25,221,127
② China	19,216,255
③ Nigeria	5,490,479
④ Pakistan	4,829,240
⑤ Indonesia	4,482,766
⑥ USA	4,290,520
⑦ Ethiopia	3,814,505
⑧ Bangladesh	3,761,967
⑨ Brazil	3,641,981
⑩ Dem. Rep. of Congo	2,996,929
World	*135,994,165*

Source: US Census Bureau, International Data Base

TOP 10 COUNTRIES WITH THE MOST CREMATIONS

	COUNTRY	% OF DEATHS	CREMATIONS*
1	China#	50.00	4,543,795
2	Japan	99.81	1,193,697
3	USA	34.89	842,467
4	UK	72.49	417,920
5	Germany	40.10	338,469
6	Thailand	80.00	318,750
7	South Korea	58.91	144,255
8	France	27.33	141,862
9	Canada	56.00	120,714
10	Russia	46.50	113,110

* Estimated in latest year for which data available
# Including Taiwan

Source: The Cremation Society of Great Britain

THE 10 COUNTRIES WITH THE MOST DEATHS

	COUNTRY	ESTIMATED DEATHS (2010)
1	China	9,567,701
2	India	7,199,270
3	USA	2,599,751
4	Nigeria	2,482,665
5	Russia	2,235,819
6	Indonesia	1,518,552
7	Bangladesh	1,435,238
8	Pakistan	1,349,241
9	Brazil	1,277,006
10	Japan	1,246,488
	Top 10 total	*30,911,731*
	World	*55,956,426*

Source: US Census Bureau, International Data Base

The Top 10 countries account for some 55 percent of all deaths in the world.

TOP 10 COUNTRIES WITH THE GREATEST POPULATION GROWTH

	COUNTRY	GROWTH RATE % (2010)
1	Niger	3.66
2 =	Uganda	3.56
=	United Arab Emirates	3.56
4	Kuwait	3.50
5	Yemen	3.44
6	Ethiopia	3.20
7	Dem. Rep. of Congo	3.17
8	Burkina Faso	3.10
9 =	Oman	3.07
=	São Tomé and Príncipe	3.07
	USA	*0.98*
	World average	*1.16*

Source: US Census Bureau, International Data Base

Baby boom
With a growth rate of three times the world average, the population of Niger doubled between 1989 and 2009.

THE 10 MOST SUICIDAL COUNTRIES

	COUNTRY	SUICIDES PER 100,000 PER ANNUM*		
		MALE	FEMALE	TOTAL
1	Lithuania	68.1	12.9	38.6
2	Belarus	63.3	10.3	35.1
3	Russia	58.1	9.8	32.2
4	Slovenia	42.1	11.1	26.3
5	Hungary	42.3	11.2	26.0
6	Kazakhstan	45.0	8.1	25.9
7	Latvia	42.0	9.6	24.5
8	South Korea	29.6	14.1	21.9
9	Guyana	33.8	11.6	22.9
10	Ukraine	40.9	7.0	22.6
	USA	*17.7*	*4.5*	*11.0*

* In those countries/latest year for which data available

Source: World Health Organization

THE 10 COUNTRIES WITH THE HIGHEST INFANT MORTALITY

	COUNTRY	ESTIMATED DEATH RATE PER 1,000 LIVE BIRTHS (2010)
1	Angola	178.13
2	Sierra Leone	152.42
3	Afghanistan	149.28
4	Liberia	136.06
5	Niger	114.50
6	Somalia	107.42
7	Mozambique	103.82
8	Mali	100.30
9	Zambia	99.92
10	Guinea-Bissau	98.05
	USA	*6.18*
	World average	*39.70*

Source: US Census Bureau, International Data Base

For Better or For Worse

TOP 10 US STATES WITH MOST MARRIAGES

	STATE	MARRIAGES (2007)
1	California	225,832
2	Texas	179,904
3	Florida	157,610
4	Nevada	131,389
5	New York	130,584
6	Illinois	75,292
7	Pennsylvania	71,094
8	Ohio	70,905
9	North Carolina	68,131
10	Tennessee	65,551

Source: National Center for Health Statistics

TOP 10 MONTHS FOR MARRIAGES IN THE USA

	MONTH	MARRIAGES (2007)
1	June	238,000
2	July	234,000
3	September	221,000
4	August	214,000
5	May	212,000
6	October	195,000
7	April	171,000
8	March	156,000
9	December	150,000
10	November	148,000

Source: National Center for Health Statistics

Estimates for 2005 from a US total of some 2,194,000—an increase of 34,000 compared with the previous year. February was at No. 11 with 138,000, and January the least popular month with 117,000 marriages.

TOP 10 COUNTRIES WITH THE MOST MARRIAGES

	COUNTRY	MARRIAGES PER ANNUM*
1	USA	2,160,000
2	Bangladesh	1,181,000
3	Russia	1,001,589
4	Vietnam	964,701
5	Japan	757,331
6	Brazil	710,120
7	Iran	650,960
8	Ethiopia	630,290
9	Mexico	570,060
10	Egypt	525,412

* In those countries/latest year for which data available

Source: United Nations

THE 10 **COUNTRIES WITH THE HIGHEST DIVORCE RATES**

	COUNTRY	DIVORCE RATE PER 1,000*
1	Russia	5.30
2	Aruba	5.27
3	USA	4.19
4	Ukraine	3.79
5	Belarus	3.77
6	Moldova	3.50
7	Cuba	3.16
8	Czech Republic	3.11
9	= Lithuania	3.05
	= South Korea	3.05

* In those countries/latest year
for which data available

Source: United Nations

THE 10 **COUNTRIES WITH THE LOWEST MARRIAGE RATE**

	COUNTRY	MARRIAGES PER 1,000 PER ANNUM*
1	Colombia	1.7
2	= Dominican Republic	2.8
	= St. Lucia	2.8
	= Venezuela	2.8
5	= Andorra	2.9
	= Peru	2.9
7	United Arab Emirates	3.1
8	= Argentina	3.2
	= Slovenia	3.2
10	Panama	3.3

* In 2005 or latest year in those countries
for which data available

Source: United Nations

THE 10 **COUNTRIES WITH THE LOWEST DIVORCE RATES**

	COUNTRY	DIVORCE RATE PER 1,000*
1	Guatemala	0.12
2	Belize	0.17
3	Mongolia	0.28
4	Libya	0.32
5	Georgia	0.40
6	Chile	0.42
7	St. Vincent and the Grenadines	0.43
8	Jamaica	0.44
9	Armenia	0.47
10	Turkey	0.49

* In those countries/latest year for which
data available

Source: United Nations

The countries that figure among those with the lowest rates represent a range of cultures and religions, which either condone or condemn divorce to varying extents, thus affecting its prevalence or otherwise. In some countries, legal and other obstacles make divorce difficult or costly, while in certain societies—such as Jamaica, where the marriage rate is also low—partners often separate without the formality of divorce.

Names of the Decades

TOP 10 FIRST NAMES IN IN THE USA
1900s

BOYS		GIRLS
John	1	Mary
William	2	Helen
James	3	Margaret
George	4	Anna
Charles	5	Ruth
Robert	6	Elizabeth
Joseph	7	Dorothy
Frank	8	Marie
Edward	9	Florence
Thomas	10	Mildred

TOP 10 FIRST NAMES IN IN THE USA
1910s

BOYS		GIRLS
John	1	Mary
William	2	Helen
James	3	Dorothy
Robert	4	Margaret
Joseph	5	Ruth
George	6	Mildred
Charles	7	Anna
Edward	8	Elizabeth
Frank	9	Frances
Thomas	10	Virginia

TOP 10 FIRST NAMES IN IN THE USA
1920s

BOYS		GIRLS
Robert	1	Mary
John	2	Dorothy
James	3	Helen
William	4	Betty
Charles	5	Margaret
George	6	Ruth
Joseph	7	Virginia
Richard	8	Doris
Edward	9	Mildred
Donald	10	Frances

TOP 10 FIRST NAMES IN IN THE USA
1930s

BOYS		GIRLS
Robert	1	Mary
James	2	Betty
John	3	Barbara
William	4	Shirley
Richard	5	Patricia
Charles	6	Dorothy
Donald	7	Joan
George	8	Margaret
Thomas	9	Nancy
Joseph	10	Helen

TOP 10 FIRST NAMES IN IN THE USA
1940s

BOYS		GIRLS
James	1	Mary
Robert	2	Linda
John	3	Barbara
William	4	Patricia
Richard	5	Carol
David	6	Sandra
Charles	7	Nancy
Thomas	8	Judith
Michael	9	Sharon
Ronald	10	Judith

TOP 10 FIRST NAMES IN IN THE USA
1950s

BOYS		GIRLS
James	1	Mary
Michael	2	Linda
Robert	3	Patricia
John	4	Susan
David	5	Deborah
William	6	Barbara
Richard	7	Debra
Thomas	8	Karen
Mark	9	Nancy
Charles	10	Donna

TOP 10 FIRST NAMES IN IN THE USA
1960s

BOYS		GIRLS
Michael	1	Lisa
David	2	Mary
John	3	Susan
James	4	Karen
Robert	5	Kimberly
Mark	6	Patricia
William	7	Linda
Richard	8	Donna
Thomas	9	Michelle
Jeffrey	10	Cynthia

TOP 10 FIRST NAMES IN IN THE USA
1970s

BOYS		GIRLS
Michael	1	Jennifer
Christopher	2	Amy
Jason	3	Melissa
David	4	Michelle
James	5	Kimberly
John	6	Lisa
Robert	7	Angela
Brian	8	Heather
William	9	Stephanie
Matthew	10	Nicole

TOP 10 FIRST NAMES IN IN THE USA
1980s

BOYS		GIRLS
Michael	1	Jessica
Christopher	2	Jennifer
Matthew	3	Amanda
Joshua	4	Ashley
David	5	Sarah
James	6	Stephanie
Daniel	7	Melissa
Robert	8	Nicole
John	9	Elizabeth
Joseph	10	Heather

Changing Fashions

US Social Security records indicate that boys' names are less susceptible to changes in fashion than those of girls. Michael, for example, has been firmly in the Top 10 since the 1940s, while long-stayer William fell out of the Top 10 in 1976, the first time since records began. Jacob, today's No. 1, has been in the Top 100 for more than 100 years. In contrast, Emily, the present decade's No. 1, was not even in the Top 100 until 1973 or Madison, now at No. 2, until 1993. Emma is a returnee to the Top 10, having last appeared in 1896.

Source (all lists): Social Security Administration

TOP 10 FIRST NAMES IN IN THE USA
1990s

BOYS		GIRLS
Michael	1	Jessica
Christopher	2	Ashley
Matthew	3	Emily
Joshua	4	Sarah
Jacob	5	Samantha
Nicholas	6	Amanda
Andrew	7	Brittany
Daniel	8	Elizabeth
Tyler	9	Taylor
Joseph	10	Megan

TOP 10 FIRST NAMES IN IN THE USA
2000s

BOYS		GIRLS
Jacob	1	Emily
Michael	2	Madison
Joshua	3	Hannah
Matthew	4	Emma
Andrew	5	Ashley
Christopher	6	Abigail
Joseph	7	Alexis
Daniel	8	Olivia
Nicholas	9	Samantha
Ethan	10	Sara

Names Around the World

TOP 10 **SURNAMES IN FRANCE**

SURNAME / NO.	
1 Martin	235,846
2 Bernard	105,132
3 Dubois	95,998
4 Thomas	95,387
5 Robert	91,393
6 Richard	90,689
7 Petit	88,318
8 Durand	84,252
9 Leroy	78,868
10 Moreau	78,177

TOP 10 **SURNAMES IN SPAIN**

SURNAME / NO.	
1 García	813,257
2 Fernández	503,142
3 González	499,596
4 Rodríguez	482,448
5 López	467,681
6 Martínez	449,954
7 Sánchez	433,030
8 Pérez	421,997
9 Martín	278,261
10 Gómez	261,776

TOP 10 **SURNAMES IN GERMANY**

NAME / NO.	
1 Müller	78,107
2 Schmidt	56,730
3 Schneider	32,887
4 Fischer	28,776
5 Meyer	27,131
6 Weber	24,665
7 = Schulz	22,199
= Wagner	22,199
= Becker	22,199
10 Hoffmann	21,377

TOP 10 **SURNAMES IN ITALY**

SURNAME
1 Rossi
2 Russo
3 Ferrari
4 Esposito
5 Bianchi
6 Romano
7 Colombo
8 Ricci
9 Marino
10 Greco

TOP 10 **SURNAMES IN DENMARK**

SURNAME / NO.	
1 Jensen	288,050
2 Nielsen	283,928
3 Hansen	238,251
4 Pedersen	178,578
5 Andersen	168,761
6 Christensen	128,168
7 Larsen	125,438
8 Sørensen	119,929
9 Rasmussen	101,154
10 Jørgensen	95,244

Source: Statistics Denmark

TOP 10 **SURNAMES IN POLAND**

SURNAME / NO.	
1 Nowak	203,506
2 Kowalski	139,719
3 Wisniewski	109,855
4 Wójcik	99,509
5 Kowalczyk	97,796
6 Kaminski	94,499
7 Lewandowski	92,449
8 Zielinski	91,043
9 Szymanski	89,091
10 Wozniak	88,039

Source: Jaroslaw Maciej Zawadzki, *1000 Najpopularniejszych Nazwisk w Polsce* (2002)

TOP 10 **SURNAMES IN THE UK**

SURNAME / NO.	
1 Smith	729,862
2 Jones	578,261
3 Taylor	458,268
4 Williams	411,385
5 Brown	380,443
6 Davies	316,982*
7 Evans	231,844
8 Wilson	227,652
9 Thomas	220,228
10 Roberts	219,694

* There are also 108,041 people bearing the surname Davis

TOP 10 **SURNAMES IN THE USA**

SURNAME / NO.	
1 Smith	2,376,206
2 Johnson	1,857,160
3 Williams	1,534,042
4 Brown	1,380,145
5 Jones	1,362,755
6 Miller	1,127,803
7 Davis	1,072,335
8 Garcia	858,289
9 Rodriguez	804,240
10 Wilson	783,051

Source: US Census Bureau, Census 2000

TOP 10 **SURNAMES IN AUSTRALIA***

SURNAME / NO.	
1 Smith	114,997
2 Jones	56,698
3 Williams	55,555
4 Brown	54,896
5 Wilson	46,961
6 Taylor	45,328
7 Johnson	33,435
8 White	31,099
9 Martin	31,058
10 Anderson	30,910

* Based on occurrences on Australian electoral rolls

TOP 10 **SURNAMES IN CHINA**

SURNAME

1 Wáng
2 Li
3 Zhang
4 Liú
5 Chén
6 Yáng
7 Huáng
8 Zhào
9 Zhou
10 Wú

Source: Ministry of Public Security

Royalty

TOP 10 **LONGEST-REIGNING QUEENS***

1 THRONE = 10 YEARS	MONARCH	COUNTRY	REIGN	AGE AT ACCESSION	REIGN		
					YRS	MTHS	DAYS
	1 Victoria	UK	Jun 20, 1837–Jan 22, 1901	18	63	7	2
	2 Wilhelmina	Netherlands	Nov 23, 1890–Sep 4, 1948	10	57	9	12
	3 Elizabeth II	UK	Feb 6, 1952–#	25	57	1	25
	4 Salote Tupou III	Tonga	Apr 5, 1918–Dec 16, 1965	18	47	8	11
	5 Elizabeth I	England	Nov 17, 1558–Mar 24, 1603	25	44	4	7
	6 Maria Theresa	Hungary	Oct 20, 1740–Nov 29, 1780	23	40	1	9
	7 Maria I	Portugal	Feb 24, 1777–Mar 20, 1816	42	39	25	0
	8 Joanna I	Naples	Jan 20, 1343–May 12, 1382	16	39	3	22
	9 Isabella II	Spain	Sep 29, 1833–Sep 30, 1868†	2	35	0	1
	10 Catharine II	Russia	Jun 28, 1762–Nov 17, 1796	32	34	4	20

* Queens and empresses who ruled in their own right, not as consorts of kings or emperors, during past 1,000 years, excluding earlier rulers of dubious authenticity
\# Current; as at March 31, 2009 † Exiled; later abdicated

TOP 10 **LONGEST-REIGNING BRITISH MONARCHS**

MONARCH	REIGN	YRS	REIGN* MTHS	DAYS
1 Victoria	Jun 20, 1837–Jan 22, 1901	63	7	2
2 George III	Oct 25, 1760–Jan 29, 1820	59	3	4
3 Elizabeth II	Feb 6, 1952–	57	1	25
4 Henry III	Oct 18, 1216–Nov 16, 1272	56	0	29
5 Edward III	Jan 25, 1327–Jun 21, 1377	50	4	27

MONARCH	REIGN	YRS	MTHS	DAYS
6 Elizabeth I	Nov 17, 1558–Mar 24, 1603	44	4	7
7 Henry VI	Aug 31, 1422–Mar 4, 1461/ Oct 31, 1470–Apr 11, 1471	38	11	15
8 Henry VIII	Apr 22, 1509–Jan 28, 1547	37	9	6
9 Charles II	Jan 30, 1649–Sep 3, 1651#/ May 29, 1660–Feb 6, 1685	36	7	0
10 Henry I	Aug 2, 1100–Dec 1, 1135	35	3	29

* As at March 31, 2009
\# Reign in Scotland; discounting 1649–60 Interregnum

Young ruler
Crowned at the age of 28, King Jigme Khesar Namgyal Wangchuck of Bhutan became the world's youngest reigning monarch and head of state.

TOP 10 LONGEST-REIGNING LIVING MONARCHS

MONARCH	COUNTRY*	ACCESSION	REIGN# YRS	MTHS	DAYS
1 Bhumibol Adulyadej	Thailand	Jun 9, 1946	62	7	28
2 Elizabeth II	UK	Feb 6, 1952	57	1	25
3 Malietoa Tanumafili II	Samoa	Jan 1, 1962†	47	1	5
4 Haji Hassanal Bolkiah	Brunei	Oct 5, 1967	41	4	1
5 Sayyid Qaboos ibn Said al-Said	Oman	Jul 23, 1970	38	6	14
6 Margrethe II	Denmark	Jan 14, 1972	37	0	23
7 Carl XVI Gustaf	Sweden	Sep 15, 1973	35	4	22
8 Juan Carlos	Spain	Nov 22, 1975	33	2	15
9 Beatrix	Netherlands	Apr 30, 1980	28	9	7
10 Mswati	Swaziland	Mar 25, 1986	22	8	12

* Sovereign states only
# As at March 31, 2009
† Sole ruler since April 15, 1963

THE 10 LATEST MONARCHS TO ASCEND THE THRONE

MONARCH	COUNTRY*	ACCESSION
1 King Jigme Khesar Namgyal Wangchuck	Bhutan	Dec 15, 2006
2 Sultan Mizan Zainal Abidin	Malaysia	Dec 13, 2006
3 King George Tupou V	Tonga	Sep 11, 2006
4 Emir Sabah Al-Ahmad Al-Jaber Al-Sabah	Kuwait	Jan 29, 2006
5 Emir Mohammed bin Rashid Al Maktoum	Dubai	Jan 4, 2006
6 King Abdullah	Saudi Arabia	Aug 1, 2005
7 Prince Albert II	Monaco	Apr 6, 2005
8 King Norodom Sihamoni	Cambodia	Oct 14, 2004
9 Grand Duke Henri	Luxembourg	Oct 7, 2000
10 Mohammed VI	Morocco	Jul 23, 1999

* Sovereign states only

Malaysia has a unique system of "revolving monarchy," which was established following Malaysia's independence from Britain in 1957. Each of the nine state sultans takes a five-year turn as king.

Politics

THE 10 YOUNGEST US PRESIDENTS

	PRESIDENT	TOOK OFFICE	AGE ON TAKING OFFICE		
			YRS	MTHS	DAYS
1	Theodore Roosevelt	Sep 14, 1901	42	10	18
2	John F. Kennedy	Jan 20, 1961	43	7	22
3	Bill Clinton	Jan 20, 1993	46	5	1
4	Ulysses S. Grant	Mar 4, 1869	46	10	5
5	Barack Obama	Jan 20, 2009	47	5	16
6	Grover Cleveland	Mar 4, 1893	47	11	14
7	Franklin Pierce	Mar 4, 1804	48	3	9
8	James A. Garfield	Mar 4, 1881	49	3	13
9	James K. Polk	Mar 4, 1845	49	4	2
10	Millard Fillmore	Jul 10, 1850	50	6	3

Roosevelt became president following the assassination of William McKinley, while Kennedy was the youngest to be elected. US presidents must be at least 35 years old.

THE 10 SHORTEST-SERVING US PRESIDENTS

	PRESIDENT / DATES	PERIOD IN OFFICE		
		YRS	MTHS	DAYS
1	William H. Harrison (1841)*	0	0	30
2	James A. Garfield (1881)*	0	6	15
3	Zachary Taylor (1849–50)*	1	4	5
4	Warren G. Harding (1921–23)*	2	4	29
5	Gerald R. Ford (1974–77)	2	5	11
6	Millard Fillmore (1850–53)	2	5	25
7	John F. Kennedy (1961–63)*	2	10	2
8	Chester A. Arthur (1881–85)	3	5	13
9	Andrew Johnson (1865–69)	3	10	17
10	John Tyler (1841–45)	3	11	0

* Died in office

Ninth and second-oldest President William Harrison caught pneumonia while delivering an inaugural address in the rain on March 8, 1841. The longest on record, its 8,400 words took him one hour 45 minutes to deliver. He was ill throughout his record shortest term in office, and became the first US president to die in office and the first to die in the White House. Outside these 10, all other presidents have served either one or the now maximum two full four-year terms. Franklin D. Roosevelt was elected to a fourth term, and died in office.

President Obama
The average age of US presidents on taking office is 55 years 1 month—only four have been younger than Barack Obama.

TOP 10 **PARLIAMENTS WITH THE HIGHEST PERCENTAGE OF WOMEN MEMBERS***

PARLIAMENT (LATEST ELECTION)	WOMEN MEMBERS	TOTAL MEMBERS	% WOMEN
1 Rwanda (2008)	45	80	56.3
2 Sweden (2006)	164	349	47.0
3 Cuba (2008)	265	614	43.2
4 Finland (2007)	83	200	41.5
5 Argentina (2007)	102	255	40.0
6 Netherlands (2003)	59	150	39.3
7 Denmark (2007)	68	179	38.0
8 Angola (2008)	82	220	37.3
9 Costa Rica (2006)	21	57	36.8
10 Spain (2008)	127	350	36.3
USA (2008)	*74*	*435*	*17.0*

* As at February 28, 2009

Source: Inter-Parliamentary Union

This list is based on the most recent general election results for 136 democratic countries, based on the lower chamber where the parliament or equivalent body comprises two chambers. A total of 102 countries have at least 10 percent female members of parliament, 57 more than 20 percent, 22 over 30 percent and five over 40 percent. Rwanda is the first—and to date only—country with more than 50 percent female members. Nine countries have no women members.

Cuban parliament
Women won 43.2 percent of the seats in the 2008 elections to Cuba's National Assembly.

THE 10 **FIRST COUNTRIES TO GIVE WOMEN THE VOTE**

	COUNTRY	YEAR
1	New Zealand	1893
2	Australia (South Australia 1894; Western Australia 1898; Australia united in 1901)	
3	Finland (then a Grand Duchy under the Russian Crown)	1902
4	Norway (restricted franchise; all women over 25 in 1913)	1906
5	Denmark and Iceland (a Danish dependency until 1918)	1907
6	= Netherlands (granted; enacted 1919)	1915
	= USSR	
8	= Austria	1917
	= Azerbaijan	1917
	= Canada	1918
	= Estonia	1918
	= Germany	1918
	= Great Britain and Ireland (Ireland part of the United Kingdom until 1921; women over 30 only, lowered to 21 in 1928)	1918
	= Latvia	1918
	= Poland	1918

Nobel Prizes

TOP 10 OLDEST NOBEL PRIZE WINNERS

WINNER / COUNTRY / AWARD	DATE OF BIRTH	AGE* YRS	MTHS	DAYS
1 Leonid Hurwicz (USA) Economics 2007	Aug 21, 1917	90	3	28
2 Raymond Davis Jr. (USA) Physics 2002	Oct 14, 1914	88	1	26
3 Doris Lessing (UK) Literature 2007	Oct 22, 1919	88	1	18
4 Yoichiro Nambu (Japan) Physics 2008	Jan 18, 1921	87	10	22
5 Vitaly L. Ginzburg (Russia) Physics 2003	Oct 4, 1916	87	2	6
6 Peyton Rous (USA) Medicine 1966	Oct 5, 1879	87	2	5
7 Joseph Rotblat (UK) Peace 1995	Nov 4, 1908	87	1	6
8 Karl von Frisch (Germany) Medicine 1973	Nov 20, 1886	87	0	20
9 Ferdinand Buisson (France) Peace 1927	Dec 20, 1841	85	11	20
10 John B. Fenn (USA) Chemistry 2002	Jun 15, 1917	85	5	25

* At date of award ceremony—prizes are announced in October, but awarded annually on December 10, Alfred Nobel's birthday

Senior scientist
American scientist Raymond Davis, Jr. (1914–2006), head of the Homestake Experiment that detected neutrinos in the Sun, became the oldest-ever winner of the Nobel Physics prize for his work.

THE 10 YOUNGEST NOBEL PRIZE WINNERS

WINNER / COUNTRY	DATE OF BIRTH	AWARD	AGE* YRS	MTHS	DAYS
1 William Lawrence Bragg (UK)	Mar 31, 1890	Physics 1915	25	8	10
2 Werner Karl Heisenberg (Germany)	Dec 5, 1901	Physics 1932	31	0	5
3 Tsung-Dao Lee (China)	Nov 24, 1926	Physics 1957	31	0	16
4 Carl David Anderson (USA)	Sept 3, 1905	Physics 1936	31	3	7
5 Paul Adrien Maurice Dirac (UK)	Aug 8, 1902	Physics 1933	31	4	2
6 Frederick Grant Banting (Canada)	Nov 14, 1891	Medicine 1923	32	0	26
7 Rudolf Ludwig Mössbauer (West Germany)	Jan 31, 1929	Physics 1961	32	10	10
8 Mairead Corrigan (UK)	Jan 27, 1944	Peace 1976	32	10	13
9 Joshua Lederberg (USA)	May 23, 1925	Medicine 1958	33	6	17
10 Betty Williams (UK)	2May 22, 1943	Peace 1976	33	6	18

* At date of award ceremony

TOP 10 NOBEL PRIZE-WINNING COUNTRIES*

COUNTRY	NOBEL PRIZES	PRIZES PER MILLION
1 Switzerland	25	3.27
2 Iceland	1	3.13
3 Sweden	28	3.04
4 Denmark	13	2.37
5 Norway	11	2.30
6 Austria	19	2.28
7 UK	114	1.86
8 Ireland	8	1.81
9 Germany	101	1.23
10 Netherlands	18	1.09

* Ranked by prizes per million of population

THE 10 **FIRST WOMEN TO WIN A NOBEL PRIZE**

WINNER	COUNTRY	PRIZE	YEAR
1 Marie Curie* (1867–1934)	Poland	Physics	1903
2 Bertha von Suttner (1843–1914)	Austria	Peace	1905
3 Selma Lagerlöf (1858–1940)	Sweden	Literature	1909
4 Marie Curie (1867–1934)	Poland	Chemistry	1911
5 Grazia Deledda (1875–1936)	Italy	Literature	1926#
6 Sigrid Undset (1882–1949)	Norway	Literature	1928
7 Jane Addams† (1860–1935)	USA	Peace	1931
8 Irène Joliot-Curie§ (1897–1956)	France	Chemistry	1935
9 Pearl Buck (1892–1973)	USA	Literature	1938
10 Gabriela Mistral (1899–1957)	Chile	Literature	1945

* Shared half with husband Pierre Curie; other half to Henri Becquerel
\# Awarded 1927
† Shared with Nicholas Murray Butler
§ Shared with husband Frédéric Joliot-Curie

Medical pioneer
Institut Pasteur virologist Françoise Barré-Sinoussi received her 2008 Nobel Prize for Medicine for her discovery of HIV/AIDS.

THE 10 **LATEST WOMEN TO WIN A NOBEL PRIZE**

	WINNER / COUNTRY	PRIZE	YEAR
1	Françoise Barré-Sinoussi (France, b. 1947) France	Medicine	2008
2	Doris Lessing (b. 1919) UK	Literature	2007
3	= Linda B. Buck (b. 1947) USA	Medicine	2004
	= Elfriede Jelinek (b. 1946) Austria	Literature	2004
	= Wangari Maathai (b. 1940) Kenya	Peace	2004
6	Shirin Ebadi (b. 1947) Iran	Peace	2003
7	Jody Williams (b. 1950) USA	Peace	1997
8	Wislawa Szymborska (b. 1923) Poland	Literature	1996
9	Christiane Nüsslein-Volhard (b. 1942) Germany	Medicine	1995
10	Toni Morrison (b. 1931) USA	Literature	1993

Women have won a total of 34 Nobel Prizes, 12 of them for Peace, 11 for Literature, seven for Physiology or Medicine, three for Chemistry, and two for Physics.

World War I

TOP 10 LARGEST ARMED FORCES OF WORLD WAR I

	COUNTRY	MOBILIZED*
1	Russia	12,000,000
2	Germany	11,000,000
3	British Empire#	8,904,467
4	France	8,410,000
5	Austria-Hungary	7,800,000
6	Italy	5,615,000
7	USA	4,355,000
8	Turkey	2,850,000
9	Bulgaria	1,200,000
10	Japan	800,000

* Total at peak strength
# Including Australia, Canada, India, New Zealand, South Africa, etc.

Russia's armed forces were relatively small in relation to the country's population— some six percent, compared with 17 percent in Germany. Several other European nations had forces that were similarly substantial in relation to their populations: Serbia's army was equivalent to 14 percent of its population. In total, more than 65,000,000 combatants were involved in fighting some of the costliest battles—in terms of numbers killed—that the world has ever known.

THE 10 SMALLEST ARMED FORCES OF WORLD WAR I

	COUNTRY	MOBILIZED*
1	Montenegro	50,000
2	Portugal	100,000
3	Greece	230,000
4	Belgium	267,000
5	Serbia	707,343
6	Romania	750,000
7	Japan	800,000
8	Bulgaria	1,200,000
9	Turkey	2,850,000
10	USA	4,355,000

* Total at peak strength

THE 10 COUNTRIES SUFFERING THE GREATEST MILITARY LOSSES IN WORLD WAR I

COUNTRY	MOBILIZED*	WOUNDED	MISSING/POW	DEAD
1 Germany	11,000,000	4,216,058	1,152,800	1,773,700
2 Russia	12,000,000	4,950,000	2,500,000	1,700,000
3 France	8,410,000	4,266,000	537,000	1,375,800
4 Austria-Hungary	7,800,000	3,620,000	2,200,000	1,200,000
5 British Empire*	8,904,467	2,090,212	191,652	908,371
6 Italy	5,615,000	947,000	600,000	650,000
7 Romania	750,000	120,000	80,000	335,706
8 Turkey	2,850,000	400,000	250,000	325,000
9 USA	4,355,000	234,300	4,526	126,000
10 Bulgaria	1,200,000	152,390	27,029	87,500

1 cross = 10,000 dead

* Total at peak strength
# Including Australia, Canada, India, New Zealand, South Africa, etc.

THE 10 COUNTRIES WITH THE HIGHEST PROPORTIONS OF MILITARY VICTIMS IN WORLD WAR I*

COUNTRY	WOUNDED (%)	MISSING/POW (%)	DEAD (%)
1 Romania	16.00	10.67	44.76
2 France	50.73	6.39	16.36
3 Germany	38.33	10.48	16.12
4 Austria-Hungary	46.41	28.21	15.38
5 Russia	41.25	20.83	14.17
6 Italy	16.87	10.69	11.58
7 Turkey	14.04	8.77	11.40
8 Great Britain	23.47	2.15	10.20
9 Bulgaria	12.70	2.25	7.29
10 Portugal	13.75	12.32	7.22
USA	*5.38*	*0.10*	*2.89*

* As percentage of troops mobilized

Memorials to the Missing

In addition to the graves of known victims of World War I, Commonwealth War Graves Commission memorials alone record a total of 526,974 names of those who have no known graves: the Thiepval Memorial (Somme) lists 72,090 names, the Menin Gate, Ypres, 54,896, and Tyne Cot, near Passendale, 34,984.

Below: Line of fire
Of all the German troops mobilized, nearly 65 percent were killed, wounded, or captured in the course of World War I.

TOP 10 AIR ACES OF WORLD WAR I

	PILOT	NATIONALITY	KILLS CLAIMED*
1	Rittmeister Manfred Albrecht Freiherr von Richthofen#	German	80
2	Capitaine René Paul Fonck	French	75
3	Major William Avery Bishop	Canadian	72
4	Major Edward Corringham "Mick" Mannock#	British	68
5	= Major Raymond Collishaw	Canadian	62†
	= Oberleutnant Ernst Udet	German	62
7	Major James Thomas Byford McCudden#	British	57
8	= Captain Anthony Wetherby Beauchamp-Proctor	South African	54
	= Captain Donald Roderick MacLaren	Canadian	54
	= Capitaine George Marie Ludovic Jules Guynemer#	French	54

* Approximate—some kills disputed
\# Killed in action
† Including two in Russian Civil War, 1919

The term "ace," a pilot who had downed at least five enemy aircraft, first appeared in print in the British newspaper *The Times*, on September 14, 1917.

Right: Red Baron
25-year-old air ace Manfred von Richthofen's reign of aerial terror ended when he was shot down on April 21, 1918.

World War II

THE 10 COUNTRIES SUFFERING THE GREATEST MILITARY LOSSES IN WORLD WAR II

COUNTRY	KILLED
1 USSR	13,600,000*
2 Germany	3,300,000
3 China	1,324,516
4 Japan	1,140,429
5 British Empire# (UK 264,000)	357,116
6 Romania	350,000
7 Poland	320,000
8 Yugoslavia	305,000
9 USA	292,131
10 Italy	279,800
Total	*21,268,992*

* Total, of which 7.8 million battlefield deaths
# Including Australia, Canada, India, New Zealand, etc.

The precise numbers of World War II military victims and civilian war deaths will never be known, these figures representing only authoritative estimates.

THE 10 SMALLEST ARMED FORCES OF WORLD WAR II

COUNTRY	PERSONNEL*
1 Costa Rica	400
2 Liberia	1,000
3 = El Salvador	3,000
= Honduras	3,000
= Nicaragua	3,000
6 Haiti	3,500
7 Dominican Republic	4,000
8 Guatemala	5,000
9 = Bolivia	8,000
= Paraguay	8,000
= Uruguay	8,000

* Total at peak strength

The smallest European force was that of Denmark, some 15,000, 13 of whom were killed during the one-day German invasion of April 9, 1940, when Denmark became the second country to be occupied.

THE 10 AREAS OF EUROPE MOST BOMBED BY ALLIED AIRCRAFT* IN WORLD WAR II

AREA / BOMBS DROPPED (TONS)

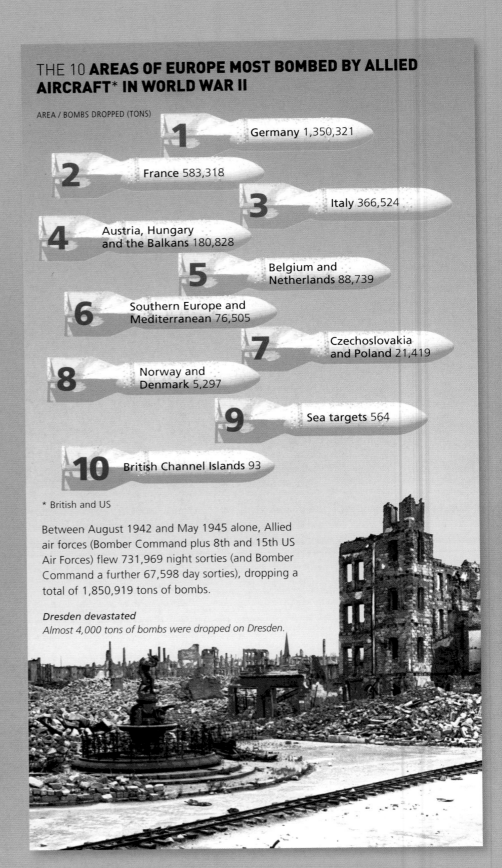

1 Germany 1,350,321

2 France 583,318

3 Italy 366,524

4 Austria, Hungary and the Balkans 180,828

5 Belgium and Netherlands 88,739

6 Southern Europe and Mediterranean 76,505

7 Czechoslovakia and Poland 21,419

8 Norway and Denmark 5,297

9 Sea targets 564

10 British Channel Islands 93

* British and US

Between August 1942 and May 1945 alone, Allied air forces (Bomber Command plus 8th and 15th US Air Forces) flew 731,969 night sorties (and Bomber Command a further 67,598 day sorties), dropping a total of 1,850,919 tons of bombs.

Dresden devastated
Almost 4,000 tons of bombs were dropped on Dresden.

THE 10 SUBMARINE FLEETS WITH THE GREATEST LOSSES IN WORLD WAR II

COUNTRY / SUBMARINES SUNK

10 Greece 4
9 Norway 5
8 Netherlands 10
7 France 23
1 Germany 787
2 Japan 130
3 USSR 103
6 USA 50
5 UK 77
4 Italy 85

U-boat loss
German submarine U-185 sank in the mid-Atlantic on August 24, 1943 after sustained attack by US aircraft.

THE 10 COUNTRIES SUFFERING THE GREATEST AIRCRAFT LOSSES IN WORLD WAR II

COUNTRY / AIRCRAFT LOST

10 New Zealand 684
9 France 2,100
8 Canada 2,389
1 Germany 116,584
2 USSR 106,652
3 USA 59,296
7 Italy 5,272
4 Japan 49,485
6 Australia 7,160
5 UK 33,090

While many reports are vague, very precise combat-loss figures exist for the Battle of Britain: during the period from July 10 to October 31, 1940, 1,065 RAF aircraft were destroyed, compared with 1,922 Luftwaffe fighters, bombers, and other aircraft.

Modern Military

TOP 10 LARGEST ARMED FORCES

COUNTRY	ARMY	ESTIMATED ACTIVE FORCES NAVY	AIR	TOTAL
1 China	1,600,000	255,000	330,000	2,185,000
2 USA	632,245	339,453	340,530	1,539,587*
3 India	1,100,000	55,000	120,000	1,281,200#
4 North Korea	950,000	46,000	110,000	1,106,000
5 Russia	360,000	142,000	160,000	1,027,000†
6 South Korea	560,000	68,000	64,000	692,000
7 Pakistan	550,000	22,000	45,000	617,000
8 Iran	350,000	18,000	30,000	523,000§
9 Turkey	402,000	48,600	60,000	510,600
10 Egypt	340,000	18,500	30,000	468,500‡

* Includes 186,661 Marine Corps and 40,698 Coast Guard
\# Includes 6,200 Coast Guard
† Includes 35,000 Airbone Army, 80,000 Strategic Deterrent Forces, and 250,000 Command and Support
§ Includes 125,000 Islamic Revolutionary Guard Corps
‡ Includes 80,000 Air Defence Command

Source: The International Institute for Strategic Studies,
The Military Balance 2008

TOP 10 MILITARY EXPENDITURE COUNTRIES

COUNTRY	% OF WORLD TOTAL	MILITARY SPENDING ($MILLION)*
1 USA	48.51	713,100
2 France	4.19	61,571
3 UK	4.17	61,281
4 China	4.16	61,000
5 Russia	3.40	50,000
6 Japan	3.32	48,860
7 Germany	3.12	45,930
8 Italy	2.72	40,050
9 Saudi Arabia	2.11	31,050
10 Turkey	2.10	30,936
Top 10 total	*77.80*	*1,143,778*
World total	*100*	*1,470,000*

* 2009 or latest available year

Show of arms
Recruits to the Jammu and Kashmir Light Infantry Regiment at a passing-out parade. The JKLIR, which celebrated its 50th anniversary in 2008, is a component of the million-plus Indian army.

Fighting force
The Chinese People's Liberation Army combines the country's serving land, sea, and air personnel in a vast organization of over two million troops.

Chinese ar...

TOP 10 RANKS OF THE US NAVY, ARMY, AND AIR FORCE

NAVY	ARMY	AIR FORCE
1 Fleet Admiral	General	General
2 Admiral	Lieutenant-General	Lieutenant-General
3 Vice-Admiral	Major-General	Major-General
4 Rear-Admiral (Upper Half)	Brigadier-General	Brigadier-General
5 Rear-Admiral (Lower Half)	Colonel	Colonel
6 Captain	Lieutenant-Colonel	Lieutenant-Colonel
7 Commander	Major	Major
8 Lieutenant Commander	Captain	Captain
9 Lieutenant	First Lieutenant	First Lieutenant
10 Lieutenant (Junior Grade)	Second Lieutenant	Second Lieutenant

US military ranks were originally derived from those of the eighteenth-century British army and navy, but have been modified over the past 200 years. Each rank is designated by insignia such as stars for the most senior ranks and braid on sleeves. Although no one has been appointed to the naval rank of Fleet Admiral since 1945, it is regarded as active, whereas General of the Army has not been conferred since Omar Bradley in 1950, and is unlikely to be used in the future. General of the Armies ranks above General of the Army, but has been awarded only to John J. Pershing in 1919 and retrospectively in 1976 to George Washington; as it has since been decreed that no one may ever outrank Washington, it is no longer valid.

TOP 10 COUNTRIES WITH THE MOST BATTLE TANKS

COUNTRY		TANKS
1 Russia		28,381
2 USA		7,821
3 China		7,580
4 Turkey		4,205
5 Syria		4,100
6 India		3,978
7 Ukraine		3,784
8 Egypt		3,680
9 Israel		3,650
10 North Korea		3,500

Fire power
The USA's main battle tank, the M1A1 Abrams. At an average cost of $3.325 million each, they represent a total cost of $26 billion.

THE 10 COUNTRIES WITH THE HIGHEST MURDER RATES

	COUNTRY	MURDERS PER 100,000 POP.*
1	El Salvador	55.3
2	Honduras	49.9
3	Jamaica	49.0
4	Venezuela	3 0
5	Guatemala	45.2
6	South Africa	38.6
7	Colombia	37.0
8	Belize	30.8
9	Trinidad & Tobago	30.4
10	Brazil	25.7

* Recorded in 2006/2007

THE 10 US STATES WITH THE HIGHEST CRIME RATES*

		CRIMES PER 100,000 (2007)	
		VIOLENT	PROPERTY
1	Arizona	482.7	4,414.0
2	South Carolina	788.3	4,271.7
3	Hawaii	272.8	4,225.4
4	Texas	510.6	4,121.2
5	Florida	722.6	4,089.3
6	Tennessee	753.3	4,088.6
7	North Carolina	466.4	4,087.3
8	Louisiana	729.5	4,076.0
9	Washington	333.1	4,030.8
10	Alabama	448.0	3,971.6

* Ranked by property crime rate

Source: US Department of Justice, *Crime in the United States 2007*

THE 10 MOST COMMON CRIMES IN THE USA

	CRIME	NO. RECORDED (2007)
1	Property crime	8,988,919
2	Larceny-theft	5,970,603
3	Burglary	1,989,593
4	Violent crime	1,305,814
5	Motor vehicle theft	1,028,723
6	Aggravated assault	789,254
7	Robbery	422,184
8	Forcible rape	78,669
9	Arson	62,000
10	Murder and nonnegligent manslaughter	15,707
	Total	*20,651,466*

Source: US Department of Justice/FBI, *Crime in the United States 2008*

THE 10 MOST CORRUPT COUNTRIES

	COUNTRY	RATING
1	Somalia	1.0
2	= Iraq	1.3
	= Myanmar	1.3
4	Haiti	1.4
5	Afghanistan	1.5
6	= Chad	1.6
	= Guinea	1.6
	= Sudan	1.6
9	= Dem. Rep. of Congo	1.7
	= Equatorial Guinea	1.7

Source: Transparency International, *Corruption Perceptions Index 2008*

THE 10 LEAST CORRUPT COUNTRIES

	COUNTRY	RATING
1	= Denmark	9.3
	= New Zealand	9.3
	= Sweden	9.3
4	Singapore	9.2
5	= Finland	9.0
	= Switzerland	9.0
7	= Iceland	8.9
	= Netherlands	8.9
9	= Australia	8.7
	= Canada	8.7
	USA	7.3

Source: Transparency International, *Corruption Perceptions Index 2008*

The Corruption Perceptions Index ranks countries by how likely they are to accept bribes, as perceived by the general public, business people, and risk analysts. They are ranked on a scale of 0–10, the higher the score, the "cleaner," or less corrupt, the country. A total of 180 countries were covered by the latest survey.

Somali pirate
With little law and order, Somalia is considered the world's most corrupt country, with piracy an ongoing threat to international shipping.

Executions

THE 10 US STATES WITH THE MOST PRISONERS ON DEATH ROW

STATE / PRISONERS UNDER DEATH SENTENCE*

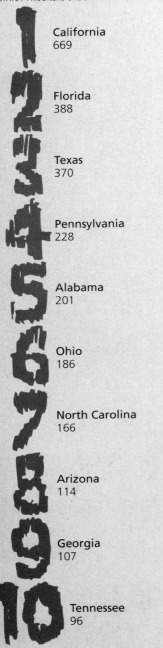

1 California
669

2 Florida
388

3 Texas
370

4 Pennsylvania
228

5 Alabama
201

6 Ohio
186

7 North Carolina
166

8 Arizona
114

9 Georgia
107

10 Tennessee
96

Total 3,263

* As at February 2008

Source: Death Penalty Information Center

THE 10 YEARS WITH THE MOST PRISONERS ON DEATH ROW

YEAR / PRISONERS UNDER DEATH SENTENCE*

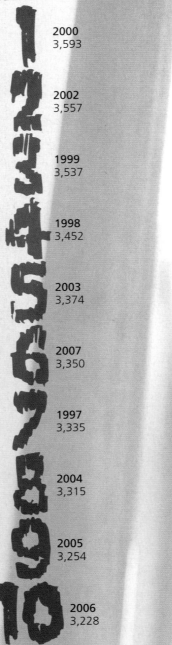

1 2000
3,593

2 2002
3,557

3 1999
3,537

4 1998
3,452

5 2003
3,374

6 2007
3,350

7 1997
3,335

8 2004
3,315

9 2005
3,254

10 2006
3,228

Source: Death Penalty Information Center

The year 1982 was the first in which the number of inmates on death row passed 1,000; it crossed the 2,000 threshold in 1988, and 3,000 in 1995.

THE 10 YEARS WITH THE MOST EXECUTIONS IN THE USA*

YEAR / EXECUTIONS

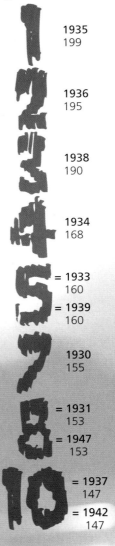

1 1935
199

2 1936
195

3 1938
190

4 1934
168

5 = 1933
160

= 1939
160

6 1930
155

7 = 1931
153

= 1947
153

8 = 1937
147

= 1942
147

* All offences, 1930–2008

Source: Department of Justice/Death Penalty Information Center

In 2007, 42 prisoners were executed, all but one of them by lethal injection.

THE 10 US STATES WITH THE MOST EXECUTIONS*

	STATE	1608–1976	EXECUTIONS SINCE 1976	TOTAL
1	Virginia	1,277	102	1,379
2	Texas	755	413	1,168
3	New York	1,130	0	1,130
4	Pennsylvania	1,040	3	1,043
5	Georgia	950	42	992
6	North Carolina	784	43	827
7	Alabama	708	38	746
8	California	709	13	722
9	South Carolina	641	39	680
10	Louisiana	632	27	659

* To September 2, 2008

Source: Death Penalty Information Center

A total of 1,116 people have been executed in the USA since 1976, when the death penalty was reintroduced after a 10-year moratorium. During this period, 17 states and Washington, D.C., have not carried out any executions.

THE 10 FIRST STATES TO USE THE ELECTRIC CHAIR

	STATE	FIRST VICTIM	DATE
1	New York	William Kemmler	Aug 6, 1890
2	Ohio	William Haas	Apr 21, 1897
3	Massachusetts	Luigi Storti	Dec 17, 1901
4	New Jersey	Saverio DiGiovanni	Dec 11, 1907
5	Virginia	Henry Smith	Jan 13, 1908
6	North Carolina	Walter Morrison	Mar 18, 1910
7	Kentucky	James Buckner	Jul 8, 1911
8	South Carolina	William Reed	Aug 6, 1912
9	Arkansas	Lee Simms	Sep 5, 1913
10	Indiana	Harry Rasico	Feb 20, 1914

In all, 26 states plus Washington, D.C., adopted the electric chair, with West Virginia being the last to do so, on March 26, 1951. It remains an optional execution method in a number of states.

THE 10 FIRST COUNTRIES TO ABOLISH CAPITAL PUNISHMENT

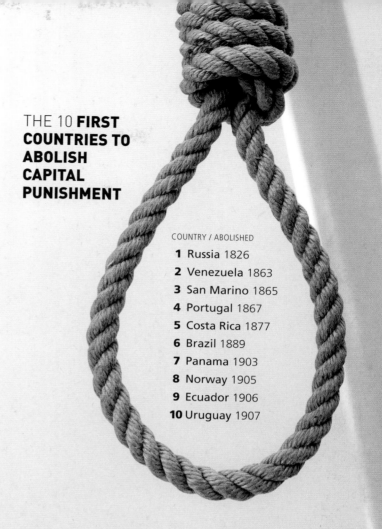

	COUNTRY / ABOLISHED
1	Russia 1826
2	Venezuela 1863
3	San Marino 1865
4	Portugal 1867
5	Costa Rica 1877
6	Brazil 1889
7	Panama 1903
8	Norway 1905
9	Ecuador 1906
10	Uruguay 1907

Fall and Rise of US Executions

The total number of executions in the USA fell below three figures for the first time in the twentieth century in 1950, when 82 prisoners were executed, and below double figures in 1965, with just seven executions. Only one prisoner was executed in 1966, and no others until 1977, when Gary Gilmore became the first person for 10 years to receive the death penalty. Double figures were again recorded in 1984 (21 executions) and in all subsequent years.

World Religions

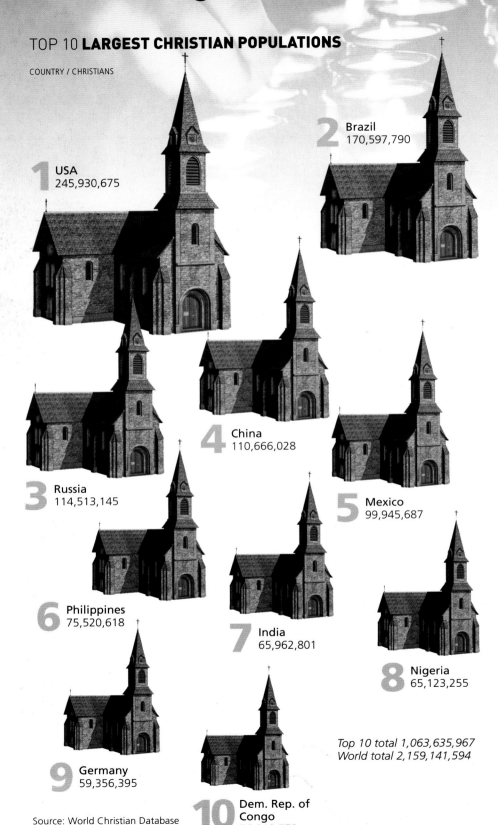

TOP 10 LARGEST CHRISTIAN POPULATIONS

COUNTRY / CHRISTIANS

1 USA
245,930,675

2 Brazil
170,597,790

3 Russia
114,513,145

4 China
110,666,028

5 Mexico
99,945,687

6 Philippines
75,520,618

7 India
65,962,801

8 Nigeria
65,123,255

9 Germany
59,356,395

10 Dem. Rep. of Congo
56,019,573

Top 10 total 1,063,635,967
World total 2,159,141,594

Source: World Christian Database

TOP 10 LARGEST JEWISH POPULATIONS

	COUNTRY	JEWS
1	USA	5,760,530
2	Israel	4,843,655
3	France	609,905
4	Argentina	512,671
5	Canada	418,315
6	UK	282,306
7	Germany	224,963
8	Russia	187,916
9	Ukraine	182,425
10	Brazil	140,925
	Top 10 total	*13,163,611*
	World total	*14,692,748*

Source: World Christian Database

Although not an independent country, the West Bank and Gaza are together reckoned to have 444,707 Jewish inhabitants.

TOP 10 LARGEST HINDU POPULATIONS

	COUNTRY	HINDUS
1	India	817,112,705
2	Nepal	18,725,504
3	Bangladesh	14,751,609
4	Indonesia	7,217,099
5	Sri Lanka	2,515,776
6	Pakistan	2,053,374
7	Malaysia	1,607,947
8	USA	1,337,734
9	South Africa	1,141,006
10	Myanmar	818,250
	Top 10 total	*867,281,004*
	World total	*872,921,745*

Source: World Christian Database

Hindus constitute some 72.03 percent of the population of India and 69.11 percent of that of Nepal, but only 9.62 percent of that of Bangladesh, and as little as 3.19 percent of Indonesia.

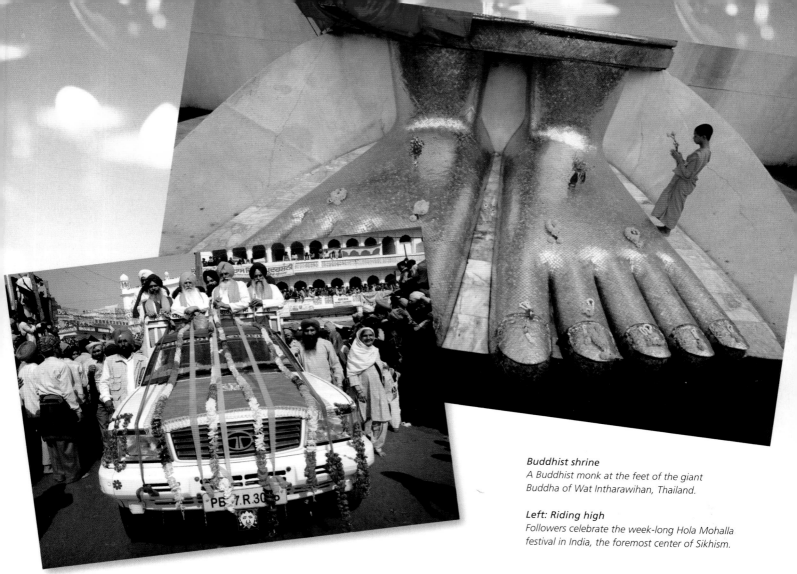

Buddhist shrine
A Buddhist monk at the feet of the giant
Buddha of Wat Intharawihan, Thailand.

Left: Riding high
Followers celebrate the week-long Hola Mohalla
festival in India, the foremost center of Sikhism.

TOP 10 **LARGEST SIKH POPULATIONS**

	COUNTRY	SIKHS
1	India	21,274,191
2	UK	384,906
3	Canada	330,773
4	USA	269,862
5	Thailand	51,032
6	Saudi Arabia	45,336
7	Malaysia	42,481
8	Pakistan	40,627
9	Australia	35,171
10	Kenya	32,566
	Top 10 total	22,506,945
	World total	22,782,827

Source: World Christian Database

TOP 10 **LARGEST MUSLIM POPULATIONS**

	COUNTRY	MUSLIMS
1	India	155,115,142
2	Pakistan	151,806,340
3	Bangladesh	135,690,886
4	Indonesia	127,753,305
5	Turkey	71,054,050
6	Iran	68,243,783
7	Nigeria	62,408,926
8	Egypt	61,769,354
9	Algeria	32,198,881
10	Morocco	29,991,256
	USA	4,749,632
	Top 10 total	896,031,923
	World total	1,358,290,337

Source: World Christian Database

TOP 10 **LARGEST BUDDHIST POPULATIONS**

	COUNTRY	BUDDHISTS
1	China	116,774,700
2	Japan	71,795,145
3	Thailand	54,158,633
4	Vietnam	41,401,771
5	Myanmar	35,476,781
6	Sri Lanka	12,999,238
7	Cambodia	11,901,352
8	India	7,789,140
9	South Korea	7,233,870
10	Laos	3,001,939
	USA	2,810,773
	Top 10 total	362,532,569
	World total	378,724,109

Source: World Christian Database

TOWN & COUNTRY

Country Facts

THE 10 **LARGEST COUNTRIES IN THE AMERICAS**

	COUNTRY	AREA SQ MILES	AREA SQ KM
1	Canada	3,855,103	9,984,670
2	USA	3,717,813	9,629,091
3	Brazil	3,287,613	8,514,877
4	Argentina	1,073,519	2,780,400
5	Mexico	758,450	1,964,375
6	Peru	496,225	1,285,216
7	Colombia	439,737	1,138,914
8	Bolivia	424,165	1,098,581
9	Venezuela	352,145	912,050
10	Chile	291,933	756,102

Source: United Nations

Geographically, Greenland—with an area of 836,331 sq miles (2,166,086 sq km), which would place it fifth in this list—is considered part of the Americas, but being under Danish control, it does not qualify as an independent country.

TOP 10 **LARGEST COUNTRIES IN EUROPE**

	COUNTRY	AREA SQ MILES	AREA SQ KM
1	Russia*	1,528,965	3,960,000
2	Ukraine	233,013	603,500
3	France	212,935	551,500
4	Spain	195,365	505,992
5	Sweden	173,860	450,295
6	Germany	137,849	357,022
7	Finland	130,559	338,145
8	Norway	125,021	323,802
9	Poland	120,728	312,685
10	Italy	116,340	301,318

* In Europe; total area 6,601,669 sq miles (17,098,242 sq km)

Source: United Nations

The United Kingdom falls just outside the Top 10 at 93,784 sq miles (242,900 sq km), the 78th largest in the world.

THE 10 **MOST RECENT INDEPENDENT COUNTRIES**

	COUNTRY	INDEPENDENCE
1	Abkhazia	Aug 26, 2008*
2	South Ossetia	Aug 8, 2008*
3	Kosovo	Feb 17, 2008*
4	= Serbia	Jun 3, 2006
	= Montenegro	Jun 3, 2006
6	East Timor	May 20, 2002
7	Palau	Oct 1, 1994
8	Eritrea	May 24, 1993
9	= Czech Republic	Jan 1, 1993
	= Slovakia	Jan 1, 1993

* Not recognized internationally

New country
Although it awaits full international recognition, Kosovo became one of the world's newest countries when it declared independence in 2008.

TOP 10 **COUNTRIES WITH MOST NEIGHBORS**

COUNTRY / NEIGHBORS

NO. OF NEIGHBORS

1 Russia
Abkhazia, Azerbaijan, Belarus, China, Estonia, Finland, Georgia, Kazakhstan, Latvia, Lithuania, Mongolia, North Korea, Norway, Poland, South Ossetia, Ukraine — 16

2 China
Afghanistan, Bhutan, India, Kazakhstan, Kyrgyzstan, Laos, Mongolia, Myanmar, Nepal, North Korea, Pakistan, Russia, Tajikistan, Vietnam — 14

3 = Brazil
Argentina, Bolivia, Colombia, Guyana, Paraguay, Peru, Suriname, Uruguay, Venezuela — 9

= Dem Rep of Congo
Angola, Burundi, Central African Republic, Congo, Rwanda, Sudan, Tanzania, Uganda, Zambia — 9

= Germany
Austria, Belgium, Czech Republic, Denmark, France, Luxembourg, Netherlands, Poland, Switzerland — 9

= Sudan
Central African Republic, Chad, Dem. Rep. of Congo, Egypt, Eritrea, Ethiopia, Kenya, Libya, Uganda — 9

7 = Austria
Czech Republic, Germany, Hungary, Italy, Liechtenstein, Slovakia, Slovenia, Switzerland — 8

= France
Andorra, Belgium, Germany, Italy, Luxembourg, Monaco, Spain, Switzerland — 8

= Serbia
Albania, Bosnia-Herzegovina, Bulgaria, Croatia, Hungary, Republic of Macedonia, Montenegro, Romania — 8

= Tanzania
Burundi, Dem. Rep. of Congo, Kenya, Malawi, Mozambique, Rwanda, Uganda, Zambia — 8

= Turkey
Armenia, Azerbaijan, Bulgaria, Georgia, Greece, Iran, Iraq, Syria — 8

= Zambia
Angola, Botswana, Dem Rep of Congo, Malawi, Mozambique, Namibia, Tanzania, Zimbabwe — 8

It should be noted that some countries have more than one discontinuous border with the same country, each of which has been counted only once. Borders with overseas territories are discounted—if included, France, with borders such as that with Brazil and French Guyana, could be considered as bordering a total of 11 countries. Countries connected only by bridges or tunnels (Bahrain/Saudi Arabia, Denmark/Sweden, Singapore/Malaysia, and UK/France) are also excluded.

TOP 10 **LARGEST COUNTRIES**

COUNTRY / AREA SQ MILES/SQ KM / % OF WORLD TOTAL

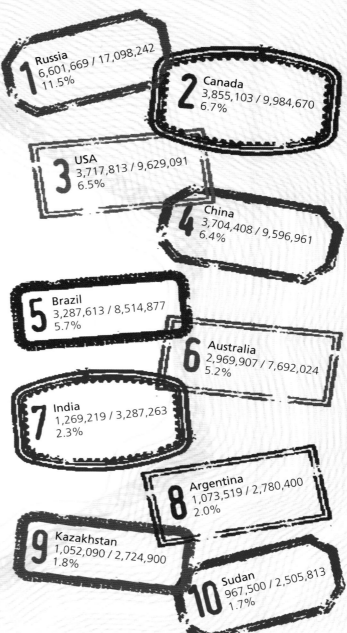

1 Russia 6,601,669 / 17,098,242 11.5%

2 Canada 3,855,103 / 9,984,670 6.7%

3 USA 3,717,813 / 9,629,091 6.5%

4 China 3,704,408 / 9,596,961 6.4%

5 Brazil 3,287,613 / 8,514,877 5.7%

6 Australia 2,969,907 / 7,692,024 5.2%

7 India 1,269,219 / 3,287,263 2.3%

8 Argentina 1,073,519 / 2,780,400 2.0%

9 Kazakhstan 1,052,090 / 2,724,900 1.8%

10 Sudan 967,500 / 2,505,813 1.7%

World 148,939,063 / 57,505,700 100.0%

Source: United Nations Statistics Division

This list is based on the total area of a country within its borders, including offshore islands, inland water such as lakes and rivers, and reservoirs. It may thus differ from versions of this list in which such features are excluded.

People Counting

Top town
London, the world's most populous city in 1910, was overtaken by New York a decade later.

Gene pool
Although one-fifth of the world's population lives in China, it is scheduled to be overtaken by India.

TOP 10 **MOST POPULATED COUNTRIES**

	COUNTRY	% OF WORLD TOTAL	POPULATION (2010 EST.)
1	China	19.62	1,347,563,498
2	India	17.24	1,184,090,490
3	USA	4.50	309,162,581
4	Indonesia	3.54	242,968,342
5	Brazil	2.93	201,103,330
6	Pakistan	2.62	179,659,223
7	Bangladesh	2.33	159,765,367
8	Nigeria	2.22	152,217,341
9	Russia	2.03	139,390,205
10	Japan	1.85	126,804,433
	Top 10 total	*58.87*	*4,042,724,810*
	World	*100.00*	*6,866,880,431*

Source: US Census Bureau, International Data Base

In 2009, the population of Nigeria overtook that of Russia, the only country in the Top 10 whose population is declining. Mexico, with a projected 2010 population of 112,468,855, is the only other country in the world with a population of more than 100 million.

TOP 10 **MOST POPULOUS CITIES IN THE WORLD, 1910**

	CITY	POPULATION
1	London, UK	6,580,616
2	Paris, France	2,763,393
3	Tokyo, Japan	2,186,079
4	Vienna, Austria	2,085,888
5	Berlin, Germany	2,040,148
6	St. Petersburg, Russia	1,678,000
7	Peking, China	1,600,000
8	Moscow, Russia	1,359,254
9	Osaka, Japan	1,226,590
10	Buenos Aires, Argentina	1,189,252

TOP 10 **URBAN POPULATION COUNTRIES**

	COUNTRY	%	URBAN POPULATION TOTAL
1	China	45	594,794,000
2	India	28	327,316,000
3	USA	79	240,544,000
4	Brazil	83	162,452,000
5	Indonesia	48	115,510,000
6	Russia	73	103,526,000
7	Japan	79	100,516,000
8	Mexico	76	82,158,000
9	Nigeria	47	69,149,000
10	Germany	73	60,280,000

Source: Population Reference Bureau, *2008 World Population Data Sheet*

World Population Milestones

The world's population 2,000 years ago is estimated to have been about 200 million. Having climbed to one billion by 1804, it took 123 years—until 1927— for it to attain two billion. It hit three billion in 1960, four billion in 1974, five billion in 1987, and six billion in 1999. It is estimated that world population will increase to 6.9 billion in 2010, seven billion in 2012, eight billion in 2025, and nine billion in 2040.

TOP 10 **COUNTRIES WITH THE BIGGEST POPULATION DECREASE**

COUNTRY / ESTIMATED POPULATION DECREASE 2008–50 (NO. / %)

1 Bulgaria
-2,648,000
-35%

2 Swaziland
-378,000
-33%

3 Guyana
-226,000
-29%

4 Georgia
-1,306,000
-28%

= Ukraine
-12,805,000
-28%

6 Tonga
-28,000
-27%

7 Japan
-32,568,000
-25%

8 Moldova
-964,000
-23%

9 Russia
-31,775,000
-22%

10 Serbia
-1,535,000
-21%

Source: Population Reference Bureau, *2008 World Population Data Sheet*

TOP 10 **COUNTRIES WITH THE BIGGEST POPULATION INCREASE**

COUNTRY / ESTIMATED POPULATION INCREASE 2008–50 (NO. / %)

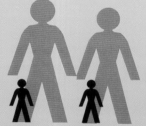

1 Uganda
76,855,000
263%

2 Niger
38,432,000
261%

3 Burundi
19,459,000
220%

4 Liberia
8,518,000
216%

5 Guinea-Bissau
3,578,000
205%

6 Dem. Rep. of Congo
122,796,000
185%

7 Timor-Leste
1,935,000
179%

8 Mayotte
325,000
174%

9 Mali
21,515,000
169%

10 Somalia
14,859,000
166%
*USA
133,667,000
44%*

Source: Population Reference Bureau, *2008 World Population Data Sheet*

TOP 10 **MOST POPULOUS CITIES IN THE USA, 1910**

CITY	POPULATION
1 New York, New York	4,766,883
2 Chicago, Illinois	2,185,283
3 Philadelphia, Pennsylvania	1,549,008
4 Saint Louis, Missouri	687,029
5 Boston, Massachusetts	670,585
6 Cleveland, Ohio	560,663
7 Baltimore, Maryland	558,485
8 Pittsburgh, Pennsylvania	533,905
9 Detroit, Michigan	465,766
10 Buffalo, New York	423,715

Source: US Census Bureau

TOP 10 **MOST POPULOUS CITIES IN THE USA AT THE 2000 CENSUS**

CITY	POPULATION
1 New York	8,018,350
2 Los Angeles	3,705,060
3 Chicago	2,896,375
4 Houston	1,977,206
5 Phoenix	1,326,879
6 Philadelphia	1,513,655
7 San Antonio	1,163,914
8 San Diego	1,227,784
9 Dallas	1,190,753
10 San Jose	898,402

Source: US Census Bureau

TOP 10 **MOST POPULATED ISLAND COUNTRIES**

COUNTRY	POPULATION (2010 EST.)
1 Indonesia	242,968,342
2 Japan	126,804,433
3 Philippines	99,900,177
4 Malaysia	26,160,256
5 Sri Lanka	21,513,990
6 Madagascar	21,281,844
7 Cuba	11,477,459
8 Dominican Republic	9,794,487
9 Haiti	9,203,083
10 Papua New Guinea	6,182,390

Source: US Census Bureau, International Data Base

Place Names

TOP 10 **LONGEST PLACE NAMES***

NAME / LETTERS

1 Krung Thep Mahanakhon Amon Rattanakosin Mahinthara Ayuthaya Mahadilok Phop Noppharat Ratchathani Burirom Udomratchaniwet Mahasathan Amon Piman Awatan Sathit Sakkathattiya Witsanukam Prasit (168)

It means "The city of angels, the great city, the eternal jewel city, the impregnable city of God Indra, the grand capital of the world endowed with nine precious gems, the happy city, abounding in an enormous Royal Palace that resembles the heavenly abode where reigns the reincarnated god, a city given by Indra and built by Vishnukarn." When the poetic name of Bangkok, capital of Thailand, is used, it is usually abbreviated to "Krung Thep" (city of angels).

2 Taumatawhakatangihangakoauauotamateaturipu kakapikimaungahoronukupokaiwhenuakitanatahu (85)

This is the longer version (the other has a mere 83 letters) of the Maori name of a hill in New Zealand. It translates as "The place where Tamatea, the man with the big knees, who slid, climbed, and swallowed mountains, known as land-eater, played on the flute to his loved one."

3 Gorsafawddachaidraigddanheddogleddollôn penrhynareurdraethceredigion (67)

A name contrived by the Fairbourne Steam Railway, Gwynedd, North Wales, for publicity purposes and in order to outdo its rival, No. 4. It means "The Mawddach station and its dragon teeth at the Northern Penrhyn Road on the golden beach of Cardigan Bay."

4 Llanfairpwllgwyngyllgogerychwyrndrobwllllanty siliogogogoch (58)

This is the place in Gwynedd famed for the length of its railway tickets. Its name means "St. Mary's Church in the hollow of the white hazel near to the rapid whirlpool of the church of St. Tysilo near the Red Cave." It appears to have been a hoax perpetrated in the 1860s by an unnamed tailor.

5 El Pueblo de Nuestra Señora la Reina de los Ángeles de la Porciúncula (57)

The site of a Franciscan mission and the full Spanish name of Los Angeles; it means "The town of Our Lady the Queen of the Angels of the Little Portion." Nowadays it is known by its initial letters, "LA," making it also one of the shortest-named cities in the world.

6 Chargoggagoggmanchaugagoggchaubunag ungamaug (43)

America's longest place name, a lake near Webster, Massachusetts, is claimed to mean "You fish on your side, I'll fish on mine, and no one fishes in the middle." It is, however, a hoax name devised in about 1921 by local journalist Larry Daly.

7 = Lower North Branch Little Southwest Miramichi = Villa Real de la Santa Fé de San Francisco de Asis (40)

Canada's longest place name—a short river in New Brunswick. The full Spanish name of Santa Fe, New Mexico, translates as, "Royal city of the holy faith of St. Francis of Assisi."

9 Te Whakatakanga-o-te-ngarehu-o-te-ahi-a-Tamatea (38)

The hyphenated or single-word Maori name of Hammer Springs, New Zealand. Like the second name in this list, it refers to a legend of Tamatea, explaining how the springs were warmed by "the falling of the cinders of the fire of Tamatea."

10 Meallan Liath Coire Mhic Dhubhghaill (32)

The longest multiple name in Scotland, a place near Aultanrynie, Highland, alternatively spelled Meallan Liath Coire Mhic Dhughaill (30 letters).

* Including single-word, hyphenated, and multiple names

Above: Brasília
The National Congress, Brasília: the purpose-built city replaced Rio de Janeiro as Brazil's capital in 1960.

Above right: South American giant
At the Rio carnival, Brazil celebrates with a float depicting Simón Bolívar, the founder of its neighbor Bolivia.

TOP 10 **LARGEST COUNTRIES WHOSE NAMES ARE INCLUDED IN THOSE OF THE CAPITAL CITY**

	CAPITAL	COUNTRY	POPULATION
1	Brasília	Brazil	188,001,000
2	Mexico City	Mexico	106,682,500
3	Algiers	Algeria	33,858,000
4	Guatemala City	Guatemala	13,354,000
5	Tunis	Tunisia	10,327,000
6	Santo Domingo	Dominican Republic	9,760,000
7	Singapore	Singapore	4,839,400
8	Panama City	Panama	3,343,000
9	Kuwait	Kuwait	2,851,000
10	Bissau	Guinea Bissau	1,695,000

These are the only 10 countries in the world with populations of more than one million where the country names are identical to or are incorporated in those of its capital cities. In some instances the city took its name from the country, while in others it was the other way round. Among smaller countries exhibiting this phenomenon are Djibouti (Djibouti), Luxembourg (Luxembourg), São Tomé (São Tomé and Príncipe), Andorra la Vella (Andorra), Monaco (Monaco), San Marino (San Marino), and Vatican City (Vatican City).

TOP 10 **LARGEST COUNTRIES NAMED AFTER REAL PEOPLE**

	COUNTRY / NAMED AFTER	AREA SQ MILES	SQ KM
1	United States of America Amerigo Vespucci (Italy; 1451–1512)	3,539,245	9,166,601
2	Saudi Arabia Abdul Aziz ibn-Saud (Nejd;1882–1953)	830,000	2,149,690
3	Bolivia Simón Bolívar (Venezuela;1783–1830)	418,685	1,084,389
4	Colombia Christopher Columbus (Italy; 1451–1506)	401,044	1,038,699
5	Philippines Philip II (Spain; 1527–98)	115,124	298,171
6	Swaziland Mswati II (Swaziland; c. 1820–68)	6,704	17,364
7	Falkland Islands Lucius Cary, 2nd Viscount Falkland (Britain; c. 1610–43)	4,700	12,173
8	Mauritius Maurice of Nassau (Orange; 1567–1625)	787	2,040
9	Kiribati Thomas Gilbert (British; fl. 1780s)	280	726
10	Northern Mariana Maria Theresa (Austria; 1717–80)	184	477

Many countries were named after mythical characters, or saints of dubious historical authenticity—often because they were discovered on the saint's day—but these are all named after real people. The origin of the name "America" is uncertain, some authorities citing a Richard Amerike (c. 1445–1503) as its true source.

Capital Cities

TOP 10 LARGEST CAPITAL CITIES

CITY / COUNTRY	ESTIMATED POPULATION (2009)
1 Tokyo Japan	33,800,000
2 Seoul, South Korea	23,900,000
3 Mexico City, Mexico	22,900,000
4 Delhi*, India	21,500,000
5 Manila, Philippines	19,200,000
6 Cairo, Egypt	14,800,000
7 Jakarta, Indonesia	15,100,000
8 Buenos Aires, Argentina	13,800,000
9 Moscow, Russia	13,500,000
10 Beijing, China	13,200,000

* Capital New Delhi

Source: Th. Brinkhoff: *The Principal Agglomerations of the World*,
www.citypopulation.de

TOP 10 LARGEST NON-CAPITAL CITIES

CITY / COUNTRY	CAPITAL	POPULATION (2009)
1 Mumbai, India	Delhi	22,300,000
2 New York, USA	Washington DC	21,900,000
3 São Paulo, Brazil	Brasília	21,000,000
4 Los Angeles, USA	Washington DC	18,000,000
5 Shanghai, China	Beijing	17,900,000
6 Osaka, Japan	Tokyo	16,700,000
7 Kolkata*, India	Delhi	16,000,000
8 Karachi*, Pakistan	Islamabad	15,700,000
9 Guangzhou, China	Beijing	15,300,000
10 Rio de Janeiro*, Brazil	Brasília	12,500,000

* Former capital

Source: Th. Brinkhoff: *The Principal Agglomerations of the World*,
www.citypopulation.de

SY

Northern Lights
Reykjavik, Iceland—the most northerly capital city—is situated 4,432 miles (7,134 km) from the North Pole.

TOP 10 **MOST NORTHERLY CAPITAL CITIES**

	CAPITAL	COUNTRY	LATITUDE
1	Reykjavik	Iceland	64° 08′ N
2	Helsinki	Finland	60° 12′ N
3	Olso	Norway	59° 56′ N
4	Tallin	Estonia	59° 26′ N
5	Stockholm	Sweden	59° 21′ N
6	Riga	Latvia	56° 58′ N
7	Moscow	Russia	55° 45′ N
8	Copenhagen	Denmark	55° 43′ N
9	Vilnius	Lithuania	54° 41′ N
10	Dublin	Ireland	53° 21′ N

TOP 10 **CAPITAL CITIES CLOSEST TO THE EQUATOR**

	CAPITAL	COUNTRY	LATITUDE
1	Quito	Ecuador	0° 15′ S
2	Kampala	Uganda	0° 19′ N
3	São Tomé	São Tomé and Príncipe	0° 20′ N
4	Libreville	Gabon	0° 23′ N
5	= Nairobi	Kenya	1° 17′ S
	= Singapore City	Singapore	1° 17′ N
7	Kigali	Rwanda	1° 57′ S
8	Mogadishu	Somalia	2° 04′ N
9	Kuala Lumpur	Malaysia	3° 08′ N
10	Bujumbura	Burundi	3° 23′ S

TOP 10 **MOST SOUTHERLY CAPITAL CITIES**

	CAPITAL	COUNTRY	LATITUDE
1	Wellington	New Zealand	41° 17′ S
2	Canberra	Australia	35° 17′ S
3	Montevideo	Uruguay	34° 53′ S
4	Buenos Aires	Argentina	34° 40′ S
5	Santiago	Chile	33° 27′ S
6	Maseru	Lesotho	29° 18′ S
7	Mbabane	Swaziland	26° 19′ S
8	Asuncíon	Paraguay	25° 16′ S
9	Maputo	Mozambique	25° 58′ S
10	Pretoria	South Africa	25° 44′ S

Although the Falkland Islands is a self-governing British Overseas Territory, rather than a country, its capital, Stanley, lies at 51° 41′—making it as far south as London is to the north (51° 30′).

Tallest by Decade

100 years ago
The world's highest building in 1909 was the Metropolitan Life Tower, New York. Since then it has been overtaken as the heights of the tallest skyscrapers have almost quadrupled, with construction of record-breaking buildings increasingly shifting to Asia.

Chrysler Building
The Chrysler Building briefly held the title of world's tallest, from May 28, 1930 to May 1, 1931.

Empire State Building
The iconic building remained the record-holder for over 40 years, from 1931 until the completion of the World Trade Center.

TOP 10 **TALLEST HABITABLE BUILDINGS IN** 1930

BUILDING / LOCATION	YEAR COMPLETED	STORIES	HEIGHT FT	HEIGHT M
1 Chrysler Building, New York, USA	1930	77	925	282
spire			*1,046*	*319*
2 40 Wall Street (Trump Building, formerly Bank of Manhattan Trust), New York, USA	1930	71	866	264
spire			*927*	*283*
3 Woolworth Building, New York, USA	1913	57	792	241
4 Terminal Tower, Cleveland, USA	1930	52	708	216
spire			*771*	*235*
5 Metropolitan Life Tower, New York, USA	1909	50	700	213
6 Lincoln Building, New York	1930	53	673	205
7 Chanin Building, New York, USA	1929	56	649	198
spire			*680*	*207*
8 Mercantile Building (10 East 40th Street), New York, USA	1929	48	632	193
9 New York Life Building, New York, USA	1928	33	615	187
spire			*665*	*203*
10 Singer Building*, New York, USA	1908	47	612	187

* Demolished 1968

TOP 10 **TALLEST HABITABLE BUILDINGS IN** 1960

BUILDING / LOCATION	YEAR COMPLETED	STORIES	HEIGHT FT	HEIGHT M
1 Empire State Building, New York, USA	1931	102	1,250	381
spire			*1,472*	*449*
2 Chrysler Building, New York, USA	1929	77	925	282
spire			*1,046*	*319*
3 40 Wall Street, New York, USA	1929	71	866	264
spire			*927*	*283*
4 GE Building (formerly RCA Building), New York, USA	1933	70	850	259
5 American International Building, New York, USA	1932	67	826	252
spire			*952*	*290*
6 1 Chase Manhattan Plaza, New York, USA	1960	60	813	248
7 Woolworth Building, New York, USA	1913	57	792	241
8 MV Lomonosov State University, Moscow, Russia	1953	39	784	239
9 Palace of Culture and Science, Warsaw, Poland	1955	42	758	231
10 City Bank-Farmers Trust Company Building (20 Exchange Place), New York, USA	1931	57	741	226
spire			*748*	*228*

Sears Tower
Chicago's Sears Tower took the world's tallest crown in 1974 and remains America's highest habitable building.

Burj Dubai
Topped off in 2009, the Burj Dubai ("Dubai Tower") has broken every height record, even overtaking the tallest mast.

TOP 10 **TALLEST HABITABLE BUILDINGS IN**

BUILDING / LOCATION	YEAR COMPLETED	STORIES	HEIGHT FT	M
1 Sears Tower, Chicago, USA *spire*	1974	108	1,450 1,730	442 527
2 1 World Trade Center*, New York, USA *spire*	1972	110	1,368 1,727	417 526
3 2 World Trade Center*, New York, USA	1973	110	1,363	415
4 Empire State Building, New York, USA *spire*	1931	102	1,250 1,472	381 449
5 Aon Center (formerly Amoco Building), Chicago, USA	1973	83	1,136	346
6 John Hancock Center, Chicago, USA *spire*	1968	100	1,127 1,500	344 427
7 Library Tower, Los Angeles, USA	1990	73	1,018	310
8 JPMorgan Chase Tower (formerly Texas Commerce Tower), Houston, USA	1982	75	1,002	305
9 Bank of China Tower, Hong Kong *spires*	1989	70	1,001 1,205	305 367
10 First Canadian Place, Toronto, Canada *spire*	1975	72	978 1,165	298 355

* Destroyed by 9/11 terrorist attacks

TOP 10 **TALLEST HABITABLE BUILDINGS IN**

BUILDING / LOCATION	YEAR COMPLETED	STORIES	HEIGHT FT	M
1 Burj Dubai, Dubai, UAE	2009	162	2,684	818
2 Taipei 101, Taipei, China *spire*	2004	101	1,470 1,671	448 509
3 Shanghai World Financial Center, Shanghai, China	2008	101	1,614	492
4 International Commerce Centre, Hong Kong, China	2010*	118	1,588	484
5 Abraj Al Bait Towers, Mecca, Saudi Arabia *spire*	2010*	76	1,509 1,952	460 595
6 Petronas Towers, Kuala Lumpur, Malaysia	1998	88	1,483	452
7 Sears Tower, Chicago, USA *spire*	1974	108	1,450 1,730	442 527
8 West Tower, Guangzhou, China	2009	110	1,417	432#
9 Jin Mao Building, Shanghai, China *spire*	1998	88	1,255 1,380	383 421
10 2 International Finance Centre, Hong Kong, China	2003	90	1,362	415

* Under construction—scheduled completion
# Helipad takes height to 1,435 ft (437.5 m)

Tallest by Type

TOP 10 **TALLEST BUILDINGS WITH NARROW BASES**

	BUILDING / LOCATION	YEAR COMPLETED	STORIES	HEIGHT FT	HEIGHT M
1	The Center, Hong Kong, China	1998	73	958	292
	spire			*1,135*	*346*
2	Citigroup Center, New York, USA	1977	59	915	279
3	Alberta Plaza, Calgary, Canada	1984	75	909	277
4	Tower 42, London, UK	1980	47	600	183
5	First National Bank, Boston, Massachussets, USA	1971	37	591	180
6	Dalian Hope Mansion, Dalian, China	1999	38	561	171
7	MCI Plaza, Denver, Colorado, USA	1981	42	522	159
8	Rainier Tower, Seattle, Washington, USA	1977	31	512	156
9	Tour du Midi, Brussels, Belgium	1967	38	492	150
10	Kwa Dukuza Egoli Hotel Tower 1, Johannesburg, South Africa	1985	40	459	140

TOP 10 **TALLEST REINFORCED CONCRETE BUILDINGS**

	BUILDING / LOCATION	YEAR COMPLETED	STORIES	HEIGHT FT	HEIGHT M
1	Mekkah Royal Hotel Tower, Mekkah, Saudi Arabia	2010*	76	1,591	485
2	Dubai Towers, Doha, Qatar	2010*	84	1,434	437
3	Trump International Hotel & Tower, Chicago, USA	2009*	96	1,362	415
4	Princess Tower, Dubai, United Arab Emirates	2009*	101	1,358	414
5 =	Al Hamra Tower, Kuwait City, Kuwait	2009*	77	1,352	412
=	Marina 101, Dubai, United Arab Emirates	2010*	101	1,352	412
7	Emirates Park Towers Hotel & Spa 1, Dubai, United Arab Emirates	2010*	77	1,296	395
8	Emirates Park Towers Hotel & Spa 2, Dubai, United Arab Emirates	2010*	77	1,296	395
9	CITIC Plaza, Guangzhou, China	1996	80	1,283	391
10	23 Marina, Dubai, United Arab Emirates	2009*	90	1,276	389

* Under construction—scheduled completion

Left: Skyscraper on stilts
New York's Citigroup Center has a distinctive stilt-like narrow base.

Right: Trumping its rivals
The Trump International Hotel and Tower, Chicago, is the USA's second tallest building.

TOP 10 **TALLEST CYLINDRICAL BUILDINGS**

BUILDING / LOCATION	YEAR COMPLETED	STORIES	HEIGHT FT	M
1 8 Shenton Way (formerly Treasury Building), Singapore	1986	52	770	235
2 Tun Abdul Razak Building, Penang, Malaysia	1985	61	760	232
3 Westin Peachtree Plaza, Atlanta, USA	1973	71	721	220
4 Renaissance Centre, Detroit, USA	1977	73	718	219
5 Hopewell Centre, Hong Kong, China	1980	64	705	215
6 Marina City Apartments (twin towers), Chicago, USA	1969	61	588	179
7 Australia Square Tower, Sydney, Australia	1968	46	560	170
8 Amartapura Condominium 1, Tangerang, Indonesia	1996	54	535	163
9 Shenzen City Plaza, Shenzen, China	1996	37	490	150
10 Amartapura Condominium 2, Tangerang, Indonesia	1997	36	445	136

TOP 10 **TALLEST BUILDINGS WITH HOLES**

BUILDING / LOCATION	YEAR COMPLETED	STORIES	HEIGHT FT	M
1 Shanghai World Financial Center, Shanghai, China	2008	101	1,614	492
2 Tuntex 85 Sky Tower, Kaohsiung, China *spire*	1997	85	1,142 *1,240*	348 *378*
3 Gate of the Orient, Suzhou, China	2009*	66	988	301
4 Kingdom Centre, Riyadh, Saudi Arabia	2002	41	984	300
5 The HarbourSide, Hong Kong, China	2003	74	837	255
6 Repsol Tower, Madrid, Spain	2008	45	823	250
7 Chelsea Tower, Dubai, United Arab Emirates *spire*	2005	49	755 *823*	230 *251*
8 CCTV Headquarters, Beijing, China	2008	51	768	234
9 The Arch, Hong Kong, China	2005	65	758	231
10 Centerpoint Energy Plaza, Houston, Texas, USA	1974	53	741	226

* Under construction—scheduled completion

Left: 12-sided structure
Also known as the KOMTAR Tower, the Tun Abdul Razak is the tallest building in Penang, Malaysia.

Right: Working space
The CCTV (Central China Television) headquarters was constructed by connecting two adjacent towers.

Megastructures

TOWER / LOCATION	YEAR COMPLETED	HEIGHT* FT	HEIGHT* M
① Tokyo Sky Tree, Tokyo, Japan	2011#	2,001	610.58
② Guangzhou TV & Sightseeing Tower, Guangzhou, China	2009#	2,001	610.0
③ Jakarta TV Tower, Jakarta, Indonesia	2010#	1,831	558.0
④ CN Tower, Toronto, Canada	1975	1,821	555.0
⑤ Ostankino Tower†, Moscow, Russia	1967	1,762	537.0
⑥ Broadcasting, Telephone and TV-tower, Xian, China	2008	1,542	470
⑦ Oriental Pearl Broadcasting Tower, Shanghai, China	1995	1,535	467.9
⑧ Borj-e Milad Telecommunications Tower, Tehran, Iran	2007	1,427	435.0
⑨ Menara Telecom Tower, Kuala Lumpur, Malaysia	1996	1,381	421.0
⑩ Tianjin Radio and Television Tower, Tianjin, China	1991	1,362	415.2

* To tip of antenna
# Under construction—scheduled completion
† Severely damaged by fire August 27, 2000, restored and reopened 2004

All the towers listed are self-supporting, rather than masts braced with guy wires, and all have observation facilities. A flurry of tower construction in recent years has evicted the Eiffel Tower (1889, 10.063 ft/324.0 m—which long headed the list—from the Top 10.

Ancient and modern
Symbolizing an early Chinese poem that refers to pearls, the Oriental Pearl Tower, Shanghai, China—a high-tech structure with a revolving restaurant—was once China's tallest structure.

Mighty Mosques

The world's tallest religious building is the Hassan II Mosque, Casablanca, Morocco. Completed in 1993, its minaret stands 689 ft (210 m) high. The world's largest mosque is the Masjid al-Haram ("Sacred Mosque"), Mecca, which covers 3,840,570 sq ft (356,800 sq m).

Gateway to the West
The Gateway Arch, St. Louis, USA, is a monument commemorating the nation's westward expansion.

TOP 10 **TALLEST MONUMENTS**

MONUMENT	LOCATION	YEAR	HEIGHT FT	M
1 Gateway Arch	St. Louis, Missouri, USA	1965	630	192
2 San Jacinto Monument	La Porte, Texas, USA	1939	570	174
3 Crazy Horse Memorial	Thunderhead Mountain, South Dakota, USA	u/c*	563	172
4 Juche Tower	Pyongyang, North, Korea	1982	558	170
5 Washington Monument	Washington, DC, USA	1884	555	169
6 Cruz de los Caidos	San Lorenzo de El Escorial, Spain	1956	492	150
7 Victory Monument	Moscow, Russia	1995	465	142
8 Pyramid of Khufu	Giza, Egypt	2560 BC	455	139
9 National Monument	Jakarta, Indonesia	1975	449	137
10 Pyramid of Khafre	Giza, Egypt	2532 BC	448	136

* Under construction

TOP 10 **HIGHEST DAMS**

DAM / RIVER / LOCATION	YEAR COMPLETED	HEIGHT FT	M
1 Rogun, Vakhsh, Tajikistan	1985	1,099	335
2 Nurek, Vakhsh, Tajikistan	1980	984	300
3 Xiaowan, Lancangjiang, China	2012*	958	292
4 Grande Dixence, Dixence, Switzerland	1962	935	285
5 Xiluodu, China	2015*	896	273
6 Inguri, Inguri, Georgia	1984	892	272
7 Vaiont, Vaiont, Italy	1961	860	262
8 = Manuel Moreno Torres, Chicoasén, Grijalva, Mexico	1981	856	261
= Tehri, Bhagirathi, India	2006	856	261
10 Álvaro Obregón, Mextiquic, Mexico	1946	853	260

* Under construction—scheduled completion

Source: International Commission on Large Dams (ICOLD), *World Register of Dams*

TOP 10 **TALLEST CHIMNEYS**

CHIMNEY / LOCATION	YEAR	HEIGHT FT	M
1 GRES-2 power station, Ekibastuz, Kazakhstan	1987	1,378	420
2 Inco Superstack, International Nickel Company, Copper, Hill Sudbury, Ontario, Canada	1971	1,250	381
3 Homer City Generating Station Unit 3, Minersville, Pennsylvania, USA	1977	1,217	371
4 = Kennecott Copper Corporation, Magna, Utah, USA	1974	1,214	370
= Beryozovskaya GRES, Shaypovo, Russia	1985	1,214	370
6 Mitchell Power Plant, Moundsville, West Virginia, USA	1971	1,207	368
7 Zasavje power station, Trbovlje, Slovenia	1976	1,181	360
8 Endesa Termic, La Coruña, Spain	1974	1,168	356
9 Phoenix Copper Smelter, Baia Mare, Romania	n/a	1,155	352
10 Syrdarya Power Plant Units 5–10, Syrdarya, Uzbekistan	1975	1,148	350

Bridges & Tunnels

TOP 10 LONGEST ARCH BRIDGES

	BRIDGE / LOCATION	YEAR COMPLETED	LENGTH OF MAIN SPAN FT	M
1	Chaotianmen, Chongqing, China	2008	1,811	552
2	Lupu, Shanghai, China	2003	1,804	550
3	New River Gorge, Fayetteville, West Virginia, USA	1977	1,699	518
4	Bayonne, Kill Van Kull, New Jersey/New York, USA	1931	1,654	504
5	Sydney Harbour, Sydney, Australia	1932	1,650	503
6	Chenab, Bakkal, India	2009	1,575	480
7	Wushan, Chongqing, China	2005	1,509	460
8	Xinguang, Guangzhou, China	2008	1,405	428
9 =	Wanxian, Wanxian, China	1997	1,378	420
=	Caiyuanba, Chongqing, China	2007	1,378	420

Over-arching
Connecting Luwan and Pudong—hence its name—the Lupu Bridge, Shanghai, China, held the record as the world's longest arch bridge from 2003–08.

Sky high
While the giant pylons of the Millau Viaduct, France, are taller, the Royal Gorge Bridge, Colorado, USA, has the highest road deck.

TOP 10 LONGEST RAIL TUNNELS

	TUNNEL / LOCATION	YEAR COMPLETED	LENGTH MILES	KM
1	AlpTransit Gotthard, Switzerland	2018*	35.6	57.1
2	Seikan, Japan	1988	33.6	53.9
3	Channel Tunnel, France/England	1994	31.5	50.5
4	Moscow Metro (Serpukhovsko-Timiryazevskaya line), Russia	2002	25.9	41.5
5	Moscow Metro (Kaluzhsko-Rizhskaya line), Russia	1990	23.4	37.6
6	Lötschberg Base, Switzerland	2007	21.6	34.6
7	Berlin U-Bahn (U7 line)	1984	19.8	31.8
8	Guadarrama, Spain	2007	17.7	28.4
9	Taihang, China	2008	17.4	27.9
10	London Underground (East Finchley/Morden, Northern Line), UK	1939	17.3	27.8

* Under construction—scheduled completion

The world's longest rail tunnel, the AlpTransit Gotthard, Switzerland, was proposed as early as 1947 and given the go-ahead in 1998 after a referendum of the Swiss electorate. When completed, trains will travel through it at 155 mph (250 km/h).

TOP 10 LONGEST ROAD AND RAIL TUNNELS IN THE USA*

	TUNNEL / LOCATION	TYPE	YEAR COMPLETED	LENGTH FT	M
1	New Cascade, Washington	Rail	1929	41,154	12,544
2	Flathead, Montana	Rail	1970	37,073	11,300
3	Moffat, Colorado	Rail	1928	32,795	9,996
4	Hoosac, Massachusetts	Rail	1875	25,082	7,645
5	BART Transbay Tubes, San Francisco, California	Rail	1974	18,996	5,790
6	Ted Williams, Boston, Massachusetts	Road	2003	13,779	4,200
7	Anton Anderson Memorial, Whittier City, Alaska	Road/rail	2000	13,727	4,184
8	Brooklyn-Battery, New York	Road	1950	9,117	2,779
9	Eisenhower-Johnson Memorial, Colorado#	Road	1979	8,959	2,731
10	Holland Tunnel, New York	Road	1927	8,556	2,608

* In use for road or rail transportation; excluding subways
# The highest elevation highway tunnel in the world

The Henderson narrow-gauge railway that operated in a 51,837-ft (15,800-m) mine tunnel in Colorado, built in 1976, was replaced in 1999 by a conveyor belt, so has been discounted.

TOP 10 **TALLEST BRIDGES**

	BRIDGE	LOCATION	YEAR	HEIGHT* FT	M
1	Royal Gorge	Colorado, USA	1929	1,053	321
2	Millau Viaduct	Millau, France	2004	886	270
3	New River Gorge	West Virginia, USA	1977	876	267
4	Foresthill	California, USA	1973	732	223
5	Mala Rijeka viaduct#	Montenegro	1973	656	200
6	Europabrücke	Patsch, Austria	1963	623	190
7	Kocher Valley	Geislingen am Kocher, Germany	1979	607	185
8	Đurđevića Tara	Montenegro	1940	564	172
9	Verrazano Narrows	New York City, USA	1964	226	69
10	Golden Gate	San Francisco, USA	1937	220	67

* Clearance above water
\# Rail; all others road

TOP 10 **LONGEST SUSPENSION BRIDGES**

	BRIDGE / LOCATION	YEAR COMPLETED	LENGTH OF MAIN SPAN FT	M
1	Akashi-Kaikyō, Kobe-Naruto, Japan	1998	6,532	1,991
2	Xihoumen, China	2007	5,413	1,650
3	Great Belt, Denmark	1997	5,328	1,624
4	Ryungyang, China	2005	4,888	1,490
5	Humber Estuary, UK	1980	4,625	1,410
6	Jiangyin, China	1998	4,543	1,385
7	Tsing Ma, Hong Kong, China	1997	4,518	1,377
8	Verrazano-Narrows, New York, USA	1964	4,260	1,298
9	= Golden Gate, San Francisco, USA	1937	4,200	1,280
	= Yangluo, Wuhan, China	2007	4,200	1,280

TOP 10 **LONGEST ROAD TUNNELS**

	TUNNEL / LOCATION	YEAR COMPLETED	LENGTH FT	M
1	Lærdal, Norway	2000	80,413	24,510
2	Zhongnanshan, China	2007	59,186	18,040
3	St Gotthard, Switzerland	1980	55,505	16,918
4	Arlberg, Austria	1978	45,850	13,972
5	Hsuehshan, Taiwan	2006	42,323	12,900
6	Fréjus, France/Italy	1980	42,306	12,895
7	Mont-Blanc, France/Italy	1965	38,094	11,611
8	Gudvangen, Norway	1991	37,493	11,428
9	Folgefonn, Norway	2001	36,417	11,100
10	Kan-Etsu II (southbound), Japan	1991	36,122	11,010

* Under construction—scheduled completion

Nos. 1, 3, 4, and 7 have all held the record as "world's longest road tunnel." Previous record-holders include the 19,206-ft (5,854-m) Grand San Bernardo (Italy-Switzerland; 1964); the 16,841-ft (5,133-m) Alfonos XIII or Viella (Spain; 1948); the 10,620-ft (3,237-m) Queensway (Mersey) Tunnel (connecting Liverpool and Birkenhead, UK; 1934); and the 10,453-ft (3,186-m) Col de Tende (France-Italy; 1882).

Going underground
Engineering advances have enabled the construction of increasingly long subterranean and underwater tunnels.

CULTURE & LEARNING

Words & Language

TOP 10 **LANGUAGES INTO WHICH MOST BOOKS ARE TRANSLATED**

LANGUAGE / TRANSLATIONS 1979–2008

1 German 270,484

2 Spanish 206,779
3 French 203,559

4 Japanese 117,769
5 English 115,710

6 Dutch 101,763

7 Portuguese 71,291

8 Polish 64,119

9 Russian 62,983
10 Danish 59,014

Source: UNESCO,
Index Translationum
(1979–2008)

TOP 10 **LANGUAGES FROM WHICH MOST BOOKS ARE TRANSLATED**

LANGUAGE / TRANSLATIONS 1979–2008

1 English 1,000,758

2 French 186,036   **3** German 169,387   **4** Russian 93,779

5 Italian
55,397

6 Spanish
43,365

7 Swedish
30,738

8 Latin
16,602

9 Danish
16,222

10 Czech
16,050

Source: UNESCO,
Index Translationum (1979–2008)

TOP 10 **LANGUAGES MOST SPOKEN IN THE USA**

LANGUAGE / NO. OF SPEAKERS

1 English 215,423,557
2 Spanish 28,101,052
3 Chinese 2,022,143
4 French 1,643,838
5 German 1,382,613
6 Tagalog 1,224,241
7 Vietnamese 1,009,627
8 Italian 1,008,370
9 Korean 894,063
10 Russian 706,242

Source: US Census Bureau,
Census 2000

TOP 10 **MOST COMMON WORDS IN ENGLISH**

WRITTEN		SPOKEN
the	1	be
of	2	the
and	3	I
a	4	you
in	5	and
to	6	it
is	7	have
was	8	a
it	9	not
for	10	do

Source: British National Corpus

A survey of a wide range of texts containing a total of almost 90 million words indicated that, in written English, one word in every 16 is "the."

TOP 10 **LANGUAGES OFFICIALLY SPOKEN IN THE MOST COUNTRIES**

LANGUAGE / COUNTRIES

English 55

French 29

Arabic 24

Spanish 20

Portuguese 10

German 7

= Albanian 4
= Italian 4
= Russian 4
= Serbian 4

World English
English has become the lingua franca in countries that have a multiplicity of local languages.

TOP 10 **MOST-SPOKEN LANGUAGES***

	LANGUAGE	SPEAKERS
1	Chinese (Mandarin)	873,014,298
2	Spanish	322,299,171
3	English	309,352,280
4	Hindi	180,764,791
5	Portuguese	177,457,180
6	Bengali	171,070,202
7	Russian	145,031,551
8	Japanese	122,433,899
9	German	95,392,978
10	Chinese (Wu)	77,175,000

* Primary speakers only

Source: Gordon, Raymond G., Jr. (ed.),
Ethnologue: Languages of the World, Fifteenth
edition. Dallas, Tex.: SIL International, 2005.
Online version: www.ethnologue.com

Schools

TOP 10 COUNTRIES WITH MOST PRIMARY SCHOOL PUPILS

	COUNTRY	PRIMARY SCHOOL PUPILS (2006)
1	India	139,170,000
2	China	108,925,000
3	Indonesia	28,983,000
4	USA	24,319,000
5	Nigeria	22,115,000
6	Brazil	18,661,000
7	Pakistan	17,979,000
8	Bangladesh	17,953,000
9	Mexico	14,595,000
10	Philippines	13,007,000
	Top 10 total	405,707,000
	World total	688,608,000

Source: UNESCO, *Global Education Digest 2008*

TOP 10 COUNTRIES WITH MOST PRIMARY SCHOOL TEACHERS

	COUNTRY	AVERAGE CLASS SIZE	PRIMARY SCHOOL TEACHERS (2006)
1	China	18	5,968,000
2	India	64	2,189,000
3	USA	14	1,761,000
4	Indonesia	20	1,428,000
5	Brazil	21	887,000
6	Nigeria	37	599,000
7	Mexico	28	521,000
8	Pakistan	40	450,000
9	Japan	19	386,000
10	Philippines	35	376,000
	World	25	27,216,000

Source: UNESCO, *Global Education Digest 2008*

A class of their own
Almost 140 million children attend primary school in India, one in eight of its population.

TOP 10 **OLDEST SCHOOLS IN THE WORLD**

	SCHOOL	FOUNDED
1	Shishi Middle School, Chengdu, China	143–141 BC
2	The King's School, Canterbury, UK	597
3	The King's School, Rochester, UK	604
4	St. Peter's School, York, UK	627
5	Beverley Grammar School, Beverley, UK	700
6	Gymnasium Paulinum, Münster, Germany	797
7	Gymnasium Carolinum, Osnabrück, Germany	804
8	Warwick School, Warwick, UK	914
9	St. Alban's School, St. Alban's, UK	948
10	The King's School, Ely, UK	970

TOP 10 **COUNTRIES WITH THE MOST SECONDARY SCHOOL PUPILS**

	COUNTRY	SECONDARY SCHOOL PUPILS (2006)
1	China	101,195,000
2	India	91,529,000
3	Brazil	24,863,000
4	USA	24,552,000
5	Indonesia	16,798,000
6	Russia	11,548,000
7	Mexico	10,883,000
8	Bangladesh	10,355,000
9	Vietnam	9,975,000
10	Egypt	8,330,000
	Top 10 total	310,028,000
	World total	513,766,000

High school
Although close behind Brazil in numbers of pupils in secondary school, the population of the USA is more than one-third higher.

Further Education

TOP 10 **LARGEST UNIVERSITIES**

UNIVERSITY / LOCATION / APPROX. ENROLMENT

Allama Iqbal Open University,
Islamabad, Pakistan
1,850,643

**Indira Gandhi National
Open University,**
New Delhi, India
1,800,000

Islamic Azad University,
Tehran, Iran
1,300,000

Anadolu University,
Eskisehir, Turkey
884,081

**Bangladesh
Open University,**
Eskisehir, Turkey
884,081

**University System
of Ohio,**
Ohio, USA
800,000

**Dr. Babasaheb
Ambedkar Open
University,**
Andhra Pradesh, India
450,000

**State University
of New York,**
New York, USA
418,000

**California State
University,**
California, USA
417,000

University of Delhi
India
400,000

High flyers
*A graduation ceremony in China, now at the
forefront of higher education.*

TOP 10 **COUNTRIES WITH THE MOST
UNIVERSITY STUDENTS**

COUNTRY / % FEMALE /
STUDENTS IN TERTIARY
EDUCATION (2006)

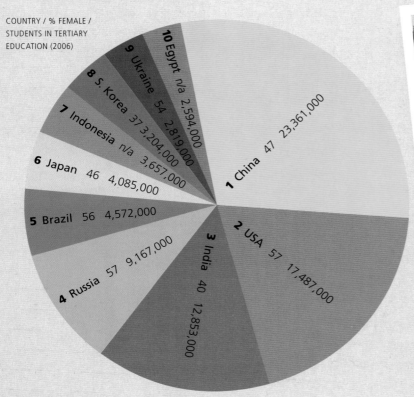

10 Egypt n/a 2,594,000
9 Ukraine 54 2,819,000
8 S. Korea 37 3,204,000
7 Indonesia n/a 3,657,000
6 Japan 46 4,085,000
5 Brazil 56 4,572,000
4 Russia 57 9,167,000
3 India 40 12,853,000
2 USA 57 17,487,000
1 China 47 23,361,000

TOP 10 **OLDEST UNIVERSITIES***

	UNIVERSITY	COUNTRY	FOUNDED
1	Parma	Italy	1064
2	Bologna	Italy	1088
3	Oxford	England	1117
4	Paris	France	1150
5	Modena	Italy	1175
6	Cambridge	England	1209
7	Salamanca	Spain	1218
8	Padua	Italy	1222
9	Naples	Italy	1224
10	Toulouse	France	1229

* Only those in continuous operation since founding

Alma mater
One of the world's oldest universities, Bologna's former students include Renaissance astronomer Nicolaus Copernicus.

TOP 10 **OLDEST UNIVERSITIES IN THE UK**

	UNIVERSITY	FOUNDED
1	Oxford	1117
2	Cambridge	1209
3	St. Andrews	1411
4	Glasgow	1451
5	Aberdeen	1495
6	Edinburgh	1583
7	Dublin*	1592
8	Durham#	1832
9	London†	1836
10	Manchester	1851

* Ireland then part of England
\# A short-lived Cromwellian establishment was set up in 1657
† Constituent colleges founded earlier:
University College 1826, King's College 1828

Although its constituent colleges were founded earlier – Lampeter 1822, Aberystwyth 1872, Cardiff 1883, Bangor 1884 – the University of Wales dates from 1893.

Dreaming spires
Oxford was Britain's first university and is the oldest outside Italy.

TOP 10 **OLDEST UNIVERSITIES AND COLLEGES IN THE USA**

	UNIVERSITY / LOCATION	YEAR CHARTERED
1	**Harvard University**, Massachusetts	1636
2	**College of William and Mary**, Virginia	1692
3	**Yale University**, Connecticut	1701
4	**University of Pennsylvania**, Pennsylvania	1740
5	**Moravian College**, Pennsylvania	1742
6	**Princeton University**, New Jersey	1746
7	**Washington and Lee University**, Virginia	1749
8	**Columbia University**, New York	1754
9	**Brown University**, Rhode Island	1764
10	**Rutgers**, the State University of New Jersey	1766

Source: National Center for Education Statistics

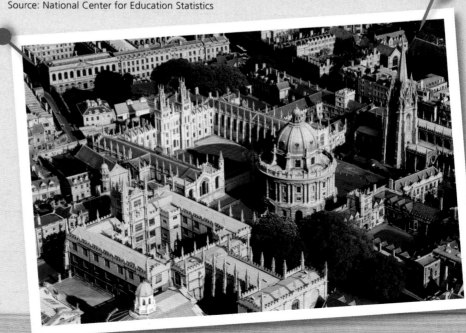

Books & Libraries

Making his mark
A hundred years after his death, Mark Twain remains one of the most-read American authors.

TOP 10 MOST DOWNLOADED ENGLISH-LANGUAGE AUTHORS

	AUTHOR	DOWNLOADS*
1	Charles Dickens	37,541
2	Mark Twain	32,273
3	Jane Austen	27,979
4	William Shakespeare	27,678
5	Sir Arthur Conan Doyle	26,007
6	J. Arthur Thomson	23,069
7	Oscar Wilde	14,551
8	Lewis Carroll	13,790
9	Edgar Allan Poe	13,563
10	L. Frank Baum	13,355

* Based on 30-day sample on Project Gutenberg

THE 10 FIRST PUBLIC LIBRARIES IN THE USA

	LIBRARY	FOUNDED
1	Peterboro Public Library, NH	1833
2	Buffalo and Erie County Public Library, NY	1836
3	New Orleans Public Library, LA	1843
4	Boston Public Library, MA	1848
5	Public Library of Cincinnati and Hamilton County, OH	1853
6	Springfield City Library, MA	1857
7	Worcester Public Library, MA	1859
8	Multnomah County Library, OR	1864
9	Detroit Public Library, MI	1865
10	Atlanta-Fulton Public Library, GA	1867

TOP 10 BESTSELLING ENGLISH-LANGUAGE AUTHORS

	AUTHOR / COUNTRY / DATES	MAX. ESTIMATED SALES
1	= Agatha Christie (UK, 1890–1976)	4,000,000,000
	= William Shakespeare (England, 1664–1616)	4,000,000,000
3	Barbara Cartland (UK, 1901–2000)	1,000,000,000
4	Harold Robbins (USA, 1916–97)	750,000,000
5	Enid Blyton (UK, 1897–1968)	600,000,000
6	Danielle Steel (USA, b. 1947)	570,000,000
7	Dr. Seuss (Theodor Seuss Geisel; USA, 1904–91)	500,000,000
8	= Horatio Alger Jr (USA, 1832–99)	400,000,000
	= Jackie Collins (UK, b. 1937)	400,000,000
	= J. K. Rowling (UK, b. 1965)	400,000,000
	= R. L. Stine (USA, b. 1943)	400,000,000

Estimates of book sales are fraught with difficulty: records have often been lost, publishers may either withhold information or exaggerate for publicity purposes, while taking account of all editions, including hardbacks, paperbacks, and translations, compounds the problem. This list should therefore be regarded as a tentative attempt to indicate the total sales of the oeuvre of some of the bestselling writers of all time in the English language, according to authorities on the respective writers and their work. The omission, through lack of sales evidence, of such writers as Charles Dickens suggests that it should not be taken as definitive.

TOP 10 **LARGEST LIBRARIES**

	LIBRARY	LOCATION	FOUNDED	BOOKS
1	Library of Congress	Washington DC, USA	1800	32,124,001
2	British Library*	London, UK	1753	29,000,000
3	Library of the Russian Academy of Sciences	St. Petersburg, Russia	1714	20,500,000
4	National Library of Canada	Ottawa, Canada	1953	19,500,000
5	Deutsche Bibliothek#	Frankfurt, Germany	1990	22,200,000
6	Russian State Library†	Moscow, Russia	1862	17,000,000
7	Harvard University Library	Cambridge, Massachusetts, USA	1638	15,826,570
8	Boston Public Library	Boston, Massachusetts, USA	1895	15,686,902
9	Vernadsky National Scientific Library of Ukraine	Kiev, Ukraine	1919	15,000,000
10	National Library of Russia	St Petersburg	1795	14,799,267

* Founded as part of the British Museum, 1753; became an independent body in 1973
# Formed in 1990 through the unification of the Deutsche Bibliothek, Frankfurt (founded 1947) and the Deutsche Bucherei, Leipzig
† Founded 1862 as Rumyantsev Library, formerly State V. I. Lenin Library

Library of Congress
The vast range of the collections of the Library of Congress is exemplified by the figures that surmount the eight columns in its reading room, which represent Religion, Commerce, History, Art, Philosophy, Poetry, Law, and Science.

TOP 10 **BOOKS FOUND IN MOST LIBRARIES**

BOOK / TOTAL LIBRARY HOLDINGS*

* Based on WorldCat listings of all editions of books held in 53,000 libraries in 96 countries

Source: OCLC (Online Computer Library Center)

1 Bible 796,882
2 US Census 460,628
3 Mother Goose 67,663
4 Dante Alighieri, Divine Comedy 62,414
5 Homer, The Odyssey 45,551
6 Homer, The Iliad 44,093
7 Mark Twain, Huckleberry Finn 42,724
8 J. R. R. Tolkien, Lord of the Rings (trilogy) 40,907
9 William Shakespeare, Hamlet 39,521
10 Lewis Carroll, Alice's Adventures in Wonderland 39,277

Literary Prizes

THE 10 **LATEST CALDECOTT MEDAL WINNERS**

YEAR	AUTHOR / TITLE
2008	Brian Selznick, The Invention of Hugo Cabret
2007	David Wiesner, Flotsam
2006	Chris Raschka, The Hello, Goodbye Window
2005	Kevin Henkes, Kitten's First Full Moon
2004	Mordicai Gerstein, The Man Who Walked Between the Towers
2003	Eric Rohmann, My Friend Rabbit
2002	David Wiesner, The Three Pigs
2001	Judith St. George (illustrated by David Small), So You Want to be President?
2000	Simms Taback, Joseph Had a Little Overcoat
1999	Jacqueline Briggs Martin (illustrated by Mary Azarian), Snowflake Bentley

The Caldecott Medal has been awarded annually since 1938.

Michael Chabon
Having received the Pulitzer Prize for Fiction in 2001, US author Michael Chabon won the 2008 Hugo Award.

THE 10 **LATEST NATIONAL BOOK AWARDS FOR NON-FICTION**

YEAR	AUTHOR / TITLE
2008	Annette Gordon-Reed, The Hemingses of Monticello: An American Family
2007	Tim Weiner, Legacy of Ashes: The History of the CIA
2006	Timothy Egan, The Worst Hard Time: The Untold Story of Those Who Survived the Great American Dust Bowl
2005	Joan Didion, The Year of Magical Thinking
2004	Kevin Boyle, Arc of Justice: A Saga of Race, Civil Rights, and Murder in the Jazz Age
2003	Carlos Eire, Waiting for Snow in Havana: Confessions of a Cuban Boy
2002	Robert A. Caro, Master of the Senate: The Years of Lyndon Johnson
2001	Andrew Solomon, The Noonday Demon: An Atlas of Depression
2000	Nathaniel Philbrick, In the Heart of the Sea: The Tragedy of the Whaleship Essex
1999	John W. Dower, Embracing Defeat: Japan in the Wake of World War II

The prestigious National Book Awards were established in 1950, with a mission "to celebrate the best of American literature, to expand its audience, and to enhance the cultural value of good writing in America."

THE 10 **LATEST WINNERS OF HUGO AWARDS FOR BEST SCIENCE FICTION NOVEL**

YEAR	AUTHOR / TITLE
2008	Michael Chabon, The Yiddish Policeman's Union
2007	Vernor Vinge, Rainbows End
2006	Robert Charles Wilson, Spin
2005	Susanna Clarke, Jonathan Strange & Mr Norrell
2004	Lois McMaster Bujold, Paladin of Souls
2003	Robert J. Sawyer, Hominids
2002	Neil Gaiman, American Gods
2001	J. K. Rowling, Harry Potter and the Goblet of Fire
2000	Vernor Vinge, A Deepness in the Sky
1999	Connie Willis, To Say Nothing of the Dog

Hugo Awards for science-fiction novels, short stories and other fiction and non-fiction works are presented by the World Science Fiction Society. Named in honor of Hugo Gernsback, the "father of magazine science fiction," they were established in 1953 as "Science Fiction Achievement Awards for the best science fiction writing." The prize in the Awards' inaugural year was presented to Alfred Bester for *The Demolished Man*.

THE 10 **LATEST WINNERS OF THE NOBEL PRIZE IN LITERATURE**

YEAR	WINNER / COUNTRY
2008	J. M. G. Le Clézio, France
2007	Doris Lessing, UK
2006	Orhan Pamuk, Turkey
2005	Harold Pinter, UK
2004	Elfriede Jelinek, Austria
2003	J. M. Coetzee, South Africa
2002	Imre Kertész, Hungary
2001	Sir V. S. Naipaul, UK
2000	Gao Xingjian, China
1999	Günter Grass, Germany

Le Clézio
Jean-Marie Gustave Le Clézio (left) receives his Nobel Prize from King Carl XVI Gustaf of Sweden.

THE 10 **LATEST WINNERS OF THE JOHN NEWBERY MEDAL**

YEAR	AUTHOR / TITLE
2008	Sebastian Barry, Good Masters! Sweet Ladies! Voices from a Medieval Village
2007	Susan Patron, The Higher Power of Lucky
2006	Lynne Rae Perkins, Criss Cross
2005	Cynthia Kadohata, Kira-Kira
2004	Kate DiCamillo, The Tale of Despereaux
2003	Avi, Crispin: The Cross of Lead
2002	Linda Sue Park, A Single Shard
2001	Richard Peck, A Year Down Yonder
2000	Christopher Paul Curtis, Bud, Not Buddy
1999	Louis Sachar, Holes

THE 10 **LATEST WINNERS OF THE PULITZER PRIZE FOR FICTION**

YEAR	AUTHOR / TITLE
2008	Junot Diaz, The Brief Wondrous Life of Oscar Wao
2007	Cormac McCarthy, The Road
2006	Geraldine Brooks, March
2005	Marilynne Robinson, Gilead
2003	Edward P. Jones, The Known World
2002	Jeffrey Eugenides, Middlesex
2001	Richard Russo, Empire Falls
2000	Michael Chabon, The Amazing Adventures of Kavalier & Clay
1999	Jhumpa Lhiri, Interpreter of Maladies
1998	Michael Cunningham, The Hours

Nobel Prize Winners

Since it was first awarded in 1901, there have been 105 recipients of the Nobel Prize in Literature. As it is in effect a lifetime achievement award, it is not presented to young writers—Rudyard Kipling (UK, 1907 winner) was the youngest at 42. The first woman to receive the Prize was Selma Lagerlöf (Sweden, 1909); since then another 10 women have won. Twelve born or naturalized American and the same number of British writers have won it.

The Press

TOP 10 **DAILY NEWSPAPERS**

NEWSPAPER	COUNTRY	AVERAGE DAILY CIRCULATION (2008)*
1 Yomiuri Shimbun	Japan	10,021,000
2 Asahi Shimbun	Japan	8,054,000
3 Mainichi Shimbun	Japan	3,945,646
4 Bild	Germany	3,548,000
5 Canako Xiaoxi (Beijing)	China	3,183,000
6 The Times of India	India	3,146,000
7 The Sun	UK	3,121,000
8 Nihon Keizai Shimbun	Japan	3,034,481
9 People's Daily	China	2,808,000
10 Chunichi Shimbun	Japan	2,763,602

* Morning edition if published twice daily

Source: World Association of Newspapers 2008 or latest Audit Bureau of Circulations figure

Yomiuri Shimbun was founded in Japan 1874. It became the country's and the world's bestselling daily newspaper when, in 1998, it achieved a record average sale of 14,532,694 copies a day, including its morning and evening editions.

The Times of India *The world's most-read English-language newspaper.*

TOP 10 **ENGLISH-LANGUAGE DAILY NEWSPAPERS**

NEWSPAPER	COUNTRY	AVERAGE DAILY CIRCULATION (2008)
1 The Times of India	India	3,146,000
2 The Sun	UK	3,121,000
3 USA Today	USA	2,284,219
4 Daily Mail	UK	2,241,788
5 The Wall Street Journal	USA	2,069,463
6 Daily Mirror	UK	1,494,000
7 Hindustan Times	India	1,143,000
8 The Hindu	India	1,102,783
9 Deccan Chronicle	India	1,003,171
10 The New York Times	USA	1,000,665

Source: World Association of Newspapers 2008 or latest Audit Bureau of Circulations figure

The world's bestselling English-language dailies represent both long-established publications and relative newcomers: the *Daily Herald*, the first paper to ever sell two million copies, was launched in 1911, became *The Sun* in 1964 and was re-launched as a tabloid in 1969. The *Daily Mail* started in 1896, absorbing the *News Chronicle* in 1960 and *Daily Sketch* in 1971. *USA Today*, launched in 1982, was one of the first newspapers to use computers and to transmit editions for simultaneous publication around the world. *The Times of India* began in 1838 as *The Bombay Times* and *Journal of Commerce*, changing to its present name in 1861.

TOP 10 DAILY NEWSPAPERS IN THE USA

NEWSPAPER	AVERAGE CIRCULATION (2008)
1 USA Today	2,284,219
2 The Wall Street Journal	2,069,463
3 The New York Times	1,077,256
4 Los Angeles Times	773,884
5 New York Daily News	703,137
6 New York Post	702,488
7 Washington Post	673,180
8 Chicago Tribune	541,663
9 Houston Chronicle	494,131
10 Arizona Republic	413,332

Source: Audit Bureau of Circulations

TOP 10 LONGEST-RUNNING MAGAZINES IN THE USA

MAGAZINE	FIRST PUBLISHED
1 Scientific American	1845
2 Town & Country	1846
3 Harper's*	1850
4 The Moravian	1856
5 The Atlantic Monthly	1857
6 Armed Forces Journal†	1863
7 The Nation	1865
8 American Naturalist	1867
9 Harper's Bazaar§	1867
10 Animals¶	1868

* Originally *The National Press* then *The Home Journal*
\# Originally *Harper's New Monthly Magazine*
† Originally *Army and Navy Journal*
§ Originally spelled *Bazar*
¶ Originally *Our Dumb Animals*

Applied Science

Founded by artist-inventor Rufus Porter, *Scientific American* was first published on 28 August 1845 and is America's longest continuously published magazine. It originally included features on non-scientific topics, but its change of focus led to its becoming the world's most popular scientific journal.

Press censorship *The military junta in Myanmar (Burma) severely restricts country's press.*

THE 10 COUNTRIES WITH THE LEAST PRESS FREEDOM

COUNTRY	RATING
1 North Korea	98
2 Myanmar	97
3 Turkmenistan	96
4 = Cuba	94
= Eritrea	94
= Libya	94
7 Uzbekistan	92
8 Belarus	91
9 = Equatorial Guinea	89
= Zimbabwe	89

Source: Freedom House

This list is based on the Freedom House 2008 survey, which takes account of laws, political pressure, economic influence on, and repressive actions against broadcast and print journalists; the higher the number, the worse the press freedom. The survey concludes that of a total of 195 countries, 72 have free press, 59 are partly free, and 64 not free. The "not free" category represents a population of 2,766,500,000, or 42 percent of the world, and "free" 1,177,090,000, or 18 percent.

Reading frenzy
India's huge and literate population is served by a vast number of newspapers and magazines catering for its multiplicity of languages.

Art on Show

TOP 10 BEST-ATTENDED EXHIBITIONS AT THE NATIONAL GALLERY, WASHINGTON, DC

	EXHIBITION / YEARS	ATTENDANCE
1	Rodin Rediscovered 1981–82	1,053,223
2	Treasure Houses of Britain 1985–86	990,474
3	The Treasures of Tutankhamun 1976–77	835,924
4	Archaeological Finds of the People's Republic of China 1974–75	684,238
5	Ansel Adams: Classic Images 1985–86	651,652
6	The Splendor of Dresden 1978	620,089
7	The Art of Paul Gauguin 1988	596,058
8	Circa 1492: Art in the Age of Exploration 1991–92	568,192
9	Andrew Wyeth: The Helga Pictures 1987	558,433
10	Post Impressionism: Cross Currents in European & American Painting 1980	557,533

TOP 10 MOST-VISITED GALLERIES AND MUSEUMS, 2008

	GALLERY	TOTAL ATTENDANCE
1	Louvre Museum, Paris, France	8,500,000
2	British Museum, London, UK	5,930,000
3	National Gallery of Art, Washington, DC, USA	4,964,061
4	Tate Modern, London, UK	4,950,003
5	Metropolitan Museum of Art, New York, USA	4,821,079
6	Vatican Museums, Vatican City	4,441,734
7	National Gallery, London, UK	4,382,614
8	Musée d'Orsay, Paris, France	3,025,141
9	Musée d'Art Moderne Prado, Paris, France	2,981,000
10	Museum of Modern Art, New York, USA	2,900,157

Source: *Art Newspaper*

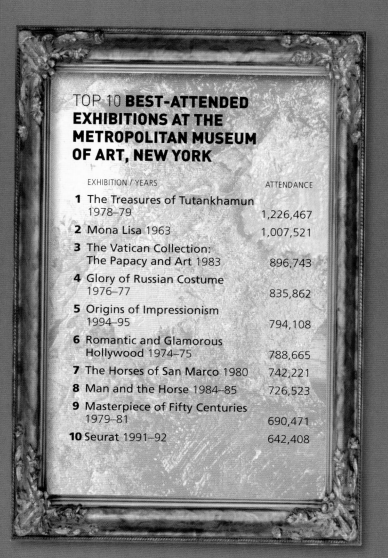

TOP 10 BEST-ATTENDED EXHIBITIONS AT THE METROPOLITAN MUSEUM OF ART, NEW YORK

EXHIBITION / YEARS	ATTENDANCE
1 The Treasures of Tutankhamun 1978–79	1,226,467
2 Mona Lisa 1963	1,007,521
3 The Vatican Collection: The Papacy and Art 1983	896,743
4 Glory of Russian Costume 1976–77	835,862
5 Origins of Impressionism 1994–95	794,108
6 Romantic and Glamorous Hollywood 1974–75	788,665
7 The Horses of San Marco 1980	742,221
8 Man and the Horse 1984–85	726,523
9 Masterpiece of Fifty Centuries 1979–81	690,471
10 Seurat 1991–92	642,408

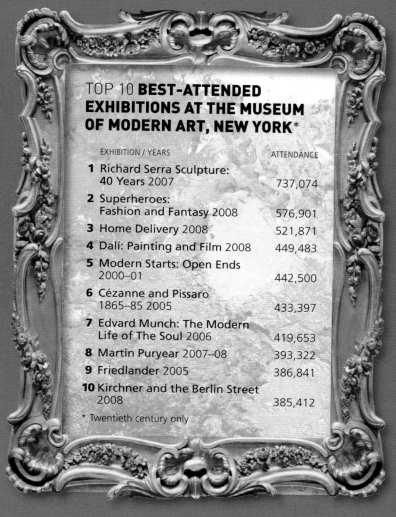

TOP 10 BEST-ATTENDED EXHIBITIONS AT THE MUSEUM OF MODERN ART, NEW YORK *

EXHIBITION / YEARS	ATTENDANCE
1 Richard Serra Sculpture: 40 Years 2007	737,074
2 Superheroes: Fashion and Fantasy 2008	576,901
3 Home Delivery 2008	521,871
4 Dalí: Painting and Film 2008	449,483
5 Modern Starts: Open Ends 2000–01	442,500
6 Cézanne and Pissaro 1865–85 2005	433,397
7 Edvard Munch: The Modern Life of The Soul 2006	419,653
8 Martin Puryear 2007–08	393,322
9 Friedlander 2005	386,841
10 Kirchner and the Berlin Street 2008	385,412

* Twentieth century only

Ancient and Modern

Although controversial when it was built in 1989, the steel and glass Louvre pyramid, the design of Chinese-born architect I. M. Pei, has attracted increasing numbers of visitors to the museum. Once a royal palace, the Louvre was opened to the public in 1793, after the French Revolution. It is famous as the home of Leonardo da Vinci's *Mona Lisa*, which has been in France since 1516, when it was acquired by King Francis I.

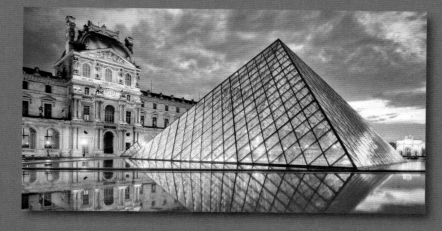

Saleroom Record-breakers

TOP 10 MOST EXPENSIVE PAINTINGS BY AMERICAN ARTISTS

PAINTING / ARTIST	SALE	PRICE ($)
1 White Center, Mark Rothko (1903–70)	Sotheby's New York, May 15, 2007	72,840,000
2 Green car crash - Green burning car I, Andy Warhol (1928–87)	Christie's New York, May 16, 2007	71,720,000
3 No. 15, Mark Rothko	Christie's New York, May 13, 2008	50,441,000
4 Untitled – Red, Blue, Orange, Mark Rothko	Christie's New York, Nov 13, 2007	34,201,000
5 Double Marlon, Andy Warhol	Christie's New York, May 13, 2008	32,521,000
6 Lemon Marilyn, Andy Warhol	Christie's New York, May 16, 2007	28,040,000
7 Polo Crowd, George Bellows (1882–1925)	Sotheby's New York, Dec 1, 1999	27,702,500
8 Untitled, Willem de Kooning* (1904–97)	Christie's New York, Nov 15, 2006	27,120,000
9 Hotel Window, Edward Hopper (1882–1967)	Sotheby's New York, Nov 29, 2006	26,896,000
10 Liz, Andy Warhol	Sotheby's London, Feb 27, 2008	22,226,645 (£11,444,500)

* Dutch-born, naturalized US citizen

TOP 10 MOST EXPENSIVE WORKS OF ART BY LIVING ARTISTS

PAINTING / ARTIST	SALE	PRICE ($)
1 Benefits Supervisor Sleeping, Lucian Freud (British; b. 1922)	Christie's New York, May 13, 2008	33,641,000
2 Balloon Flower – Magenta, Jeff Koons (American; b. 1955)	Christie's London, Jun 30, 2008	25,796,067 (£12,921,250)
3 Hanging Heart – Magenta/Gold, Jeff Koons	Sotheby's New York, Nov 14, 2006	23,561,000
4 Naked Portrait with Reflection, Lucian Freud	Christie's London, Jun 30, 2008	23,560,091 (£11,801,250)
5 IB and Her Husband, Lucian Freud	Christie's New York, May 16, 2007	19,361,000
6 Lullaby Spring, Damien Hirst (British; b. 1965)	Sotheby's London, Jun 21, 2007	19,075,098 (£9,652,000)
7 The Golden Calf, Damien Hirst	Sotheby's London, Sep 15, 2008	19,003,030 (£10,345,250)
8 The Kingdom, Damien Hirst	Sotheby's London, Sep 15, 2008	17,562,913 (£9,561,250)
9 Figure 4, Jasper Johns (American; b. 1930),	Christie's New York, May 16, 2007	17,400,000
10 False Start, Jasper Johns	Sotheby's New York, Nov 10, 1988	17,050,000

PRIVATE SALE RECORD-BREAKERS

The precise details of private (as contrasted with public auction) sales of works of art range from those that are totally secret to others where the vendor or purchaser deliberately publishes—and perhaps exaggerates—them in order to derive maximum publicity. In 2006, three paintings that were sold privately were claimed to have been the most expensive of all time: music mogul David Geffen sold Jackson Pollock's action painting *No. 5, 1948* for $140 million and Willem De Kooning's *Woman III* for $137.5 million, while Maria Altmann sold Gustav Klimt's *Portrait of Adele Bloch-Bauer I* to cosmetics magnate Ronald Lauder for $135 million. In the same year Pablo Picasso's *Le rêve* hit the headlines when its owner, Las Vegas casino owner Steve Wynn, agreed to sell it in a private transaction for $139 million. The sale was abandoned when Wynn accidentally damaged it by poking his elbow through the canvas. Picasso's *Garçon à la pipe* is the only other painting ever sold either privately or at auction for more than $100 million.

Monet market
Monet's waterlily painting was sold in 2008 for a record $80 million.

TOP 10 **MOST EXPENSIVE PAINTINGS EVER SOLD AT AUCTION**

PAINTING / ARTIST	SALE	PRICE ($)
1 Garçon à la pipe, Pablo Picasso (Spanish; 1881–1973)	Sotheby's New York, May 5, 2004	104,168,000
2 Dora Maar au chat, Pablo Picasso	Sotheby's New York, May 3, 2006	95,216,000
3 Portrait of Adele Bloch-Bauer II, Gustav Klimt (Austrian; 1862–1918)	Christie's New York, Nov 8, 2006	87,936,000
4 Triptych, Francis Bacon (Irish; 1909–92)	Sotheby's New York, May 14, 2008	86,281,000
5 Portrait du Dr Gachet, Vincent van Gogh (Dutch; 1853–90)	Christie's New York, May 15, 1990	82,500,000
6 Le Bassin aux Nymphéas, Claude Monet (French; 1840–1926)	Christie's London, Jun 24, 2008	80,379,591 (£40,921,250)
7 Bal au Moulin de la Galette, Montmartre Pierre-Auguste Renoir (French; 1841–1919)	Sotheby's New York, May 17, 1990	78,100,000
8 The Massacre of the Innocents, Sir Peter Paul Rubens (Flemish; 1577–1640)	Sotheby's London, Jul 10, 2002	75,930,440 (£49,506,648)
9 White Center (Yellow, pink and lavender on rose), Mark Rothko (American; 1903–70)	Sotheby's New York, May 15, 2007	72,840,000
10 Green Car Crash – Green Burning Car I, Andy Warhol (American; 1928–87)	Christie's New York, May 16, 2007	71,720,000

TOP 10 **MOST EXPENSIVE PAINTINGS BY WOMEN ARTISTS**

PAINTING / ARTIST		SALE PRICE ($)
1 Les Fleurs, Natalia Goncharova (Russian;1881–1962)	Christie's London, Jun 24, 2008	10,860,832 (£5,529,250)
2 Picking Apples, Natalia Goncharova	Christie's London, Jun 18, 2007	9,778,656 (£4,948,000)
3 The Visitor, Marlene Dumas (South African; b. 1953)	Sotheby's London, Jul 1, 2008	6,343,082 (£3,177,250)
4 Bluebells, Natalia Goncharova	Sotheby's London, Nov 26, 2007	6,229,793 (£3,044,500)
5 Children Playing with a Dog, Mary Cassatt (American; 1844–1926)	Christie's New York, May 24, 2007	6,200,000
6 Calla Lilies with Red Anemone, Georgia O'Keeffe (American; 1887–1986)	Christie's New York, May 23, 2001	6,166,000
7 Roots, Frida Kahlo (Mexican; 1907–54)	Sotheby's New York, May 24, 2006	5,616,000
8 Danseuses Espagnoles, Natalia Goncharova	Christie's London, Jun 18, 2007	5,573,122 (£2,820,000)
9 Cache-cache, Berthe Morisot (French; 1841–95)	Sotheby's New York, Nov 2, 2005	5,168,000
10 Chant 2, Bridget Riley (British; b. 1931)	Sotheby's London, Jul 1, 2008	5,113,296 (£2,561,250)

MUSIC

Singles

TOP 10 **SINGLES OF ALL TIME**

	TITLE / ARTIST	YEAR OF ENTRY	SALES EXCEED
1	"Candle in the Wind (1997)"/"Something About the Way You Look Tonight," Elton John	1997	37,000,000
2	"White Christmas," Bing Crosby	1942	30,000,000
3	"Rock Around the Clock," Bill Haley and His Comets	1954	17,000,000
4	"I Want to Hold Your Hand," The Beatles	1963	12,000,000
5 =	"It's Now or Never," Elvis Presley	1960	10,000,000
=	"Hey Jude," The Beatles	1968	10,000,000
=	"I Will Always Love You," Whitney Houston	1992	10,000,000
8 =	"Diana," Paul Anka	1957	9,000,000
=	"Hound Dog"/"Don't Be Cruel," Elvis Presley	1956	9,000,000
10 =	"(Everything I Do) I Do It For You," Bryan Adams	1991	8,000,000
=	"I'm a Believer," The Monkees	1966	8,000,000

Source: Music Information Database

In many countries, statistics on record sales were unavailable until recent times. Global sales are therefore notoriously difficult to calculate, with "worldwide" customarily taken to mean minimum "western world" sales. It took 55 years for a record to overtake Bing Crosby's 1942 "White Christmas," although including cover versions and sheet-music sales would place the song first in any list of bestsellers.

TOP 10 **SINGLES OF 1960 IN THE USA**

	TITLE	ARTIST
1	"It's Now or Never"	Elvis Presley
2	"Are You Lonesome Tonight?"	Elvis Presley
3	"Theme from 'A Summer Place'"	Percy Faith
4	"Cathy's Clown"	Everly Brothers
5	"Stuck on You"	Elvis Presley
6	"I'm Sorry"	Brenda Lee
7	"The Twist"	Chubby Checker
8	"Save the Last Dance for Me"	Drifters
9	"Running Bear"	Johnny Preston
10	"El Paso"	Marty Robbins

Source: Music Information Database

Out of the army in the spring of 1960, Elvis Presley wasted no time in re-establishing his preeminence, with his first three post-army singles among the year's top five US sellers. Elvis was now noticeably ballad-oriented, however, and elsewhere uptempo R & B and dance records were supplanting rock 'n' roll as the major teenage fare, along with commercialized Nashville country music.

King of the charts
Elvis Presley's US chart hits span over 50 years, with No. 1s from "All Shook Up" (1956) to the re-released "Heartbreak Hotel" (2006).

TOP 10 **ARTISTS WITH THE MOST NO. 1 SINGLES IN THE USA**

	ARTIST*	NO. 1 SINGLES
1	Elvis Presley (131)	22
2	The Beatles (72)	20
3	Mariah Carey (37)	18
4	Michael Jackson (47)	13
5 =	Madonna (54)	12
=	The Supremes (45)	12
7	Whitney Houston (38)	11
8	Janet Jackson (37)	10
9 =	The Bee Gees (43)	9
=	Paul McCartney/Wings (46)	9
=	Stevie Wonder (61)	9

* Figures in brackets denote total chart hits

Source: Music Information Database

TOP 10 **SINGLES IN THE USA IN 2008**

	TITLE / ARTIST	SALES
1	"Bleeding Love," Leona Lewis	3,420,000
2	"Lollipop," Lil Wayne feat. Static Major	3,161,000
3	"Low," Flo Rida feat. T-Pain	2,979,000
4	"I Kissed a Girl," Katy Perry	2,977,000
5	"Viva La Vida," Coldplay	2,914,000
6	"Disturbia," Rihanna	2,766,000
7	"Whatever You Like," T.I.	2,682,000
8	"I'm Yours," Jason Mraz	2,655,000
9	"No Air," Jordin Sparks duet with Chris Brown	2,612,000
10	"So What," Pink	2,590,000

Source: Nielsen SoundScan

Hot licks
Madonna achieved the first of her 12 US No. 1s in 1984 and the most recent in 2000.

TOP 10 **SINGLES IN THE USA IN THE PAST 10 YEARS**

YEAR	TITLE	ARTIST
2008	"Bleeding Love"	Leona Lewis
2007	"Crank That"	Soulja Boy Tell 'Em
2006	"Bad Day"	Daniel Powter
2005	"Hollaback Girl"	Gwen Stefani
2004	"I Believe"	Fantasia
2003	"Bridge Over Troubled Water"	Clay Aiken
2002	"Before Your Love"/ "A Moment Like This"	Kelly Clarkson
2001	"Loverboy"	Mariah Carey
2000	"Maria Maria"	Santana feat. the Product G&B
1999	"Believe"	Cher

Source: Music Information Database

The bestselling singles of 2002, 2003, and 2004 were all by the participants of the TV show *American Idol*.

TOP 10 **SINGLES THAT STAYED LONGEST IN THE US CHARTS**

	TITLE / ARTIST*	FIRST CHART ENTRY	WEEKS IN CHART
1	"How Do I Live," LeAnn Rimes (69)	1997	69
2	"Foolish Games"/"You Were Meant For Me," Jewel (41)	1996	65
3	"Before He Cheats," Carrie Underwood (64)	2006	64
4	"Macarena (Bayside Boys Mix)," Los Del Rio (60)	1996	60
5	"Smooth," Santana feat. Rob Thomas (58)	1999	58
6	"Higher," Creed (57)	1999	57
7	= "I Don't Want to Wait," Paula Cole (56)	1997	56
	= "The Way You Love Me," Faith Hill (56)	2000	56
9	= "Amazed," Lonestar (55)	1999	55
	= "Barely Breathing," Duncan Sheik (55)	1996	55
	= "Missing," Everything But The Girl (55)	1996	55

* Numbers in brackets denote longest consecutive run on the charts

Source: Music Information Database

Albums

Golden age
Sales of Michael Jackson's Thriller *album were overtaken, but it remains the world's bestselling.*

TOP 10 **ALBUMS IN THE USA IN 2008**

TITLE / ARTIST / SALES

1 Noel
Josh Groban
3,699,000

2 High School Musical 2
Soundtrack
2,957,000

3 Long Road out of Eden
Eagles
2,608,000

4 As I Am
Alicia Keys
2,543,000

5 Daughtry
Daughtry
2,497,000

6 Hannah Montana 2 –
Meet Miley, Soundtrack
2,489,000

7 Minutes to Midnight
Linkin Park
2,099,000

8 Dutchess
Fergie
2,064,000

9 Taylor Swift
Taylor Swift
1,951,000

10 Graduation
Kanye West
1,892,000

Source: Nielsen SoundScan

TOP 10 **ALBUMS IN THE USA IN THE PAST 10 YEARS**

YEAR	TITLE	ARTIST
2008	The Carter III	Lil Wayne
2007	Noel	Josh Groban
2006	High School Musical	Soundtrack
2005	The Emancipation of Mimi	Mariah Carey
2004	Confessions	Usher
2003	Get Rich or Die Tryin'	50 Cent
2002	The Eminem Show	Eminem
2001	Hybrid Theory	Linkin Park
2000	No Strings Attached	*NSync
1999	Millennium	Backstreet Boys

Source: Nielsen SoundScan

TOP 10 **ARTISTS WITH THE MOST CHART ALBUMS IN THE USA**

	ARTIST	CHART ALBUMS
1	Elvis Presley	113
2	Frank Sinatra	83
3	Johnny Mathis	69
4	Willie Nelson	55
5	Bob Dylan	53
6	= James Brown	50
	= Ray Conniff	50
8	The Temptations	49
9	= The Beach Boys	48
	= The Beatles	48

Source: Music Information Database

Strong Rumours
Stevie Nicks and Lindsey Buckingham of Fleetwood Mac, whose
Rumours is one of the bestselling albums of all time in the USA.

TOP 10 **ALBUMS OF ALL TIME IN THE USA**

	TITLE / ARTIST / YEAR	ESTIMATED SALES
1	Their Greatest Hits, 1971–1975, Eagles, 1976	29,000,000
2	Thriller, Michael Jackson, 1982	27,000,000
3	Led Zeppelin IV, Led Zeppelin, 1971	23,000,000
4	Back in Black, AC/DC, 1980	22,000,000
5	Come on Over, Shania Twain, 1997	20,000,000
6	Rumours, Fleetwood Mac, 1977	19,000,000
7	Appetite for Destruction, Guns 'N Roses	18,000,000
8 =Boston, Boston, 1976	17,000,000
	=No Fences, Garth Brooks, 1990	17,000,000
	=The Bodyguard, Soundtrack, 1992	17,000,000

Source: RIAA

TOP 10 **ALBUMS THAT STAYED LONGEST AT NO. 1 IN THE US CHARTS**

	TITLE / ARTIST / YEAR	WEEKS AT NO. 1
1	Thriller, Michael Jackson, 1982	37
2 =Calypso, Harry Belafonte, 1956	31
	=Rumours, Fleetwood Mac, 1977	31
4 =Purple Rain (Soundtrack), Prince, 1984	24*
	=Saturday Night Fever, Soundtrack, 1978	24*
6	Please Hammer Don't Hurt 'Em, MC Hammer, 1990	21
7 =Blue Hawaii (Soundtrack), Elvis Presley, 1962	20*
	=The Bodyguard (Soundtrack), Whitney Houston, 1992	20
9 =Ropin' the Wind, Garth Brooks, 1991	18
	=More of the Monkees, The Monkees, 1967	18*
	=Dirty Dancing, Soundtrack, 1988	18

* Continuous runs

Source: Music Information Database

TOP 10 **ALBUMS THAT STAYED LONGEST IN THE US CHARTS**

	TITLE / ARTIST*	FIRST CHART ENTRY	WEEKS IN CHART
1	The Dark Side of the Moon, Pink Floyd (593)	1973	741
2	Johnny's Greatest Hits, Johnny Mathis (208)	1958	490
3	My Fair Lady, Original Cast (192)	1956	480
4	Highlights from the Phantom of The Opera, Original Cast (331)	1990	331
5	Oklahoma!, Soundtrack (95)	1955	305
6	Tapestry, Carole King (302)	1971	302
7	Heavenly, Johnny Mathis (155)	1959	295
8	MCMXC A.D., Enigma (252)	1991	282
9	Metallica, Metallica (281)	1991	281
10	The King and I, Soundtrack (96)	1956	277

* Numbers in brackets denote longest consecutive run on the charts

Source: Music Information Database

Stayin' alive
Although it was released in 1977, no subsequent album has stayed
longer at No. 1 than the Saturday Night Fever soundtrack.

Record Firsts

TOP 10 SINGLES IN THE FIRST US TOP 10

TITLE / ARTIST

1 "I'll Never Smile Again"
Tommy Dorsey

2 "The Breeze and I"
Jimmy Dorsey

3 "Imagination"
Glenn Miller

4 "Playmates"
Kay Kyser

5 "Fools Rush In"
Glenn Miller

6 "Where Was I"
Charlie Barnet

7 "Pennsylvania 6-5000"
Glenn Miller

8 "Imagination"
Tommy Dorsey

9 "Sierra Sue"
Bing Crosby

10 "Make-Believe Island"
Mitchell Ayres

Source: Billboard

This was the first "Best Sellers In Store" chart compiled by *Billboard* magazine, for its issue dated July 20, 1940. Since the 7-inch 45-rpm single was still the best part of a decade in the future, all these would have been 10-inch 78-rpm disks.

THE 10 FIRST SIMULTANEOUS US/UK CHART TOPPERS

	TITLE	ARTIST	DATE
1	"Oh Mein Papa"	Eddie Calvert	Jan 9, 1954
2	"Cherry Pink and Apple Blossom White"	Perez Prado	May 7, 1955
3	"Memories are Made of This"	Dean Martin	Feb 18, 1956
4	"Singing the Blues"	Guy Mitchell	Jan 5, 1957
5	"It's All in the Game"	Tommy Edwards	Nov 8, 1958
6	"Cathy's Clown"	Everly Brothers	May 28, 1960
7	"Can't Buy Me Love"	The Beatles	Apr 4, 1964
8	"A Hard Day's Night"	The Beatles	Aug 1, 1964
9	"Oh, Pretty Woman"	Roy Orbison	Oct 10, 1964
10	"Baby Love"	The Supremes	Nov 21, 1964

Source: Music Information Database

THE 10 **FIRST FEMALE SINGERS TO HAVE A NO. 1 HIT IN THE US DURING THE ROCK ERA**

	ARTIST	TITLE	DATE AT NO. 1
1	Joan Weber	"Let Me Go Lover"	Jan 22, 1955
2	Georgia Gibbs	"Dance With Henry (Wallflower)"	May 21, 1955
3	Kay Starr	"Rock and Roll Waltz"	Feb 18, 1956
4	Gogi Grant	"The Wayward Wind"	Jun 16, 1956
5	Debbie Reynolds	"Tammy"	Aug 31, 1957
6	Connie Francis	"Everybody's Somebody's Fool"	Jul 2, 1960
7	Brenda Lee	"I'm Sorry"	Jul 23, 1960
8	Shelley Fabares	"Johnny Angel"	Apr 7, 1962
9	Little Eva	"The Loco-motion"	Aug 25, 1962
10	Little Peggy March	"I Will Follow Him"	Apr 27, 1963

Source: Music Information Database

By the time Little Peggy March had her first No. 1, Connie Francis had had two more and Brenda Lee one.

Transatlantic triumph
The Everly Brothers (above) and Guy Mitchell (below) were two of only 10 artists in a span of more than 12 years to achieve simultaneous US and UK chart-toppers.

THE 10 **FIRST US ARTISTS TO TOP THE UK SINGLES CHART**

	ARTIST	TITLE	DATE AT NO. 1
1	Al Martino	"Here in My Heart"	Nov 15, 1952
2	Jo Stafford	"You Belong to Me"	Jan 17, 1953
3	Kay Starr	"Comes A-Long A-Love"	Jan 24, 1953
4	Eddie Fisher	"Outside of Heaven"	Jan 31, 1953
5	Perry Como	"Don't Let the Stars Get in Your Eyes"	Feb 7, 1953
6	Guy Mitchell	"She Wears Red Feathers"	Mar 14, 1953
7	Frankie Laine	"I Believe"	Apr 25, 1953
8	Doris Day	"Secret Love"	Apr 17, 1954
9	Johnnie Ray	"Such A Night"	May 1, 1954
10	Kitty Kallen	"Little Things Mean a Lot"	Sep 11, 1954

Source: Music Information Database

THE 10 **FIRST RECORDS TO ENTER THE US CHART AT NO. 1**

	ARTIST	TITLE	DATE AT NO. 1
1	Michael Jackson	"You Are Not Alone"	Sep 2, 1995
2	Mariah Carey	"Fantasy"	Sep 20, 1995
3	Whitney Houston	"Exhale (Shoop Shoop)"	Nov 25, 1995
4	Mariah Carey & Boyz II Men	"One Sweet Day"	Dec 2, 1995
5	Mariah Carey	"Honey"	Sep 13, 1997
6	Elton John	"Candle in the Wind 1997"	Oct 11, 1997
7	Celine Dion	"My Heart Will Go On"	Feb 28, 1998
8	Aerosmith	"I Don't Want to Miss a Thing"	Sep 5, 1998
9	Lauryn Hill	"Doo Wop (That Thing)"	Nov 14, 1998
10	R. Kelly & Celine Dion	"I'm Your Angel"	Dec 5, 1998

Source: Music Information Database

The introduction of Nielsen SoundScan, using new methodology to compile the Hot 100 (*Billboard* published its first under this system on November 1, 1991), first made it possible for a single to enter the chart at the summit.

Record Lasts

THE 10 **LAST NATIONALITIES TO TOP THE US SINGLES CHART***

	NATIONALITY / ARTIST	TITLE	DATE AT NO. 1
1	Barbadian Rihanna	"Disturbia"	Aug 30, 2008
2	Canadian Avril Lavigne	"Girlfriend"	May 5, 2007
3	Senegalese, Akon	"I Wanna Love You"	Dec 9, 2006
4	Colombian Shakira	"Hips Don't Lie"	Jun 24, 2006
5	Jamaican Sean Paul	"Temperature"	Apr 1, 2006
6	Spanish Enrique Iglesias	"Be With You"	Jul 8, 2000
7	Australian Savage Garden	"I Knew I Loved You"	Feb 12, 2000
8	Swedish, Roxette	"It Must Have Been Love"	Jun 23, 1990
9	Irish Sinead O'Connor	"Nothing Compares 2 U"	May 12, 1990
10	Cuban Gloria Estefan	"Don't Wanna Lose You"	Sep 16, 1989

Source: Music Information Database

A possible candidate for this list is Carlos Santana, whose single "Smooth," featuring Rob Thomas, hit US No. 1 on January 8, 2000: Santana is Mexican, but the rest of his band is American.

Rihanna
Barbadian singer Rihanna's "Take a Bow" reached US and UK No. 1 in 2008, the year in which she also won her first Grammy Award.

THE 10 **LAST SINGLES TO ENTER THE US CHART AT NO. 1**

	TITLE / ARTIST	DATE AT NO. 1
1	"Do I Make You Proud," Taylor Hicks	Jul 1, 2006
2	"Inside Your Heaven," Carrie Underwood	Jul 2, 2005
3	"I Believe," Fantasia	Jul 10, 2004
4	"This is the Night," Clay Aiken	Jun 28, 2003
5	"I'm Your Angel," R. Kelly & Celine Dion	Dec 5, 1998
6	"Doo Wop (That Thing)," Lauryn Hill	Nov 14, 1998
7	"I Don't Want to Miss a Thing," Aerosmith	Sep 5, 1998
8	"My Heart Will Go On," Celine Dion	Feb 28, 1998
9	"Candle in the Wind 1997," Elton John	Oct 11, 1997
10	"Honey," Mariah Carey	Sep 13, 1997

Source: Music Information Database

Nos. 1 through 4 were all *American Idol* winners.

THE 10 **LAST FEMALE SINGERS TO HAVE A NO. 1 HIT IN THE USA**

	TITLE / ARTIST	DATE AT NO. 1
1	"Womanizer," Britney Spears	Oct 25, 2008
2	"Disturbia," Rihanna	Aug 30, 2008
3	"I Kissed a Girl," Katy Perry	Aug 16, 2008
4	"Bleeding Love," Leona Lewis	Apr 5, 2008
5	"Touch My Body," Mariah Carey	Apr 19, 2008
6	"No One," Alicia Keys	Dec 29, 2007
7	"Big Girls Don't Cry," Fergie	Sep 8, 2007
8	"Girlfriend," Avril Lavigne	May 5, 2007
9	"Say it Right," Nelly Furtado	Feb 24, 2007
10	"Irreplaceable," Beyonce	Feb 17, 2007

Source: Music Information Database

Katy Perry
"I Kissed a Girl" was one of only two records to achieve simultaneous UK and US No. 1 positions in 2008.

Right: Coldplay
Coldplay's "Viva la Vida" was the first US No. 1 single by a British group since the Spice Girls over 11 years earlier.

THE 10 **LAST US ARTISTS TO TOP THE UK SINGLES CHART**

	ARTIST	TITLE	DATE AT NO. 1
1	Pink	"So What"	Oct 19, 2008
2	Kings of Leon	"Sex on Fire"	Sep 28, 2008
3	Katy Perry	"I Kissed a Girl"	Sep 7, 2008
4	Kid Rock	"All Summer Long"	Aug 3, 2008
5	Ne-Yo	"Closer"	Jun 29, 2008
6	Madonna*	"4 Minutes"	May 11, 2008
7	Eva Cassidy#	"What a Wonderful World"	Dec 16, 2007
8	Sean Kingston	"Beautiful Girls"	Sep 23, 2007
9	Kanye West	"Stronger"	Aug 26, 2007
10	Timbaland†	"The Way I Are"	Aug 5, 2007

* Featuring Justin Timberlake and Timbaland
# With Katie Melua
† Featuring Keri Hilson and D.O.E.

Source: Music Information Database

THE 10 **LAST SIMULTANEOUS UK/US CHART TOPPERS***

	TITLE / ARTIST	DATE AT NO. 1
1	"Just Dance," Lady GaGa feat. Colby O'Donis	Jan 31, 2009
2	"I Kissed a Girl," Katy Perry	Aug 16, 2008
3	"Viva la Vida," Coldplay	Jun 28, 2008
4	"Umbrella," Rihanna feat. Jay-Z	May 26, 2007
5	"Give It to Me," Timbaland featuring Nelly Furtado	Apr 21, 2007
6	"Sexyback," Justin Timberlake	Sep 9, 2006
7	"Burn," Usher	Jul 17, 2004
8	"Yeah," Usher feat. Ludacris & Lil Jon	Mar 27, 2004
9	"Crazy in Love," Beyonce feat. Jay-Z	Jul 12, 2003
10	"Lose Yourself," Eminem	Dec 14, 2002

* As at March 25, 2009

Source: Music Information Database

Male Singers

Platinum for Diamond
Home Before Dark *went platinum in 2008.*

TOP 10 **MALE ARTISTS WITH THE MOST PLATINUM ALBUMS IN THE USA**

ARTIST / GOLD TOTALS	PLATINUM ALBUMS*
1 Garth Brooks (16)	111
2 Elvis Presley (81)	89
3 Billy Joel (18)	68
4 Elton John (37)	63
5 Michael Jackson (9)	59
6 Bruce Springsteen (20)	54
7 George Strait (37)	53
8 Kenny G (15)	46
9 Kenny Rogers (27)	41
10 Neil Diamond (40)	39

* By number of album awards, rather than number of albums qualifying for awards

Source: RIAA

TOP 10 **BESTSELLING ALBUMS BY A MALE ARTIST IN THE USA**

	TITLE / ARTIST / YEAR	SALES
1	Thriller, Michael Jackson, 1982	27,000,000
2	No Fences, Garth Brooks, 1990	17,000,000
3	Greatest Hits, Elton John, 1974	16,000,000
4	Born in the USA, Bruce Springsteen, 1984	15,000,000
5 =	Bat Out of Hell, Meat Loaf, 1977	14,000,000
=	Ropin' the Wind, Garth Brooks, 1991	14,000,000
7 =	Greatest Hits, Kenny Rogers, 1980	12,000,000
=	No Jacket Required, Phil Collins, 1985	12,000,000
=	Breathless, Kenny G, 1992	12,000,000
10 =	James Taylor's Greatest Hits, James Taylor, 1976	11,000,000
=	Devil Without a Cause, Kid Rock, 1999	11,000,000

Source: RIAA

Within two years of its release, Michael Jackson's *Thriller* album had sold a record total of 20 million copies, but it continued to sell into its second and third decades, being certified for record sales of 27 million copies in 2005. To these US sales must be added those in other countries, bringing the world total to more than 50 million.

Yellow Brick Road
Elton John has sustained a long run of hits, with US chart albums spanning 1970 to 2007, including nine-times multi-platinum The Very Best of Elton John.

TOP 10 **MALE SOLO ALBUMS IN THE USA IN THE PAST 10 YEARS**

YEAR / TITLE / ARTIST

2008 The Carter III, Lil Wayne

2007 Noel, Josh Groban

2006 Futuresex/Love Sounds, Justin Timberlake

2005 The Massacre, 50 Cent

2004 Confessions, Usher

2003 Get Rich or Die Tryin', 50 Cent

2002 The Eminem Show, Eminem

2001 Hotshot, Shaggy

2000 The Marshall Mathers LP, Eminem

1999 Ricky Martin, Ricky Martin

Source: Nielsen SoundScan

THE 10 **LAST US NO. 1 RECORDS BY A FOREIGN MALE ARTIST***

	TITLE / ARTIST / NATIONALITY	DATE
1	"Bad Day," Daniel Powter (Canadian)	Apr 8, 2006
2	"Temperature," Sean Paul (Jamaican)	Apr 1, 2006
3	"Get Busy," Sean Paul (Jamaican)	Mar 10, 2003
4	"Angel," Shaggy feat. Rayvon (Jamaican)	Mar 31, 2001
5	"It Wasn't Me," Shaggy feat. Ricardo "Rikrok" Ducent (Jamaican)	Feb 3, 2001
6	"Be With You," Enrique Iglesias (Spanish)	Jun 24, 2000
7	"Livin' La Vida Loca," Ricky Martin (Puerto Rican)	May 8, 1999
8	"Bailamos," Enrique Iglesias (Spanish)	Sep 4, 1999
9	"Have You Ever Really Loved a Woman?," Bryan Adams (Canadian)	Jun 3, 1995
10	"Here Comes The Hotstepper," Ini Kamoze (Jamaican)	Dec 16, 1994

* Excluding UK acts

Source: Music Information Database

TOP 10 **SINGLES BY MALE SOLO SINGERS IN THE USA**

	TITLE / ARTIST	YEAR
1	"Candle in the Wind (1997)"/"Something About the Way You Look Tonight," Elton John	1997
2	"White Christmas," Bing Crosby	1942
3	"Hound Dog"/"Don't Be Cruel," Elvis Presley	1956
4	"Gangsta's Paradise," Coolio featuring L.V.	1995
5	"(Everything I Do) I Do It For You," Bryan Adams	1991
6	"Love Me Tender"/"Any Way You Want Me," Elvis Presley	1956
7	"All Shook Up," Elvis Presley	1957
8	"Jailhouse Rock," Elvis Presley	1957
9	"Heartbreak Hotel"/"I Was the One," Elvis Presley	1956
10	"Baby Got Back," Sir Mix-A-Lot	1992

Source: Music Information Database

Shaggy
Jamaican artists such as Shaggy dominate the list of foreign No. 1s in the USA.

Female Singers

Man eater
As well as her solo 2006 and 2007
US No. 1s, Nelly Furtado featured on
Timbaland's "Give It to Me" in 2007.

THE 10 LAST US NO. 1 SINGLES BY A FOREIGN FEMALE ARTIST*

	TITLE / ARTIST / NATIONALITY	DATE
1	"Disturbia," Rihanna (Barbadian)	Aug 30, 2008
2	"Umbrella," Rihanna	Jun 9, 2007
3	"Girlfriend," Avril Lavigne (Canadian)	May 5, 2007
4	"Say It Right," Nelly Furtado (Canadian)	Feb 24, 2007
5	"Promiscuous," Nelly Furtado	Jul 8, 2006
6	"Hips Don't Lie," Shakira (Colombian)	Jun 17, 2006
7	"SOS," Rihanna	May 13, 2006
8	"My Heart Will Go On," Celine Dion (Canadian)	Feb 28, 1998
9	"Because You Loved Me," Celine Dion	Mar 23, 1996
10	"The Power of Love," Celine Dion	Feb 12, 1994

* Excluding UK acts
Source: Music Information Database

TOP 10 FEMALE SOLO SINGERS IN THE USA

	SINGER	TOTAL CHART HITS
1	Aretha Franklin	70
2	Connie Francis	53
3	Madonna	51
4	Brenda Lee	50
5	Dionne Warwick	49
6	= Diana Ross	34
	= Barbra Streisand	34
8	Patti Page	33
9	= Cher	32
	= Olivia Newton-John	32

Source: Music Information Database

TOP 10 FEMALE ARTISTS WITH THE MOST PLATINUM ALBUMS IN THE USA

	ARTIST / GOLD TOTALS	PLATINUM ALBUMS
1	Madonna (18)	64
2	Mariah Carey (13)	61
3	Barbra Streisand (44)	59
4	Whitney Houston (8)	54
5	Shania Twain (4)	52
6	Celine Dion (13)	49
7	Reba McEntire (26)	37
8	Britney Spears (4)	31
9	Linda Ronstadt (17)	28
10	Janet Jackson (8)	26

TOP 10 **SINGLES BY FEMALE SOLO SINGERS IN THE USA**

	TITLE / ARTIST	YEAR
1	**"I Will Always Love You,"** Whitney Houston	1992
2	**"How Do I Live,"** LeAnn Rimes	1997
3	**"Un-break My Heart,"** Toni Braxton	1996
4	**"Fantasy,"** Mariah Carey	1995
5	**"Vogue,"** Madonna	1990
6	**"You're Still the One,"** Shania Twain	1998
7	**"The First Night,"** Monica	1998
8	**"You're Makin' Me High"/ "Let It Flow,"** Toni Braxton	1996
9	**"Because You Loved Me,"** Celine Dion	1996
10	**"You Were Meant For Me,"** Jewel	1997

Source: Music Information Database

TOP 10 **BESTSELLING ALBUMS BY A FEMALE ARTIST IN THE USA**

	TITLE / ARTIST	YEAR
1	**Come on Over**, Shania Twain	1997
2	**The Bodyguard,** Whitney Houston	1992
3	**Jagged Little Pill,** Alanis Morissette	1995
4	**...Baby One More Time,** Britney Spears	1999
5	**Whitney Houston,** Whitney Houston	1986
6	**Pieces of You**, Jewel	1996
7	**The Woman in Me,** Shania Twain	1995
8	**Up!**, Shania Twain	2002
9	**Falling Into You**, Celine Dion	1996
10	**The Immaculate Collection,** Madonna	1991

Source: RIAA

Ross's record
Diana Ross's record span between US No. 1s extends from 1976 to 1980.

Mariah Carey
Mariah Carey has had a US chart hit almost every year since 1990.

TOP 10 **FEMALE SINGERS WITH THE LONGEST GAPS BETWEEN NO. 1 HIT SINGLES IN THE USA**

	ARTIST	PERIOD	YRS	GAP MTHS	DAYS
1	Cher	Mar 23, 1974–Mar 13, 1999	24	11	21
2	Aretha Franklin	Jun 10, 1967–Apr 11, 1987	19	10	1
3	Alicia Keys	Oct 13, 2001–Dec 1, 2007	6	1	18
4	Madonna	Apr 15, 1995–Sep 9, 2000	5	4	25
5	Mariah Carey	Feb 19, 2000–Jun 4, 2005	5	3	16
6	Jennifer Warnes	Nov 27, 1982–Nov 21, 1987	4	11	25
7	Diana Ross	Jul 10, 1976–Aug 30, 1980	4	1	20
8	Janet Jackson	Dec 25, 1993–Jan 24, 1998	4	0	30
9	Olivia Newton-John	Mar 15, 1975–Jun 3, 1978	3	2	19
10	Barbra Streisand	Feb 9, 1974–Feb 26, 1977	3	0	17

Source: Music Information Database

Groups & Duos

TOP 10 **SINGLES OF ALL TIME BY GROUPS AND DUOS IN THE USA**

TITLE / ARTIST	YEAR
1 "We Are the World," USA for Africa	1985
2 "Hey Jude," The Beatles	1968
3 "Whoomp! (There it Is)," Tag Team	1993
4 "Macarena," Los Del Rio	1996
5 "I'll Be Missing You," Puff Daddy and Faith Evans (featuring 112)	1997
6 "The Boy Is Mine," Brandy & Monica	1998
7 "Come Together"/"Something," The Beatles	1969
8 "Let It Be," The Beatles	1970
9 "Eye of the Tiger," Survivor	1982
10 "Get Back," The Beatles with Billy Preston	1969

Source: Music Information Database

The USA for Africa's 1985 charity single "We Are the World" had a host of special circumstances surrounding it, launching it into the élite four-million mega-seller league. The appearance of "Hey Jude" at No. 2 is perhaps surprising. An unusually long track (7 mins 12 secs) that disqualified it from airplay on some radio stations, it does not even figure among the Top 100 of all time in the Beatles' home country (although did reach No. 1 in both the UK and US). It nonetheless sold more than four million copies in the USA.

Rockstar
Nickelback's "Rockstar"
took up residence in the
charts for 50 weeks up
to October 2008.

TOP 10 **ALBUMS BY GROUPS AND DUOS IN THE USA, 2008**

TITLE	GR
1 Viva La Vida (Or Death and All His Friends)	Coldp
2 Black Ice	AC/[
3 Death Magnetic	Metall
4 Little Bit Longer	The Jonas Broth
5 Love on the Inside	Sugarla
6 Dark Horse	Nickelba
7 The Jonas Brothers	The Jonas Broth
8 Daughtry	Daugh
9 3 Doors Down	3 Doors Dov
10 In Rainbows	Radiohe

Source: Nielsen SoundScan

TOP 10 **DIGITAL TRACKS BY GROUPS AND DUOS IN THE USA, 2008**

TITLE	GR
1 "Shake It"	Metro Stati
2 "Viva La Vida"	Coldp
3 "When I Grow Up"	Pussycat Dc
4 "Stop and Stare"	OneRepub
5 "Burnin' Up"	The Jonas Broth
6 "Damaged"	Danity Ka
7 "Sorry"	Buckcher
8 "It's Not My Time"	3 Doors Dov
9 "Paralyzer"	Finger Eleٰ
10 "Shadow of the Day"	Linkin Pa

Source: Nielsen SoundScan

TOP 10 GROUPS AND DUOS WITH THE LONGEST SINGLES CHART CAREERS IN THE USA

	GROUP/DUO	CHART SPAN	YRS	MTHS	DAYS
1	The Isley Brothers	Sep 26, 1959–Aug 16, 2003	43	10	21
2	The Rolling Stones	May 2, 1964–Oct 4, 2003	39	5	2
3	Santana	Oct 25, 1969–Nov 19, 2005	36	0	24
4	The Beatles	Jan 18, 1964–May 4, 1996	32	3	16
5	Bee Gees	May 27, 1967–Feb 7, 1998	30	8	11
6	The Righteous Brothers	May 11, 1963–Mar 23, 1991	27	10	12
7	The Beach Boys	Feb 17, 1962–Sep 9, 1989	27	6	23
8	The Everly Brothers	Jun 1, 1957–Nov 17, 1984	27	5	16
9	The Five Satins	Oct 13, 1956–Mar 27, 1982	25	5	14
10	Steve Miller Band	Nov 23, 1968–Aug 28, 1993	24	9	5

Source: Music Information Database

TOP 10 ALBUMS BY GROUPS IN THE USA

	TITLE / GROUP	YEAR
1	Their Greatest Hits, 1971–1975, Eagles	1976
2	Led Zeppelin IV (untitled), Led Zeppelin	1971
3	Back in Black, AC/DC	1980
4	Rumours, Fleetwood Mac	1977
5	Appetite For Destruction, Guns N' Roses	1987
6	Boston, Boston	1976
7	Hotel California, Eagles	1977
8	Cracked Rear View, Hootie and the Blowfish	1995
9	Supernatural, Santana	1999
10	The Dark Side of the Moon, Pink Floyd	1973

Source: Music Information Database

Rolling on
In addition to their sustained chart success, the Rolling Stones have been performing for over 47 years.

The Beatles

THE 10 FIRST BEATLES ALBUMS RELEASED IN THE USA

TITLE / RELEASE DATE

1 Introducing The Beatles
Jul 22, 1963

2 Meet The Beatles!
Jan 20, 1964

3 Jolly What! The Beatles
and Frank Ifield on Stage
Feb 26, 1964

4 The Beatles' Second Album
Apr 10, 1964

5 A Hard Day's Night
Jun 26, 1964

6 Something New
Jul 20, 1964

7 The International Battle of
The Century – The Beatles
vs The Four Seasons
Oct 1, 1964

8 The Beatles' Story
Nov 23, 1964

9 Beatles' 65
Dec 15, 1964

10 Beatles VI
Jun 14, 1965

Source (all lists): Music Information Database

TOP 10 BESTSELLING BEATLES SINGLES IN THE USA

TITLE / YEAR

1 "Hey Jude"
1968

2 "Get Back"
1969

3 "Let It Be"
1970

4 "Something"
1969

5 "Lady Madonna"
1968

6 "The Long and Winding
Road" 1970

7 "I Want to Hold Your Hand"
1964

8 "Help!"
1965

9 "Can't Buy Me Love"
1964

10 "Yesterday"
1965

40 years ago
*The Beatles era spanned the period from their
first recordings in 1962 to their breakup in
1969. The singles and albums they produced
in that period remain popular today.*

Iconic album
The Beatles' Sgt. Pepper *album has sold over 11 million copies in the USA.*

THE 10 FIRST BEATLES SINGLES RELEASED IN THE USA

TITLE / RELEASE DATE

1 Please Please Me/
Ask Me Why
Feb 7, 1963

2 From Me To You/
Thank You Girl
May 27, 1963

3 She Loves You/I'll Get You
Sep 16, 1963

4 I Want to Hold Your Hand/
I Saw Her Standing There
Jan 13, 1964

5 Please Please Me/
From Me to You
Jan 3, 1964

6 Twist and Shout/
There's a Place
Mar 2, 1964

7 Can't Buy Me Love/
You Can't Do That
Mar 16, 1964

8 Do You Want to Know
a Secret/Thank You Girl
Mar 23, 1964

9 Love Me Do/
P.S. I Love You
Apr 27, 1964

10 Sie Liebt Dich (She Loves
You)/I'll Get You
May 21, 1964

THE 10 FIRST SOLO BEATLE TOP 10 HITS IN THE USA

TITLE / FORMER BEATLE / YEAR

1 "Instant Karma (We All
Shine On)" John Lennon
1970

2 "Back Off Boogaloo"
Ringo Starr
1970

3 "My Sweet Lord"/"Isn't
It a Pity" George Harrison
1970

4 "What Is Life"
George Harrison
1971

5 "Another Day"/"Oh Woman
Oh Why" Paul McCartney
1971

6 "It Don't Come Easy"
Ringo Starr
1971

7 "Imagine"
John Lennon
1971

8 "Give Me Love (Give Me Peace
on Earth)" George Harrison
1973

9 "Photograph"
Ringo Starr
1973

10 "You're Sixteen"
Ringo Starr
1974

TOP 10 ALBUMS THAT STAYED LONGEST IN THE US CHARTS

TITLE / WEEKS

1 Sgt. Pepper's Lonely Hearts
Club Band
176

2 The Beatles 1967–1970
171

3 The Beatles
('The White Album')
170

4 The Beatles 1962–1966
161

5 Abbey Road
129

6 1
104

7 Magical Mystery Tour
89

8 Revolver
77

9 Love
73

10 = Beatles '65
71

= Meet the Beatles!
71

Background: Beatlemania
Fans besiege Buckingham Palace in 1965 as they arrive to receive their MBEs. John Lennon returned his in 1969.

Right: Stamp of success
Abbey Road, one of six Beatles album cover stamps issued in 2007.

Music Greats

All-Time Greats

In issues published between 2003 and 2008, *Rolling Stone* magazine listed artists, songs, albums, and performances in a variety of categories, ranked according to votes cast by their peers—fellow musicians, critics, and prominent music-industry figures. The listings are dominantly Anglo-American: of the "500 Greatest Songs," 357 are by US singers and 117 by British artists.

TOP 10 **GREATEST SINGERS OF ALL TIME**

SINGER / COUNTRY / DATES

1 Aretha Franklin (USA; b. 1942)
2 Ray Charles (USA; 1930–2004)
3 Elvis Presley (USA; 1935–77)
4 Sam Cooke (USA; 1931–64)
5 John Lennon (UK; 1940–80)
6 Marvin Gaye (USA; 1939–84)
7 Bob Dylan (USA; b. 1941)
8 Otis Redding (USA; 1941–67)
9 Stevie Wonder (USA; b. 1950)
10 James Brown (USA; 1933–2006)

Source: *Rolling Stone*

Vocal perfection
Aretha Franklin topped the list of "Greatest Singers" nominated by a panel of almost 200 experts.

TOP 10 **GREATEST ALBUMS OF ALL TIME**

ALBUM / ARTIST(S) / YEAR

1 Sgt. Pepper's Lonely Hearts Club Band, The Beatles (1967)
2 Pet Sounds, The Beach Boys (1966)
3 Revolver, The Beatles (1966)
4 Highway 61 Revisited, Bob Dylan (1965)
5 Rubber Soul, The Beatles (1965)
6 What's Going On, Marvin Gaye (1971)
7 Exile on Main Street, The Rolling Stones (1972)
8 London Calling, The Clash (1979)
9 Blonde on Blonde, Bob Dylan (1966)
10 The Beatles ('The White Album'), The Beatles (1968)

Source: *Rolling Stone*

TOP 10 **GREATEST MUSIC DVDS OF ALL TIME**

DVD / PRINCIPAL ARTIST / YEAR*

1 The Last Waltz, Bob Dylan (1976)
2 Monterey Pop, Various artists (1967)
3 A Hard Day's Night, The Beatles (1964)
4 Woodstock: Three Days of Peace and Music, Various artists (1969)
5 Metallica: Some Kind of Monster, Metallica (2004)
6 Gimme Shelter, Rolling Stones (1970)
7 Wild Style, Grandmaster Flash, *et al* (1983)
8 Stop Making Sense, Talking Heads (1983)
9 Purple Rain, Prince (1984)
10 No Direction Home, Bob Dylan (1966)

* Of original event or film; DVD release later

Source: *Rolling Stone*

Slow hand
Eric Clapton is the highest-ranked British guitarist on the Rolling Stone list.

TOP 10 **GREATEST GUITARISTS OF ALL TIME**

GUITARIST / COUNTRY / DATES

1 Jimi Hendrix (USA; 1942–70)
2 Duane Allman (USA; 1946–71)
3 B.B. King (USA; b. 1925)
4 Eric Clapton (UK; b. 1945)
5 Robert Johnson (USA; 1911–38)
6 Chuck Berry (USA; b. 1926)
7 Stevie Ray Vaughan (USA; 1954–90)
8 Ry Cooder (USA; b. 1947)
9 Jimmy Page (UK; b. 1944)
10 Keith Richards (UK; b. 1943)

Source: *Rolling Stone*

TOP 10 **GREATEST SONGS OF ALL TIME**

SONG / SINGER / FIRST RECORDING

1 "Like a Rolling Stone,"
Bob Dylan (1965)
2 "Satisfaction,"
The Rolling Stones (1965)
3 "Imagine," John Lennon (1971)
4 "What's Going On,"
Marvin Gaye (1970)
5 "Respect," Aretha Franklin (1967)
6 "Good Vibrations,"
The Beach Boys (1966)
7 "Johnny B. Goode,"
Chuck Berry (1958)
8 "Hey Jude," The Beatles (1968)
9 "Smells Like Teen Spirit,"
Nirvana (1991)
10 "What'd I Say," Ray Charles (1959)

Source: *Rolling Stone*

TOP 10 **IMMORTALS**

ARTIST / COUNTRY / DATES

1 The Beatles (UK; 1960–70)
2 Bob Dylan (USA; b. 1941)
3 Elvis Presley (USA; 1935–77)
4 The Rolling Stones (UK; 1962–)
5 Chuck Berry (USA; b. 1926)
6 Jimi Hendrix (USA; 1942–70)
7 James Brown (USA; 1933–2006)
8 Little Richard (USA; b. 1932)
9 Aretha Franklin (USA; b. 1942)
10 Ray Charles (USA; 1930–2004)

Source: *Rolling Stone*

Immortal Hendrix
Jimi Hendrix features both as the "Greatest Guitarist" and among rock 'n' roll's "Immortals."

Music Awards

THE 10 FIRST ARTISTS TO RECEIVE GRAMMY LIFETIME ACHIEVEMENT AWARDS

	ARTIST	YEAR
1	Bing Crosby	1962
2	Frank Sinatra	1965
3	Duke Ellington	1966
4	Ella Fitzgerald	1967
5	Irving Berlin	1968
6	Elvis Presley	1971
7	= Louis Armstrong	1972
	= Mahalia Jackson	1972
9	= Chuck Berry	1984
	= Charlie Parker	1984

Source: NARAS

Grammy veterans
Bing Crosby (below), winner of the first Grammy Lifetime Achievement Award, and Quincy Jones (below right), who has been nominated for a record 79 Grammys with 27 wins.

TOP 10 AMERICAN MUSIC AWARDS WINNERS

	ARTIST	AWARDS*
1	Alabama	23
2	Michael Jackson	20
3	= Whitney Houston	17
	= Kenny Rogers	17
5	Garth Brooks	16
6	= Reba McEntire	13
	= Lionel Richie	13
8	= Janet Jackson	11
	= Willie Nelson	11
	= Stevie Wonder	11

* For lyrics, excluding shared, merit, and other awards

Source: American Music Awards

THE 10 ARTISTS WITH MOST GRAMMY AWARDS

	ARTIST	AWARDS
1	Sir Georg Solti	31
2	Quincy Jones	27
3	= Pierre Boulez	26
	= Alison Krauss	26
5	= Vladimir Horowitz	25
	= Stevie Wonder	25
7	U2	22
8	John Williams	21
9	Henry Mancini	20
10	Bruce Springsteen	19

Source: NARAS

The Grammy Awards ceremony has been held annually in the USA since its inauguration on May 4, 1959, and is considered the most prestigious in the music industry. The presence of classical artists in this Top 10 (not least conductor Sir George Solti) is largely attributable to the large number of classical award categories. Grammy winners are selected annually by the 7,000-member Recording Academy of NARAS (the National Academy of Recording Arts & Sciences).

THE 10 LATEST GRAMMY RECORDS OF THE YEAR

YEAR / RECORD / ARTIST(S)

2009
"Please Read the Letter"
Robert Plant and Alison Krauss

2008
"Rehab"
Amy Winehouse

2007
"Not Ready to Make Nice"
Dixie Chicks

2006
"Boulevard of Broken Dreams"
Green Day

2005
"Here We Go Again"
Ray Charles and Norah Jones

2004
"Clocks"
Coldplay

2003
"Don't Know Why"
Norah Jones

2002
"Walk On"
U2

2001
"Beautiful Day"
U2

2000
"Smooth"
Santana feat. Rob Thomas

The Grammys are awarded retrospectively. Thus the 51st awards presented in 2009 were in recognition of musical accomplishment during 2008.

THE 10 LATEST WINNERS OF THE ASCAP SONGWRITER OF THE YEAR*

YEAR	SONGWRITER(S)
2009	Mikkel Eriksen & Tor Hermansen
2008	Timbaland
2007	Johntá Austin, Jermaine Dupti
2006	50 Cent
2005	Scott Storch
2004	50 Cent; Graham Edwards; Nelly
2003	Nelly; Seven
2002	Beyoncé Knowles
2001	Andreas Carlsson; Max Martin
2000	Max Martin

* Pop category

Source: American Society of Composers, Authors, and Publishers

Amy's Grammys
In 2008, Amy Winehouse was nominated for Grammy Awards in six categories, winning in five, including Record of the Year for "Rehab."

TOP 10 BILLBOARD MUSIC AWARDS WINNERS

	ARTIST	AWARDS*
1	Garth Brooks	16
2	Usher	11
3	= 50 Cent	9
	= Mariah Carey	9
	= Destiny's Child	9
6	= R. Kelly	8
	= Alicia Keys	8
	= LeAnn Rimes	8
9	= Dixie Chicks	7
	= Next	7

* For lyrics, excluding shared, merit, and other awards

Movie Music

Dancing on ice
Recorded by Cab Calloway in 1930, Happy Feet *was aptly used as the title of the animated film featuring tap-dancing penguins.*

TOP 10 MOVIES WITH TITLES DERIVED FROM SONG TITLES

	FILM	SONG*	FILM
1	Mamma Mia!	1975	2008
2	Happy Feet	1930	2006
3	American Pie	1972	1999
4	Walk the Line	1956	2005
5	Sweet Home Alabama	1976	2002
6	Bad Boys	1983	1995
7	Forever Young	1970	1992
8	Sea of Love	1959	1989
9	One Fine Day	1963	1996
10	My Girl	1965	1991

* Release of first hit version

Movies with titles derived from those of songs date back to "How Would You Like to Be the Ice Man?" a popular song before being appropriated for a movie released on April 21, 1899. "White Christmas," one of the most successful songs of all time, appeared in the film *Holiday Inn* (1942) before becoming the title of the 1954 film. Movies with titles that are coincidentally the same as song titles, or not identical to those of the songs that inspired them, have been disregarded.

TOP 10 BESTSELLING BEST SONG OSCAR-WINNING SINGLES IN THE USA

	ARTIST / SONG TITLE / MOVIE (IF DIFFERENT)	YEAR
1	Debby Boone, "You Light Up My Life"	1977
2	Joe Cocker and Jennifer Warnes, "Up Where We Belong," *An Officer and a Gentleman*	1982
3	Barbra Streisand, "Evergreen," Love Theme from *A Star is Born*	1976
4	Celine Dion, "My Heart Will Go On," *Titanic*	1997
5	Stevie Wonder, "I Just Called to Say I Love You," *The Woman in Red*	1984
6	Christopher Cross, "Arthur's Theme (Best that You Can Do)," *Arthur*	1981
7	Barbra Streisand, "The Way We Were"	1973
8	Peabo Bryson and Regina Belle, "A Whole New World," *Aladdin*	1992
9	B.J. Thomas, "Raindrops Keep Falling on My Head," *Butch Cassidy and the Sundance Kid*	1969
10	Bill Medley and Jennifer Warnes, "(I've had the) Time of My Life," *Dirty Dancing*	1987

Source: Music Information Database

TOP 10 JAMES BOND MOVIE THEMES IN THE USA

	TITLE / ARTIST / MOVIE (IF DIFFERENT)	YEAR
1	"A View to a Kill," Duran Duran	1985
2	"Nobody Does It Better," Carly Simon, *The Spy Who Loved Me*	1977
3	"Live and Let Die," Paul McCartney and Wings	1973
4	"For Your Eyes Only," Sheena Easton	1981
5	"Goldfinger," Shirley Bassey	1965
6	"Thunderball," Tom Jones	1966
7	"All Time High," Rita Coolidge, *Octopussy*	1983
8	"You Only Live Twice," Nancy Sinatra	1967
9	"Diamonds Are Forever," Shirley Bassey	1972
10	"Die Another Day," Madonna	2002

Source: Music Information Database

By no means have all the James Bond themes been major US hits, especially those from the later movies, some of which failed to chart at all. Every song listed here reached the Top 100, but only the first seven made the Top 40 and only Duran Duran have had a Bond-associated US No. 1 hit.

TOP 10 **MUSICAL MOVIES**

	FILM	YEAR
1	Mamma Mia!	2008
2	Grease	1978
3	Chicago	2002
4	Saturday Night Fever	1977
5	High School Musical 3: Senior Year	2008
6	Hairspray	2007
7	Moulin Rouge!	2001
8	The Sound of Music	1965
9	The Phantom of the Opera	2004
10	Sweeney Todd: The Demon Barber of Fleet Street	2007

In recent years, animated films with an important musical content appear to have taken over from traditional musicals (films in which the cast actually sing), with *Beauty and the Beast*, *Aladdin*, *The Lion King*, *Pocahontas*, *The Prince of Egypt*, *Tarzan* and *Monsters, Inc.* all winning Best Original Song Oscars. However, the success of *Chicago* and *Mamma Mia!* suggests that the age of the blockbuster musical movie is not yet over.

Money, money, money
With global box office income of almost $600 million, Mamma Mia! is the highest-earning musical of all time.

TOP 10 **MUSICAL MOVIES OF THE 1960s**

	MOVIE	YEAR
1	The Sound of Music	1965
2	Mary Poppins	1964
3	My Fair Lady	1964
4	Funny Girl	1968
5	Let's Make Love	1960
6	West Side Story	1961
7	Oliver!	1968
8	Thoroughly Modern Millie	1967
9	Hello Dolly!	1969
10	Paint Your Wagon	1969

TOP 10 **ORIGINAL SOUNDTRACK ALBUMS IN THE USA**

	TITLE	YEAR OF RELEASE
1	The Bodyguard	1992
2	Purple Rain	1984
3	Forrest Gump	1994
4 =	Dirty Dancing	1987
=	Titanic	1997
6	The Lion King	1994
7 =	Top Gun	1986
=	Footloose	1984
9 =	Grease	1978
=	O Brother Where Art Thou?	2000

Source: RIAA

Classical Music & Opera

TOP 10 CLASSICAL ALBUMS IN THE USA

	TITLE	PERFORMER / ORCHESTRA	YEAR
1	The Three Tenors In Concert	José Carreras, Placido Domingo, Luciano Pavarotti	1990
2	Romanza	Andrea Bocelli	1997
3	Sogno	Andrea Bocelli	1999
4	Voice of an Angel	Charlotte Church	1999
5	Chant	Benedictine Monks of Santo Domingo De Silos	1994
6	The Three Tenors— In Concert 1994	José Carreras, Placido Domingo, Luciano Pavarotti, Zubin Mehta	1994
7	Sacred Arias	Andrea Bocelli	1999
8	Tchaikovsky: Piano Concerto No. 1	Van Cliburn	1958
9	Amore	Andrea Bocelli	2006
10	Cieli Di Toscana	Andrea Bocelli	2001

Source: Music Information Database

Classical recordings held far greater sway in the early years of the US album chart, and most notably during the 1950s, than they have in subsequent decades, and this is partly reflected in the vintage nature of much of the Top 10. The two film soundtracks contained short pieces or excerpts by a number of composers, including Bach, Beethoven, and Stravinsky in *Fantasia*, and Richard and Johann Strauss in *2001: A Space Odyssey*. According to some criteria, the soundtrack album of *Titanic* is regarded as a "classical" album; if accepted as such, it would appear at No. 1 in this Top 10.

TOP 10 MOST PROLIFIC CLASSICAL COMPOSERS

	COMPOSER / NATIONALITY / DATES	HOURS OF MUSIC
1	Joseph Haydn (Austrian; 1732–1809)	340
2	George Friedrich Handel (German-English; 1685–1759)	303
3	Wolfgang Amadeus Mozart (Austrian; 1756–91)	202
4	Johann Sebastian Bach (German; 1685–1750)	175
5	Franz Schubert (German; 1797–1828)	134
6	Ludwig van Beethoven (German; 1770–1827)	120
7	Henry Purcell (English; 1659–95)	116
8	Giuseppe Verdi (Italian; 1813–1901)	87
9	Anton Dvorák (Czech; 1841–1904)	79
10 =	Franz Liszt (Hungarian; 1811–86)	76
=	Pyotr Ilyich Tchaikovsky (Russian; 1840–93)	76

This list is based on a survey conducted by *Classical Music* magazine, which ranked classical composers by the total number of hours of music each composed. If the length of the composer's working life is brought into the calculation, Schubert wins: his 134 hours were composed in a career of 18 years, giving an average of 7 hours 27 minutes per annum.

Most Prolific?

Georg Philipp Telemann (German; 1681–1767) has a claim as the most prolific composer of all time, with up to 3,000 works including more than 100 concertos and 50 operas, but since he lost count himself, only a proportion have survived and many misattributions have been discovered, his place in the world ranking must remain open to debate.

TOP 10 COMPOSERS

COMPOSER / WORKS*

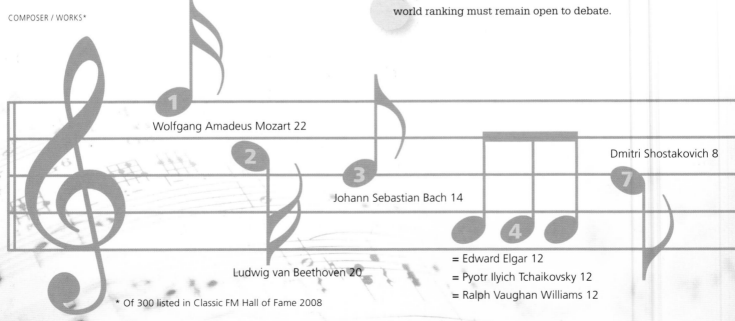

Wolfgang Amadeus Mozart 22

Ludwig van Beethoven 20

Johann Sebastian Bach 14

Dmitri Shostakovich 8

= Edward Elgar 12
= Pyotr Ilyich Tchaikovsky 12
= Ralph Vaughan Williams 12

* Of 300 listed in Classic FM Hall of Fame 2008

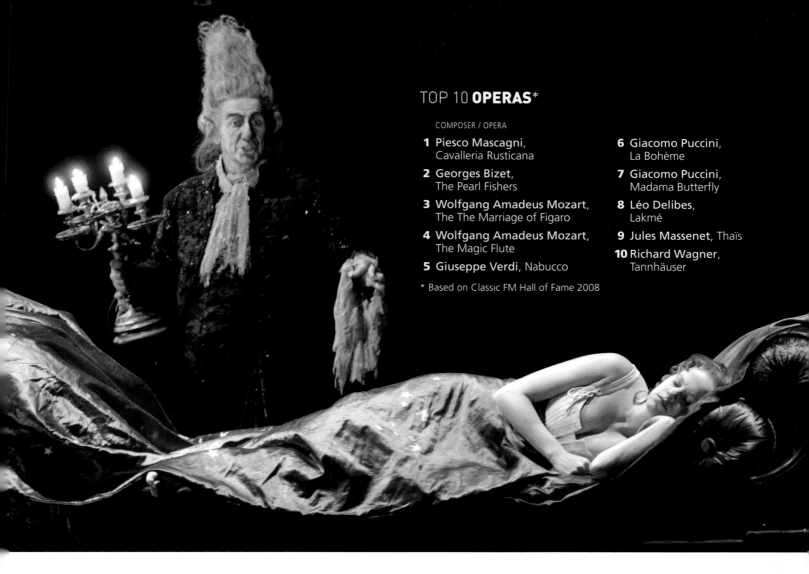

TOP 10 **OPERAS***

COMPOSER / OPERA

1 Piesco Mascagni,
Cavalleria Rusticana

2 Georges Bizet,
The Pearl Fishers

3 Wolfgang Amadeus Mozart,
The The Marriage of Figaro

4 Wolfgang Amadeus Mozart,
The Magic Flute

5 Giuseppe Verdi, Nabucco

6 Giacomo Puccini,
La Bohème

7 Giacomo Puccini,
Madama Butterfly

8 Léo Delibes,
Lakmé

9 Jules Massenet, Thaïs

10 Richard Wagner,
Tannhäuser

* Based on Classic FM Hall of Fame 2008

Mozart's magic
Mozart's first opera, Apollo et Hyacinthus, *had its debut in 1767, when he was just 11 years old. He died, aged 35, two months after the first performance of his last,* The Magic Flute, *since ranked as one his most-performed and most popular works.*

THE 10 **LAST MOZART OPERAS**

OPERA*	FIRST VENUE	PERFORMANCE
1 The Magic Flute (Die Zauberflöte)	Theater auf der Wieden, Vienna	Sep 30, 1791
2 La Clemenza di Tito	Estates Theatre, Prague	Sep 6, 1791
3 Così fan Tutte	Burgtheater, Vienna	Jan 26, 1790
4 Don Giovanni	Estates Theatre, Prague	29 Oct 1787
5 The Marriage of Figaro	Burgtheater, Vienna	1 May 1786
6 The Impresario	Orangerie, Schönbrunn	7 Feb 1786
7 Die Entführung aus dem Serail	Burgtheater, Vienna	16 Jul 1782
8 Idomeneo	Court Theatre, Munich	29 Jan 1781
9 Die Gärtnerin aus Liebe	Komödienstadl, Augsburg	1 May 1780
10 Il re pastore	Archbishop's Palace, Salzburg	23 Apr 1775

* Works performed during his lifetime only

8

10

= Franz Schubert 6
= John Williams 6

= George Friedrich Handel 7
= Sergei Rachmaninov 7

ENTERTAINMENT

On Stage

TOP 10 **LONGEST-RUNNING RODGERS & HAMMERSTEIN PRODUCTIONS ON BROADWAY**

SHOW / RUN	PERFORMANCES
1 Oklahoma! (Mar 31, 1943–May 29, 1948)	2,212
2 South Pacific (Apr 7, 1949–Jan 16, 1954)	1,925
3 The Sound of Music (Nov 16, 1959–Jun 15, 1963)	1,443
4 The King and I (Mar 29, 1951–Mar 20, 1954)	1,246
5 Carousel (Apr 19, 1945–May 24, 1947)	890
6 The King and I (Apr 11, 1996–Feb 22, 1998)	780
7 The King and I (May 2, 1977–Dec 30, 1978)	695
8 Flower Drum Song (Dec 1, 1958–May 7, 1960)	600
9 The Sound of Music (Mar 12, 1998–Jun 20, 1999)	533
10 Oklahoma! (Mar 21, 2002–Feb 23, 2003)	388

Dracula
Frank Langella took the title role in the long-running Broadway production of Dracula and went on to reprise the part in the 1979 film version.

Oklahoma!
The original 1943–48 Broadway production of Oklahoma! broke theater records before embarking on a 10-year tour.

TOP 10 **LONGEST-RUNNING MYSTERIES AND THRILLERS ON BROADWAY**

SHOW / RUN	PERFORMANCES
1 Deathtrap (Feb 26, 1978–Jul 13, 1982)	1,793
2 Arsenic and Old Lace (Jan 10, 1941–Jun 17, 1944)	1,444
3 Angel Street (Dec 5, 1941–Dec 30, 1944)	1,295
4 Sleuth (Nov 12, 1970–Oct 13, 1973	1,222
5 The Bat (Aug 23, 1920–Sep 1922)	867
6 Dracula (Oct 20, 1977–Jan 6, 1980)	925
7 Witness for the Prosecution (Dec 16, 1954–Jun 30, 1956)	645
8 Dial "M" for Murder (Oct 29, 1952–Feb 27, 1954)	552
9 Sherlock Holmes (Nov 12, 1974–Jan 4, 1976)	471
10 An Inspector Calls (Apr 27, 1994–May 28, 1995)	454

Deathtrap by Ira Levin opened at the Music Box Theatre. Though nominated for four Tony Awards it failed to win any, but went on to achieve a record four-year run. Marian Seldes appeared in almost every one of its 1,793 performances. The film version of *Deathtrap*, released the year the play closed, starred Michael Caine—who also starred in *Sleuth*, also originally a long-running Broadway thriller.

TOP 10 LONGEST RUNNING COMEDIES* ON BROADWAY

	COMEDY / RUN	PERFORMANCES
1	Life with Father (Nov 8, 1939–Jul 12, 1947)	3,224
2	The Producers (Apr 19, 2001–Apr 22, 2007)	2,502
3	Abie's Irish Rose (May 23, 1922–Oct 1, 1927)	2,327
4	Gemini (May 21, 1977–Sep 6, 1981)	1,819
5	Harvey (Nov 1, 1944– Jan 15, 1949)	1,775
6	Born Yesterday (Feb 4, 1946–Dec 31, 1949)	1,642
7	Mary, Mary (Mar 8, 1961–Dec 12, 1964)	1,572
8	The Voice of the Turtle (Dec 8, 1943–Jan 3, 1948)	1,557
9	Barefoot in the Park (Oct 23, 1963–Jun 25, 1967)	1,530
10	Spamalot (Mar 17, 2005–)	1,511#

* Including musical comedies
\# Still running—total as at November 11, 2008

Shown at the Empire Theatre, Howard Lindsay and Russel Crouse's *Life with Father*, adapted from stories in *New Yorker*, owed its success in part to the show's nostalgic view of bygone America that appeared under threat as it opened soon after the outbreak of World War II.

TOP 10 LONGEST-RUNNING MUSICALS ON BROADWAY

	SHOW / RUN	PERFORMANCES
1	The Phantom of the Opera (Jan 26, 1988–)	8,651*
2	Cats (Sep 23, 1982–Sep 10, 2000)	7,485
3	Les Misérables (Mar 12, 1987–May 18, 2003)	6,680
4	A Chorus Line (Jul 25, 1975–Apr 28, 1990)	6,137
5	Beauty and the Beast (Mar 9, 1994– Jul 28, 2007)	5,461
6	Rent (Apr 29, 1996–Sep 7, 2008)	5,123
7	Chicago (Nov 14, 1996–)	4,980*
8	The Lion King (Nov 13, 1997–)	4,565*
9	Miss Saigon (Apr 11, 1991–Jan 28, 2001)	4,092
10	42nd Street (Aug 18, 1980–Jan 8, 1989)	3,486

* Still running, total as at November 16, 2008

Phantom phenomenon
The Phantom of the Opera *has become the longest-running musical on Broadway.*

Below: The play's the thing
David Tennant appeared in 2008–09 in the critically acclaimed title role of the much-performed Hamlet.

TOP 10 PRODUCTIONS OF SHAKEPEARE ON BROADWAY

	TITLE (FIRST/LATEST PRODUCTION)	PRODUCTIONS
1	Hamlet (Nov 26, 1761–1995)	64
2	The Merchant of Venice (Jan 28, 1768–1990)	49
3	Macbeth (May 3, 1768–2008)	46
4	Romeo and Juliet (Jan 28, 1754–1987)	32
5	Twelfth Night (Jun 11, 1804–1998)	30
6	= The Taming of the Shrew (Jan 8, 1768–1951)	23
	= As You Like It (Jul 14, 1786–1987)	23
8	= Richard III (Mar 5, 1750–1979)	20
	= Othello (Dec 23, 1751–1982)	20
	= Julius Caesar (Mar 14, 1794–2005)	20

Richard III was the first Shakespeare play performed in America, at the Nassau Street Theatre from March 5–12, 1750, with Thomas Kean in the title role.

Box-office Blockbusters

TOP 10 **MOVIES OF ALL TIME**

MOVIE / YEAR / WORLD GROSS ($)

1 **Titanic*** 1997
1,848,813,795

2 **The Lord of the Rings: The Return of the King** 2003
1,133,027,325

3 **Pirates of the Caribbean: Dead Man's Chest** 2006
1,066,179,725

4 **The Dark Knight** 2008
1,001,842,429

5 **Harry Potter and the Socerer's Stone** 2001
985,817,659

6 **Pirates of the Caribbean: At World's End** 2007
961,002,663

7 **Harry Potter and the Order of the Phoenix** 2007
938,468,864

8 **The Lord of the Rings: The Two Towers** 2002
926,287,400

9 **Star Wars: Episode I – The Phantom Menace** 1999
924,317,554

10 **Shrek 2**# 2004
920,665,658

* Won Best Picture Oscar
# Animated

Only *Titanic* and *The Dark Knight* have earned more than $500 million in the USA alone.

Final role
Heath Ledger (The Joker) died before The Dark Knight *was released.*

TOP 10 **MOVIE BUDGETS**

	MOVIE	YEAR	ESTIMATED BUDGET ($)
1	Pirates of the Caribbean: At World's End	2007	300,000,000
2	Superman Returns	2006	270,000,000
3	Spider-Man 3	2007	258,000,000
4	=Pirates of the Caribbean: Dead Man's Chest	2006	225,000,000
	=Quantum of Solace	2008	225,000,000
6	X-Men: The Last Stand	2006	210,000,000
7	King Kong	2005	207,000,000
8	=Titanic	1997	200,000,000
	=Terminator 3: Rise of the Machines	2003	200,000,000
	=Spider-Man 2	2004	200,000,000
	=The Chronicles of Narnia: Prince Caspian	2008	200,000,000

FRANCHISE	NO. OF FILMS	YEARS	TOTAL WORLD GROSS ($)*
1 James Bond	22#	1963–2008	4,901,539,441
2 Harry Potter	5	2001–07	4,494,832,233
3 Star Wars†	6	1977–2005	4,309,312,004
4 The Lord of the Rings	3	2001–03	2,926,875,016
5 Pirates of the Caribbean	3	2003–07	2,681,446,403
6 Batman†	6	1989–2008	2,644,655,068
7 Spider-Man	3	2002–04	2,496,544,674
8 Indiana Jones	4	1981–2008	1,998,655,564
9 Shrek	2	2001–04	2,204,031,957
10 Jurassic Park	3	1993–2001	1,902,110,926

* Cumulative global earnings of the original film and all its sequels to March 31, 2009
# Excluding "unofficial" *Casino Royale* and *Never Say Never Again*
† Excluding animated versions

Bond begins
Sean Connery took the title role in six official James Bond films. With the release of the 22nd movie, it has become the highest-earning series ever.

TOP 10 **SEQUELS**

MOVIE (YEAR)	US GROSS ($)	SEQUEL (YEAR)	IMPROVEMENT US GROSS ($)	(%)
1 Night of the Living Dead (1990)	5,835,247	Dawn of the Dead (2004)	59,020,957	911.5
2 The Terminator (1984)	38,371,200	Terminator 2: Judgment Day (1991)	204,843,345	433.8
3 Austin Powers: International Man of Mystery (1997)	53,883,989	Austin Powers: The Spy Who Shagged Me (1999)	206,040,086	282.4
4 First Blood (1982)	47,212,904	Rambo: First Blood Part II (1985)	150,415,432	218.6
5 Mad Max (1980)	8,750,000	Mad Max 2: The Road Warrior (1981)	23,667,907	170.5
6 Highlander (1986)	5,900,000	Highlander II: The Quickening (1991)	15,556,340	163.7
7 Batman Begins (2005)	205,343,774	The Dark Knight	533,345,358	159.7
8 The Evil Dead (1983)	2,400,000	Evil Dead 2 (1987)	5,923,044	146.8
9 Lethal Weapon (1987)	65,207,127	Lethal Weapon 2 (1989)	147,253,986	125.8
10 Bad Boys (1995)	65,807,024	Bad Boys II (2003)	138,608,444	110.6

FILM FLOPS

The Adventures of Pluto Nash (2002) is considered the greatest financial flop ever: its estimated budget was $100 million, but it earned only $7,103,972, a return of just 7.1 percent. *Cutthroat Island* (1995) had a budget of $98 million but earned little more than $10 million on its US release. More recently, $100 million-plus budget films *Treasure Planet* (2002), *The Alamo* (2004), *Around the World in 80 Days* (2004), and *Stealth* (2005), incurred substantial losses, though reduced when foreign and video earnings are taken into account. *Waterworld* (1995), with a budget of $175 million, is often cited as a flop, but earned over $264 million globally.

Movies of the Decades

TOP 10 **MOVIES OF THE** 1920s

	MOVIE	YEAR
1	The Big Parade	1925
2	The Four Horsemen of the Apocalypse	1921
3	Ben-Hur	1926
4	The Ten Commandments	1923
5	What Price Glory?	1926
6	The Covered Wagon	1923
7	Way Down East	1921
8	The Singing Fool	1928
9	Wings	1927
10	The Gold Rush	1925

The Birth of a Nation (1915) was the highest-earning movie of the silent era.

Silent success
The Big Parade, *top 1920s film.*

TOP 10 **MOVIES OF THE** 1930s

	MOVIE	YEAR
1	Gone With the Wind*	1939
2	Snow White and the Seven Dwarfs	1937
3	King Kong	1933
4	The Wizard of Oz	1939
5	Frankenstein	1931
6	San Francisco	1936
7	= Hell's Angels	1930
	= Lost Horizon	1937
	= Mr. Smith Goes to Washington	1939
10	Maytime	1937

* Winner of Best Picture Oscar

Gone With the Wind and *Snow White and the Seven Dwarfs* have generated more income than any prewar film.

TOP 10 **MOVIES OF THE** 1940s

	MOVIE	YEAR
1	Bambi*	1942
2	Pinocchio*	1940
3	Fantasia*	1940
4	Song of the South#	1946
5	Mom and Dad	1944
6	Samson and Delilah	1949
7	The Best Years of Our Lives†	1946
8	The Bells of St Mary's	1945
9	Duel in the Sun	1946
10	This Is the Army	1943

* Animated
# Part animated/part live-action
† Winner of Best Picture Oscar

Four classic Disney cartoons offered colorful escapism during and after the austerity of the war years.

TOP 10 **MOVIES OF THE** 1950s

	MOVIE	YEAR
1	Lady and the Tramp*	1955
2	Peter Pan*	1953
3	Cinderella*	1950
4	The Ten Commandments	1956
5	Ben-Hur#	1959
6	Sleeping Beauty*	1959
7	Around the World in 80 Days	1956
8	This is Cinerama	1952
9	South Pacific	1958
10	The Robe	1953

* Animated
# Winner of Best Picture Oscar

As in the 1940s, feature-length animated films dominated the 1950s, along with popular biblical epics.

TOP 10 **MOVIES OF THE** 1960s

	MOVIE	YEAR
1	One Hundred and One Dalmatians*	1961
2	The Jungle Book*	1967
3	2001: A Space Odyssey	1968
4	The Sound of Music#	1965
5	Thunderball	1965
6	Goldfinger	1964
7	Doctor Zhivago	1965
8	You Only Live Twice	1967
9	The Graduate	1968
10	Butch Cassidy and the Sundance Kid	1969

* Animated
# Winner of Best Picture Oscar

For the first time, each of the Top 10 movies earned more than $100 million around the world.

TOP 10 MOVIES OF THE 1970s

MOVIE	YEAR
1 Star Wars*	1977
2 Jaws	1975
3 The Exorcist	1973
4 Grease	1978
5 Close Encounters of the Third Kind	1977
6 Superman	1978
7 Saturday Night Fever	1977
8 The Godfather	1972
9 Rocky	1976
10 Moonraker	1979

* Later retitled *Star Wars: Episode IV— A New Hope*

Blockbusters from Steven Spielberg and George Lucas hit the screens, with *Star Wars* once the all-time highest-earning.

TOP 10 MOVIES OF THE 1980s

MOVIE	YEAR
1 E.T.: the Extra-Terrestrial	1982
2 Return of the Jedi*	1983
3 The Empire Strikes Back#	1980
4 Indiana Jones and the Last Crusade	1989
5 Rain Man†	1988
6 Batman	1989
7 Raiders of the Lost Ark	1981
8 Back to the Future	1985
9 Top Gun	1986
10 Indiana Jones and the Temple of Doom	1984

* Later retitled *Star Wars: Episode VI—Return of the Jedi*
\# Later retitled *Star Wars: Episode V—The Empire Strikes Back*
† Winner of Best Picture Oscar

TOP 10 MOVIES OF THE 1990s

MOVIE	YEAR
1 Titanic*	1997
2 Star Wars: Episode I— The Phantom Menace	1999
3 Jurassic Park	1993
4 Independence Day	1996
5 The Lion King#	1994
6 Forrest Gump*	1994
7 The Sixth Sense	1999
8 The Lost World: Jurassic Park	1997
9 Men in Black	1997
10 Armageddon	1998

* Winner of Best Picture Oscar
\# Animated

A king's ransom
The Lord of the Rings: The Return of the King *became the second film to earn over $1 billion.*

TOP 10 MOVIES OF THE* 2000s

MOVIE	YEAR
1 The Lord of the Rings: The Return of the King	2003
2 Pirates of the Caribbean: Dead Man's Chest	2006
3 The Dark Knight	2008
4 Harry Potter and the Sorcerer's Stone	2001
5 Pirates of the Caribbean: At World's End	2007
6 Harry Potter and the Order of the Phoenix	2007
7 The Lord of the Rings: The Two Towers	2002
8 Shrek 2	2004
9 Harry Potter and the Goblet of Fire	2005
10 Spider-Man 3	2007

* As at March 31, 2009

AFI Hits

Since 1998 the American Film Institute has been compiling its "100 Years of..." lists, selected by a panel of prominent individuals in the film community and presenting Top 100s in a variety of categories ("Thrills," "Laughs," "Songs," etc.). In 2008, the AFI identified its Top 10s in a range of genres. Among them, Steven Spielberg and Stanley Kubrick each directed three films, while Tom Hanks, Gene Hackman, and Diane Keaton each appeared in (or, in the case of Hanks and the animated *Toy Story*, provided a voice for) a total of four of the movies shown in these lists.

TOP 10 **GANGSTER MOVIES**

	MOVIE	YEAR
1	The Godfather*	1972
2	Goodfellas	1990
3	The Godfather Part II*	1974
4	White Heat	1949
5	Bonnie and Clyde	1967
6	Scarface: The Shame of the Nation	1932
7	Pulp Fiction	1994
8	The Public Enemy	1931
9	Little Caesar	1931
10	Scarface	1983

* Won Best Picture Oscar

TOP 10 **WESTERNS**

	MOVIE	YEAR
1	The Searchers	1956
2	High Noon	1952
3	Shane	1953
4	Unforgiven*	1992
5	Red River	1948
6	The Wild Bunch	1969
7	Butch Cassidy and the Sundance Kid	1969
8	McCabe and Mrs Miller	1971
9	Stagecoach	1939
10	Cat Ballou	1965

* Won Best Picture Oscar

TOP 10 **FANTASY FILMS**

	MOVIE	YEAR
1	The Wizard of Oz	1939
2	The Lord of the Rings: The Fellowship of the Ring	2001
3	It's a Wonderful Life	1946
4	King Kong	1933
5	Miracle on 34th Street	1947
6	Field of Dreams	1989
7	Harvey	1950
8	Groundhog Day	1993
9	The Thief of Bagdad	1924
10	Big	1988

The Wizard of Oz
The movie's "Somewhere Over the Rainbow" previously topped the AFI "100 Years... 100 Songs" list.

TOP 10 **EPICS**

MOVIE	YEAR
1 Lawrence of Arabia*	1962
2 Ben-Hur*	1959
3 Schindler's List*	1993
4 Gone with the Wind*	1939
5 Spartacus	1960
6 Titanic*	1997
7 All Quiet on the Western Front*	1930
8 Saving Private Ryan*	1998
9 Reds	1981
10 The Ten Commandments	1956

* Won Best Picture Oscar

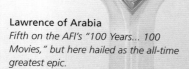

Lawrence of Arabia
Fifth on the AFI's "100 Years... 100 Movies," but here hailed as the all-time greatest epic.

TOP 10 **ROMANTIC COMEDIES**

MOVIE	YEAR
1 City Lights	1931
2 Annie Hall*	1977
3 It Happened One Night*	1934
4 Roman Holiday	1953
5 The Philadelphia Story	1940
6 When Harry Met Sally...	1989
7 Adam's Rib	1949
8 Moonstruck	1987
9 Harold and Maude	1971
10 Sleepless in Seattle	1993

* Won Best Picture Oscar

TOP 10 **SCIENCE-FICTION FILMS**

MOVIE	YEAR
1 2001: A Space Odyssey	1968
2 Star Wars: Episode IV— A New Hope	1977
3 E.T.: the Extra-Terrestrial	1982
4 A Clockwork Orange	1971
5 The Day the Earth Stood Still	1951
6 Blade Runner	1982
7 Alien	1979
8 Terminator 2: Judgment Day	1991
9 Invasion of the Body Snatchers	1956
10 Back to the Future	1985

TOP 10 **ANIMATED MOVIES**

MOVIE	YEAR
1 Snow White and the Seven Dwarfs	1937
2 Pinocchio	1940
3 Bambi	1942
4 The Lion King	1994
5 Fantasia	1940
6 Toy Story	1995
7 Beauty and the Beast	1991
8 Shrek*	2001
9 Cinderella	1950
10 Finding Nemo	2003

* DreamWorks; all others Disney

Animated Hits

TOP 10 ANIMATED MOVIES IN THE USA

MOVIE / YEAR / US TOTAL GROSS ($)

1 Shrek 2* 2004
441,226,247

2 Finding Nemo# 2003
339,714,978

3 The Lion King# 1994
328,541,776

4 Shrek the Third* 2007
322,719,944

5 Shrek* 2001
267,665,011

6 The Incredibles# 2004
261,441,092

7 Monsters, Inc.# 2001
255,873,250

8 Toy Story 2# 1999
245,852,179

9 Cars# 2006
244,082,982

10 WALL-E 2008
220,917,577

* DreamWorks
# Disney
† 20th Century Fox Animation

Just for kicks
Kung Fu Panda *had a production budget of $130 million, but earned almost five times as much worldwide.*

TOP 10 ANIMATED MOVIES

MOVIE / YEAR / GROSS ($)

1 Shrek 2*
2004
920,665,658

2 Finding Nemo#
2003
864,625,978

3 Shrek the Third*
2007
798,957,081

4 The Lion King#
1994
783,841,776

5 Ice Age: The Meltdown†
2006
651,564,512

6 Kung Fu Panda*
2008
631,908,951

7 The Incredibles#
2004
631,442,092

8 Ratatouille#
2007
621,426,008

9 Madagascar: Escape 2 Africa*
2008
584,316,050

10 WALL-E#
2008
534,745,866

* DreamWorks
# Disney
† 20th Century Fox Animation

Animated automata
During the past decade, films such as Robots *have benefited from advances in CGI.*

TOP 10 ANIMATED MOVIES BASED ON TV SERIES

	FILM	TV SERIES*	MOVIE YEAR
1	The Simpsons Movie	1987	2007
2	Pokémon: The First Movie	1997	1999
3	The Rugrats Movie	1991	1998
4	The SpongeBob SquarePants Movie	1999	2004
5	Pokémon: The Movie 2000	1997	2000
6	Rugrats in Paris: The Movie—Rugrats II	1991	2000
7	TMNT	1987	2007
8	South Park: Bigger, Longer & Uncut	1997	1999
9	Beavis and Butthead Do America	1993	1996
10	Pokémon 3: The Movie	1997	2001

* Launched on TV in USA

Many TV animated series established substantial fan-bases before they hit the big screen. *The Simpsons Movie* has made over $527 million and the Top 10 a cumulative global total of over $1.5 billion.

Animated Film Budgets

Snow White and the Seven Dwarfs (1937) had a then-record animated film budget of $1.49 million. The $2.28 million of *Fantasia* (1940) was the biggest of the 1940s, and the $6 million of *Sleeping Beauty* (1959) the highest of the 1950s. Fifty years on, budgets of $100 million or more are common, with *WALL-E* (2008) setting a record of $180 million.

TOP 10 ANIMATED SCIENCE-FICTION MOVIES

	MOVIE	YEAR	WORLDWIDE TOTAL GROSS ($)
1	WALL-E	2008	534,745,866
2	Lilo & Stitch	2002	273,144,470
3	Robots	2005	260,718,330
4	Atlantis: The Lost Empire	2001	186,053,745
5	Meet the Robinsons	2007	169,332,978
6	Pokémon: The First Movie	1999	163,644,662
7	Pokémon: The Movie 2000	2000	133,949,270
8	Treasure Planet	2002	109,578,115
9	Jimmy Neutron: Boy Genius	2001	102,992,536
10	Final Fantasy: The Spirits Within	2001	85,131,830

TOP 10 MOVIES WITH CGI STARS*

	MOVIE	YEAR	WORLDWIDE TOTAL GROSS ($)
1	King Kong	2005	550,517,357
2	Godzilla	1998	379,014,294
3	Alvin and the Chipmunks	2007	359,656,974
4	Stuart Little	1999	300,235,367
5	Casper	1995	287,928,194
6	Scooby-Doo	2002	275,650,703
7	The Incredible Hulk	2008	263,427,064
8	Hulk	2003	245,360,480
9	Garfield: The Movie	2004	198,964,900
10	Scooby-Doo 2: Monsters Unleashed	2004	181,466,833

* Main or title-named character created by computer-generated imagery

Actors

TOP 10 **HARRISON FORD MOVIES**

MOVIE	YEAR
1 Indiana Jones and the Kingdom of the Crystal Skull	2008
2 Star Wars: Episode IV— A New Hope	1977
3 Star Wars: Episode VI— Return of the Jedi	1983
4 Star Wars: Episode V— The Empire Strikes Back	1980
5 Indiana Jones and the Last Crusade	1989
6 Raiders of the Lost Ark	1981
7 The Fugitive	1993
8 Indiana Jones and the Temple of Doom	1984
9 Air Force One	1997
10 What Lies Beneath	2000

TOP 10 **CLINT EASTWOOD MOVIES**

MOVIE	YEAR
1 Million Dollar Baby*	2004
2 Gran Torino	2008
3 The Bridges of Madison County	1995
4 In the Line of Fire	1993
5 Unforgiven*	1992
6 A Perfect World	1993
7 Space Cowboys	2000
8 Every Which Way But Loose	1978
9 Absolute Power	1997
10 Any Which Way You Can	1980

* Won Best Director and Best Picture Oscars

Clint Eastwood
Unforgiven earned Clint Eastwood the first of two Best Director Oscars. His second was awarded for Best Picture Million Dollar Baby, which made over $200 million.

TOP 10 **PAUL NEWMAN MOVIES**

MOVIE	YEAR
1 Road to Perdition	2002
2 The Sting	1973
3 Message in a Bottle	1999
4 The Towering Inferno	1974
5 Butch Cassidy and the Sundance Kid	1969
6 The Verdict	1982
7 The Color of Money*	1986
8 Nobody's Fool	1994
9 Absence of Malice	1981
10 Fort Apache the Bronx	1981

* Won Best Picture Oscar

In addition to the movies in his Top 10, Paul Newman (1925–2008) appeared briefly as himself in *Silent Movie* (1976), which, if it were included, would be in ninth place. He also provided the voice of Doc Hudson in the animated film *Cars* (2006), which would appear first in his personal Top 10 by a considerable margin.

Whip-hand
Harrison Ford's Top 10 films—most notably the Indiana Jones *and* Star Wars *series—have earned a total of almost $5 billion worldwide.*

TOP 10 **JOHNNY DEPP MOVIES**

MOVIE	YEAR
1 Pirates of the Caribbean: Dead Man's Chest	2006
2 Pirates of the Caribbean: At World's End	2007
3 Pirates of the Caribbean: The Curse of the Black Pearl	2003
4 Charlie and the Chocolate Factory	2004
5 Sleepy Hollow	1999
6 Platoon	1986
7 Chocolat	2000
8 Sweeney Todd: The Demon Barber of Fleet Street	2007
9 Donnie Brasco	1997
10 Finding Neverland	2004

All Johnny Depp's Top 10 movies have earned more than $100 million each, his run of successes led—by a considerable margin—by the three *Pirates of the Caribbean* films, which have made $2.7 billion in total, with a fourth scheduled for release in 2012.

TOP 10 **MATT DAMON MOVIES**

MOVIE	YEAR
1 Saving Private Ryan	1998
2 Ocean's Eleven	2001
3 The Bourne Ultimatum	2007
4 Ocean's Twelve	2004
5 Ocean's Thirteen	2006
6 The Departed	2006
7 The Bourne Supremacy	2004
8 Good Will Hunting	1997
9 The Bourne Identity	2002
10 The Talented Mr Ripley	1999

Pirate treasure
The three Pirates of the Caribbean *movies to date head Johnny Depp's personal Top 10, having earned $2.7 billion globally.*

TOP 10 **BRAD PITT MOVIES**

MOVIE	YEAR
1 Troy	2004
2 Mr. & Mrs. Smith	2005
3 Ocean's Eleven	2001
4 Ocean's Twelve	2004
5 Se7en	1995
6 The Curious Case of Benjamin Button	2008
7 Ocean's Thirteen	2007
8 Interview with the Vampire: The Vampire Chronicles	1994
9 Twelve Monkeys	1995
10 Sleepers	1996

Troy weight
Troy, in which Brad Pitt took the role of Achilles, added to his run of box-office hits, making a world total of almost $500 million.

Actresses

TOP 10 **MERYL STREEP** MOVIES

	MOVIE	YEAR
1	Mamma Mia!	2008
2	The Devil Wears Prada	2006
3	Out of Africa	1985
4	Lemony Snicket's A Series of Unfortunate Events	2004
5	The Bridges of Madison County	1995
6	Death Becomes Her	1992
7	The Hours	2002
8	Kramer vs. Kramer	1979
9	The Manchurian Candidate	2004
10	The River Wild	1994

Meryl Streep has been nominated for Academy Awards on a total of 14 occasions, winning for her supporting role in *Kramer vs. Kramer*, and Best Actress for *Sophie's Choice* (1982), which falls outside her personal Top 10 in terms of box-office revenue. She provided the voice of the Blue Fairy in *A.I.: Artificial Intelligence* (2001) which, were it taken into account, would be in fourth place.

TOP 10 **SIGOURNEY WEAVER** MOVIES

	MOVIE	YEAR
1	Ghostbusters	1984
2	The Village	2004
3	Ghostbusters II	1989
4	Aliens	1986
5	Alien: Resurrection	1997
6	Alien3	1992
7	Vantage Point	2008
8	Alien	1979
9	Galaxy Quest	1999
10	Holes	2003

Sigourney Weaver has made a speciality of playing vulnerable-but-tough parts, her roles in the two *Ghostbusters* and four *Alien(s)* films bringing her both fame and fortune. She provided the voice of the Ship's Computer in the animated film *WALL-E* (2008); if included it would rank first in her Top 10.

TOP 10 **TILDA SWINTON** MOVIES

	MOVIE	YEAR
1	The Chronicles of Narnia: The Lion, the Witch and the Wardrobe	2005
2	The Chronicles of Narnia: Prince Caspian	2008
3	The Curious Case of Benjamin Button	2008
4	Constantine	2005
5	Vanilla Sky	2001
6	Burn After Reading	2008
7	The Beach	2000
8	Michael Clayton	2007
9	Adaptation.	2002
10	Broken Flowers	2005

British actress Tilda Swinton won a Best Supporting Actress Oscar for her role in *Michael Clayton*.

Fighting fit
Tilda Swinton took the role of the White Witch in the first two Narnia movies, which have earned $1.2 billion worldwide.

TOP 10 CATE BLANCHETT MOVIES

	MOVIE	YEAR
1	The Lord of the Rings: The Return of the King	2003
2	The Lord of the Rings: The Two Towers	2002
3	The Lord of the Rings: The Fellowship of the Ring	2001
4	Indiana Jones and the Kingdom of the Crystal Skull	2008
5	The Curious Case of Benjamin Button	2008
6	The Aviator	2004
7	Babel	2006
8	The Talented Mr Ripley	1999
9	Elizabeth	1998
10	Elizabeth: The Golden Age	2007

TOP 10 SCARLETT JOHANSSON MOVIES

	MOVIE	YEAR
1	The Horse Whisperer	1998
2	The Island	2005
3	He's Just Not That Into You	2009
4	Lost in Translation	2003
5	The Prestige	2006
6	Vicky Cristina Barcelona	2008
7	Match Point	2005
8	Home Alone 3	1997
9	The Other Boleyn Girl	2008
10	Just Cause	1995

Shooting ahead
Sci-fi thriller The Island *is one of a number of high-earning Scarlett Johansson movies.*

X-rated
Among Berry's highest-earning films, the three *X-Men* have earned a global total of $1.2 billion.

TOP 10 HALLE BERRY MOVIES

	MOVIE	YEAR
1	X-Men: The Last Stand	2006
2	Die Another Day	2002
3	X2: X-Men United	2003
4	The Flintstones	1994
5	X-Men	2000
6	Swordfish	2001
7	Gothika	2003
8	Boomerang	1992
9	Executive Decision	1996
10	Catwoman	2004

Oscar Stars & Directors

STAR	FIRST WIN	YEAR	SECOND WIN	YEAR
1 Sean Penn	Mystic River	2003	Milk	2008
2 Daniel Day-Lewis	My Left Foot	1989	There Will Be Blood	2007
3 Hilary Swank	Boys Don't Cry	1999	Million Dollar Baby*	2004
4 Jack Nicholson	One Flew over the Cuckoo's Nest*	1975	As Good as it Gets	1997
5 Tom Hanks	Philadelphia	1993	Forrest Gump*	1994
6 Jodie Foster	The Accused	1988	The Silence of the Lambs*	1991
7 Dustin Hoffman	Kramer vs. Kramer*	1979	Rain Man*	1988
8 Sally Field	Norma Rae	1979	Places in the Heart	1984
9 Katharine Hepburn	The Lion in Winter	1968	On Golden Pond	1981
10 Jane Fonda	Klute	1971	Coming Home	1978

* Film won Best Picture Oscar

Uniquely, Katharine Hepburn had already won two Best Actress Oscars, for *Morning Glory* in 1932/33 and *Guess Who's Coming to Dinner?* in 1967, which would also place her at No. 11 in this list.

Devil in disguise
Meryl Streep was nominated for a Best Actress Oscar for The Devil Wears Prada *(2006).*

TOP 10 **ACTORS AND ACTRESSES WITH THE MOST OSCAR NOMINATIONS***

ACTOR / WINS:SUPPORTING/BEST / NOMINATIONS			
1 Meryl Streep	1	1	15
2 = Katharine Hepburn	0	4	12
= Jack Nicholson	1	2	12
4 = Bette Davis	0	2	10
= Laurence Olivier	0	1	10
6 = Paul Newman	0	1	9
= Spencer Tracy	0	2	9
8 = Marlon Brando	0	2	8
= Jack Lemmon	1	1	8
= Peter O'Toole	0	0	8
= Al Pacino	0	1	8
= Geraldine Page	0	1	8

* In all acting categories

THE 10 **LATEST DIRECTORS TO WIN TWO BEST DIRECTOR OSCARS**

DIRECTOR	FIRST WIN	YEAR	SECOND WIN	YEAR
1 Clint Eastwood	Unforgiven	1992	Million Dollar Baby	2004
2 Steven Spielberg	Schindler's List	1993	Saving Private Ryan	1998
3 Oliver Stone	Platoon	1986	Born on the Fourth of July	1989
4 Milos Forman	One Flew Over the Cuckoo's Nest	1975	Amadeus	1984
5 Fred Zinnemann	From Here to Eternity	1953	A Man for All Seasons	1966
6 Robert Wise	West Side Story	1961	The Sound of Music	1965
7 David Lean	The Bridge on the River Kwai	1957	Lawrence of Arabia	1962
8 Billy Wilder	The Lost Weekend	1945	The Apartment	1960
9 George Stevens	A Place in the Sun	1951	Giant	1956
10 Elia Kazan	Gentleman's Agreement	1947	On the Waterfront	1954

John Ford is the only director to win four Best Director Oscars (from 1935 to 1952), while Frank Capra and William Wyler each reached a tally of three, with these the most recent of the relatively rare double winners.

Dream come true
Jennifer Hudson's debut Dreamgirls *won her the Best Supporting Actress Oscar.*

THE 10 **LATEST YEARS IN WHICH BEST PICTURE AND BEST DIRECTOR OSCARS WERE WON BY DIFFERENT FILMS**

	BEST PICTURE	BEST DIRECTOR FILM	YEAR
1	Crash	Brokeback Mountain	2005
2	Chicago	The Pianist	2002
3	Gladiator	Traffic	2000
4	Shakespeare in Love	Saving Private Ryan	1998
5	Driving Miss Daisy	Born on the Fourth of July	1989
6	Chariots of Fire	Reds	1981
7	The Godfather	Cabaret	1972
8	In the Heat of the Night	The Graduate	1967
9	Around the World in 80 Days	Giant	1956
10	The Greatest Show on Earth	The Quiet Man	1952

THE 10 **LATEST WINNERS OF AN OSCAR FOR THEIR DEBUT FILM***

	ACTOR/ACTRESS	FILM	FILM YEAR
1	Jennifer Hudson#	Dreamgirls	2006
2	Anna Paquin#	The Piano	1993
3	Marlee Matlin†	Children of a Lesser God	1986
4	Haing S. Ngor#	The Killing Fields	1984
5	Timothy Hutton#	Ordinary People	1980
6	Tatum O'Neal#	Paper Moon	1973
7	Barbra Streisand†	Funny Girl	1968
8 =	Julie Andrews†	Mary Poppins	1964
=	Lila Kedrova#	Zorba the Greek	1964
10	Miyoshi Umeki#	Sayonara	1957

* In a film eligible for a Best or Best Supporting Actor/Actress Oscar win (hence excluding previous TV movies, etc.)
\# Best Actor/Actress in a Supporting Role
† Best Actor/Actress in a Leading Role

Oscar Films & Studios

TOP 10 STUDIOS WITH THE MOST OSCAR* WINS IN ALL CATEGORIES

	STUDIO	WINS
1	MGM	191
2	20th Century Fox	187
3	Paramount	186
4	Warner Bros.	182
5	Columbia	155
6	United Artists	151
7	Universal	87
8	RKO Radio Pictures	56
9	Miramax	52
10	Buena Vista	47

* Oscar® is a Registered Trade Mark

THE 10 LATEST FILMS TO WIN THE BEST PICTURE OSCAR BUT NO OTHER MAJOR AWARD*

	FILM	YEAR
1	Crash	2005
2	Chariots of Fire	1981
3	Around the World in 80 Days	1956
4	The Greatest Show on Earth	1952
5	An American in Paris	1951
6	Rebecca	1940
7	Mutiny on the Bounty	1935
8	Grand Hotel	1932
9	Cimarron	1931
10	The Broadway Melody	1929

* In directing or acting categories

THE 10 FILMS WITH THE MOST NOMINATIONS WITHOUT A SINGLE WIN

	FILM	YEAR	NOMINATIONS
1 =	The Turning Point	1977	11
=	The Color Purple	1985	11
3	Gangs of New York	2002	10
4 =	The Little Foxes	1941	9
=	Peyton Place	1957	9
6 =	Quo Vadis	1951	8
=	The Nun's Story	1959	8
=	The Sand Pebbles	1966	8
=	The Elephant Man	1980	8
=	Ragtime	1981	8
=	The Remains of the Day	1993	8

TOP 10 STUDIOS WITH THE MOST BEST PICTURE OSCARS

STUDIO / WINS

In the 80 years of the Academy Awards, up to the 2009 ceremony (awarded for films released the previous year), these, along with RKO Radio Pictures with two wins (*Cimarron*, 1931 and *The Best Years of Our Lives*, 1946), are the only studios to have won multiple Best Picture Oscars. Six other studios have each achieved a single win.

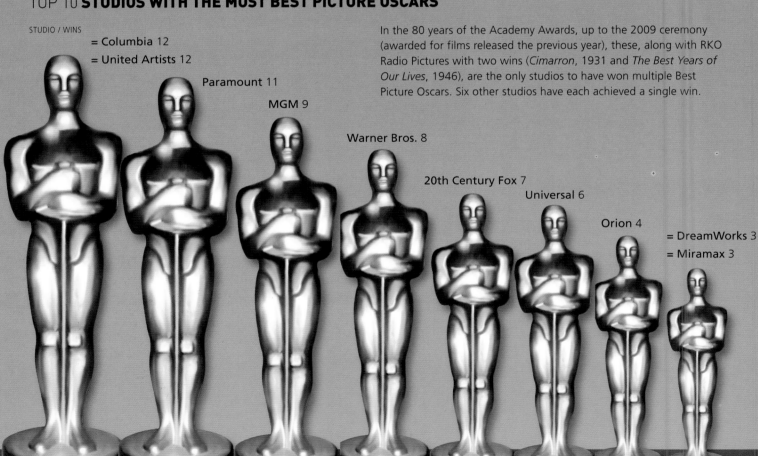

= Columbia 12
= United Artists 12
Paramount 11
MGM 9
Warner Bros. 8
20th Century Fox 7
Universal 6
Orion 4
= DreamWorks 3
= Miramax 3

1 3 4 5 6 7 8 9

Racing ahead
Ben-Hur's 11 Oscars, including Best Picture, Best Director and Best Actor for
Charlton Heston, stood as a record for 38 years.

TOP 10 **FILMS TO WIN THE MOST OSCARS**

	FILM	YEAR	NOMINATIONS	AWARDS
1 =	Ben-Hur	1959	12	11
=	Titanic	1997	14	11
=	The Lord of the Rings: The Return of the King	2003	11	11
4	West Side Story	1961	11	10
5 =	Gigi	1958	9	9
=	The Last Emperor	1987	9	9
=	The English Patient	1996	12	9
8 =	Gone With the Wind	1939	13	8*
=	From Here to Eternity	1953	13	8
=	On the Waterfront	1954	12	8
=	My Fair Lady	1964	12	8
=	Cabaret#	1972	10	8
=	Gandhi	1982	11	8
=	Amadeus	1984	11	8
=	Slumdog Millionaire	2008	10	8

* Plus two special awards
\# Did not win Best Picture Oscar

TOP 10 **HIGHEST-EARNING BEST PICTURE OSCAR-WINNERS**

	FILM	YEAR*	WORLD BOX OFFICE ($)
1	Titanic	1997	1,848,813,795
2	The Lord of the Rings: The Return of the King	2003	1,129,219,252
3	Forrest Gump	1994	677,386,686
4	Gladiator	2000	457,640,427
5	Dances With Wolves	1990	424,208,842
6	Rain Man	1988	416,011,462
7	Gone With the Wind	1939	400,176,459
8	American Beauty	1999	356,296,601
9	Schindler's List	1993	321,267,179
10	A Beautiful Mind	2001	313,542,341

* Of release; Oscars are awarded the following year

Radio & TV

TOP 10 **RADIO FORMATS IN THE USA**

FORMAT / AUDIENCE SHARE (%)

1	2	3	4	5	6	7	8	9	10
News/talk/ information 17.4	Adult Contemp- orary 14.0	Spanish 11.0	Contemp- orary hits 10.9	Urban 9.8	Country 9.7	Rock 7.9	Oldies 5.5	Alternative 3.4	New adult contemporary/ smooth jazz 2.8

Source: Arbitron, American Radio Listening Trends, 2007

TOP 10 **LONGEST-RUNNING PROGRAMS ON NATIONAL PUBLIC RADIO**

PROGRAM / FIRST BROADCAST

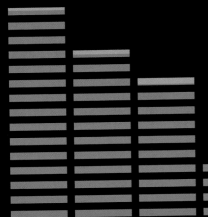    

All Things Considered 1971

Fresh Air with Terry Gross 1975

Weekend All Things Considered 1977

Marian McPartland's Piano Jazz 1978

Morning Edition 1979

Weekend Edition/ Saturday with Scott Simon 1985

Weekend Edition/ Sunday with Liane Hansen 1987

Car Talk 1987

Talk of the Nation 1991

Wait Wait... Don't Tell Me! 1998

* Produced or co-produced by NPR, excluding syndicated programs

Source: National Public Radio

TOP 10 **TELEVISION AUDIENCES IN THE USA**

	PROGRAM	DATE	TOTAL	VIEWERS %
1	M*A*S*H Special	Feb 28, 1983	50,150,000	60.2
2	Dallas	Nov 21, 1980	41,470,000	53.3
3	Roots Part 8	Jan 30, 1977	36,380,000	51.1
4	Super Bowl XVI	Jan 24, 1982	40,020,000	49.1
5	Super Bowl XVII	Jan 30, 1983	40,480,000	48.6
6	XVII Winter Olympics	Feb 23, 1994	45,690,000	48.5
7	Super Bowl XX	Jan 26, 1986	41,490,000	48.3
8	Gone With the Wind Pt.1	Nov 7, 1976	33,960,000	47.7
9	Gone With the Wind Pt.2	Nov 8, 1976	33,750,000	47.4
10	Super Bowl XII	Jan 15, 1978	34,410,000	47.2

Source: Nielsen Media Research

In 2009 there were an estimated 114.5 million television households in the USA, so a single ratings point would represent one percent, or 1,145,000 households, and so on. Historically, as more households acquired television sets, audiences generally increased, but the rise in channel choice and use of recording has checked this trend, and it is unlikely that such high percentages will ever again be attained. The two and a half hour feature-length "Goodbye, Farewell, and Amen" episode of *M*A*S*H* was the last in a series that had run for more than 10 years. An estimated 50.15 million households, or almost 106 million individual viewers, tuned in, making it the most-watched broadcast of all time.

TOP 10 **TELEVISION AUDIENCES IN THE UK**

	PROGRAM	BROADCAST	AUDIENCE
1	1966 World Cup Final: England v West Germany	Jul 30, 1966	32,300,000
2	Funeral of Diana, Princess of Wales	Sep 6, 1997	32,100,000
3	The Royal Family documentary	Jun 21, 1969	30,690,000
4	EastEnders Christmas episode (Den divorces Angie)	Dec 25, 1986	30,150,000
5	Apollo 13 splashdown	Apr 17, 1970	28,600,000
6	Cup Final Replay: Chelsea v. Leeds United	Apr 28, 1970	28,490,000
7	Wedding of Prince Charles and Lady Diana Spencer	Jul 29, 1981	28,400,000
8	Wedding of Princess Anne and Capt Mark Phillips	Nov 14, 1973	27,600,000
9	Coronation Street (Alan Bradley killed by a tram)	Mar 19, 1989	26,930,000
10	Only Fools and Horses (Batman and Robin episode)	Dec 29, 1996	24,350,000

Source: British Film Institute

China watching
Boosted by the 2008 Beijing Olympics, TV ownership in China now leads the world.

TOP 10 **TV COUNTRIES**

	COUNTRY	TV HOUSEHOLDS*
1	China	380,559,800
2	India	133,891,800
3	USA	118,035,600
4	Indonesia	55,665,400
5	Russia	51,272,700
6	Brazil	50,929,800
7	Japan	49,396,100
8	Germany	39,041,400
9	UK	26,819,500
10	Mexico	25,666,600

* Households with color TVs, 2010 forecast

Source: Euromonitor International

DVDs & Film Downloads

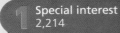

TOP 10 DVD RELEASES BY GENRE IN THE USA

GENRE / REGION 1 TITLES RELEASED*

1. **Special interest** 2,214
2. **Music, opera, stage performances** 1,033
3. **Foreign language feature films** 910
4. **Theatrical catalogue** (pre-1997) 906
5. **Direct to video feature films** 926
6. **New theatrical** (1997–) 445
7. **TV series** (multi-disk sets) 428
8. **Children's** (non-feature) 396
9. **Anime** 375
10. **Adult-themed** (non-feature) 236

* During the first three quarters of 2007
Source: *DVD Release Report/Screen Digest*

TOP 10 BESTSELLING DVDS OF ALL TIME IN THE USA

1. Finding Nemo
2. Shrek 2
3. Transformers
4. Pirates of the Caribbean: Dead Man's Chest
5. The Incredibles
6. The Chronicles of Narnia: The Lion, the Witch, and the Wardrobe
7. The Lord of the Rings: The Two Towers
8. Pirates of the Caribbean: At World's End
9. Cars
10. The Lord of the Rings: The Fellowship of the Ring

Source: Video Business

TOP 10 MOST DOWNLOADED MOVIES, 2007*

MOVIE / DOWNLOADS

1. **Transformers** 569,259
2. **Knocked Up** 509,314
3. **Shooter** 399,960
4. **Pirates of the Caribbean: At World's End** 379,749
5. **Ratatouille** 359,904
6. **300** 358,226
7. **Next** 354,044
8. **Hot Fuzz** 352,905
9. **The Bourne Ultimatum** 336,326
10. **Zodiac** 334,699

* On Mininova

As at October 3, 2008, Netherlands-based torrent download site Mininova (founded 2005) recorded a total of 6,085,866,928 downloads (films and other categories)—equivalent to almost one for every person on the planet.

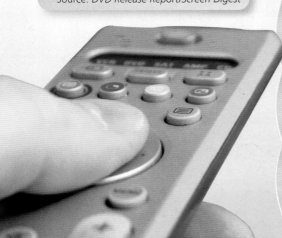

Prime mover
Transformers, *one of the bestselling DVDs and most downloaded movies of 2007,*
is set to repeat its success with its 2009 sequel, Transformers: Revenge of the Fallen.

TOP 10 **PIRATED DOWNLOADS IN THE USA, 2008**

MOVIE / ESTIMATED DOWNLOADS

1	The Dark Knight	7,030,000
2	The Incredible Hulk	5,840,000
3	The Bank Job	5,410,000
4	You Don't Mess with the Zohan	5,280,000
5	National Treasure: Book of Secrets	5,240,000
6	Juno	5,190,000
7	Tropic Thunder	4,900,000
8	I Am Legend	4,870,000
9	Forgetting Sarah Marshall	4,400,000
10	Horton Hears a Who!	4,360,000

Source: BitTorrent/Torrentfreak.com

TOP 10 **DVD SALES IN THE USA, 2008**

DVD

1 Dark Knight
2 Iron Man
3 Alvin and the Chipmunks
4 I Am Legend
5 Kung Fu Panda
6 WALL-E
7 National Treasure 2: Book of Secrets
8 Indiana Jones and the Kingdom of the Crystal Skull
9 Enchanted
10 Bee Movie

TOP 10 **DVD RENTALS IN THE USA, 2008**

DVD

1 I Am Legend
2 The Bucket List
3 3:10 to Yuma
4 No Country for Old Men
5 Juno
6 National Treasure 2: Book of Secrets
7 American Gangster
8 Good Luck Chuck
9 Fool's Gold
10 27 Dresses

THE COMMERCIAL WORLD

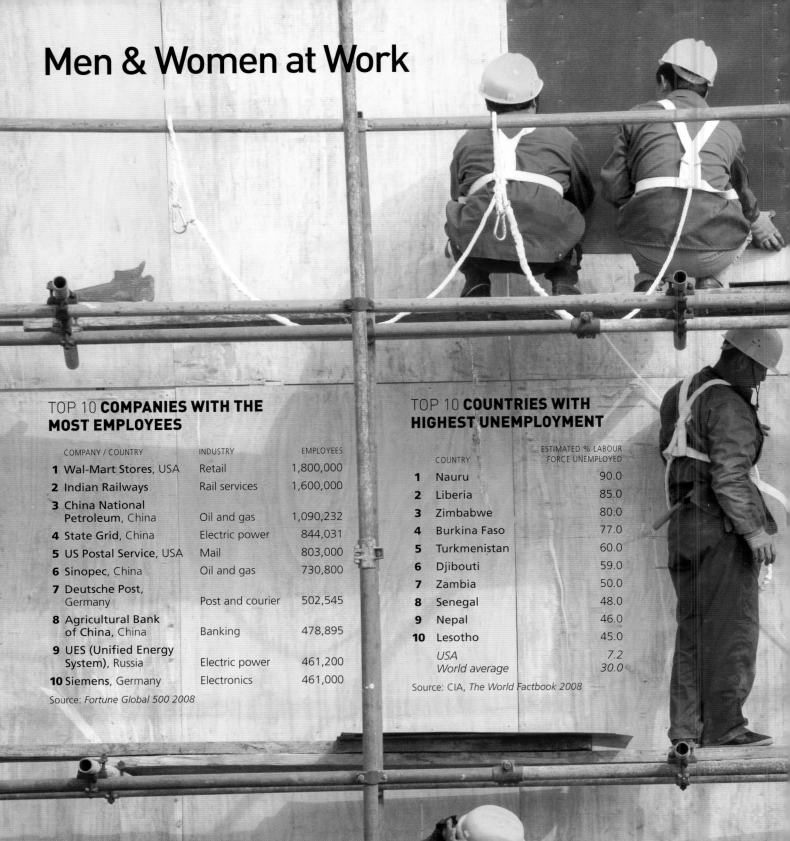

Men & Women at Work

TOP 10 COMPANIES WITH THE MOST EMPLOYEES

COMPANY / COUNTRY	INDUSTRY	EMPLOYEES
1 Wal-Mart Stores, USA	Retail	1,800,000
2 Indian Railways	Rail services	1,600,000
3 China National Petroleum, China	Oil and gas	1,090,232
4 State Grid, China	Electric power	844,031
5 US Postal Service, USA	Mail	803,000
6 Sinopec, China	Oil and gas	730,800
7 Deutsche Post, Germany	Post and courier	502,545
8 Agricultural Bank of China, China	Banking	478,895
9 UES (Unified Energy System), Russia	Electric power	461,200
10 Siemens, Germany	Electronics	461,000

Source: *Fortune Global 500 2008*

TOP 10 COUNTRIES WITH HIGHEST UNEMPLOYMENT

COUNTRY	ESTIMATED % LABOUR FORCE UNEMPLOYED
1 Nauru	90.0
2 Liberia	85.0
3 Zimbabwe	80.0
4 Burkina Faso	77.0
5 Turkmenistan	60.0
6 Djibouti	59.0
7 Zambia	50.0
8 Senegal	48.0
9 Nepal	46.0
10 Lesotho	45.0
USA	*7.2*
World average	*30.0*

Source: CIA, *The World Factbook 2008*

Chinese workforce
China's predominantly rural (744.3 million) and urban (607.2 million) population includes a labor force of 807.7 million—those aged 15 to 64 currently employed and unemployed, but excluding unpaid groups such as students and retired people.

Woman's work
Garment manufacture is one of Cambodia's principal industries, traditionally employing a high proportion of women, making the country one of few where female employees outnumber male.

TOP 10 **COUNTRIES WITH THE MOST WORKERS**

	COUNTRY	WORKERS*
1	China	807,700,000
2	India	523,500,000
3	USA	155,200,000
4	Indonesia	112,000,000
5	Brazil	100,900,000
6	Russia	75,700,000
7	Bangladesh	70,860,000
8	Japan	66,150,000
9	Nigeria	51,040,000
10	Pakistan	50,580,000
	Top 10 total	*2,013,630,000*
	World total	*3,167,000,000*

* 2008 or latest year available; based on people aged 15–64 who are currently employed; excluding unpaid groups

Source: CIA, *World Factbook 2008*/International Labour Organization

As defined by the ILO, the "labor force" includes people aged 15 to 64 currently employed and those who are unemployed, but excludes unpaid groups such as students, housewives, and retired people.

Child labor
Despite legislation, issues of exploitation, health and safety, and depriving children of access to education, child workers continue to be employed in countries such as Nepal.

TOP 10 **COUNTRIES WITH THE HIGHEST PROPORTION OF FEMALE WORKERS**

	COUNTRY	LABOR FORCE %*
1	Mozambique	53.4
2 =	Burundi	51.4
=	Rwanda	51.4
4	Cambodia	50.7
5	Malawi	50.0
6	Tanzania	49.7
7	Kazakhstan	49.4
8	Mali	49.2
9	Belarus	49.1
10	Lithuania	49.0
	USA	*45.9*
	World average	*39.9*

* Aged 15–64 who are currently employed; unpaid groups are not included

Source: World Bank, *World Development Indicators 2008*

TOP 10 **COUNTRIES WITH THE HIGHEST PROPORTION OF CHILD WORKERS**

	COUNTRY	7-14-YEAR OLDS AT WORK (%)*
1	Mali	70.9
2	Guinea-Bissau	67.5
3	Central African Republic	67.0
4	Sierra Leone	65.0
5	Chad	60.4
6	Ethiopia	56.0
7	Nepal	52.4
8	Cambodia	52.3
9	Burkina Faso	50.0
10	Guinea	48.3

* In latest year available; excludes unpaid work

Source: World Bank, *World Development Indicators 2008*/International Labor Organization

In Good Company

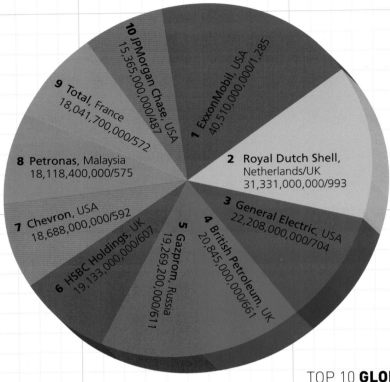

1 ExxonMobil, USA
40,510,000,000/1,285

2 Royal Dutch Shell,
Netherlands/UK
31,331,000,000/993

3 General Electric, USA
22,208,000,000/704

4 British Petroleum, UK
20,845,000,000/661

5 Gazprom, Russia
19,269,200,000/611

6 HSBC Holdings, UK
19,133,000,000/607

7 Chevron, USA
18,688,000,000/592

8 Petronas, Malaysia
18,118,400,000/575

9 Total, France
18,041,700,000/572

10 JPMorgan Chase, USA
15,365,000,000/487

Macro Microsoft
In the 30 years since its founding, US software company Microsoft has grown to become the world's largest computer-technology corporation.

TOP 10 **GLOBAL COMPANIES BY REVENUE**

REVENUE 2008   40 = 400,000,000,000 ($)

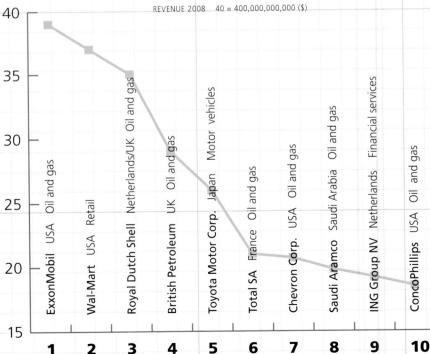

ExxonMobil USA Oil and gas	Wal-Mart USA Retail	Royal Dutch Shell Netherlands/UK Oil and gas	British Petroleum UK Oil and gas	Toyota Motor Corp. Japan Motor vehicles	Total SA France Oil and gas	Chevron Corp. USA Oil and gas	Saudi Aramco Saudi Arabia Oil and gas	ING Group NV Netherlands Financial services	ConocoPhillips USA Oil and gas
1	**2**	**3**	**4**	**5**	**6**	**7**	**8**	**9**	**10**

Gas giant
By various measures, oil and gas conglomerate ExxonMobil, created by the merger of Exxon and Mobil in 1999, is the world's biggest company.

TOP 10 **GLOBAL COMPANIES BY MARKET VALUE**

1. ExxonMobil USA Oil and gas 403,366,000,000
2. Petrochina China Oil and gas 325,320,000,000
3. General Electric USA Conglomerate 253,674,000,000
4. Microsoft USA Software 243,687,000,000
5. Wal-Mart USA Retail 235,605,000,000
6. Procter & Gamble USA Consumer goods 211,460,000,000
7. Industrial and Commercial Bank of China China Banking 208,397,000,000
8. Berkshire Hathaway USA Insurance 202,901,000,000
9. China Mobile China Telecommunications 198,558,000,000
10. Johnson & Johnson USA Healthcare 193,602,000,000

Wal-Mart, China
US retail leviathan Wal-Mart has over 7,000 stores in 14 countries. In 1996 it opened its first store in China, where it now has more than 100 outlets.

TOP 10 **OLDEST-ESTABLISHED BUSINESSES IN THE USA**

COMPANY* / LOCATION	BUSINESS	FOUNDED
1 White Horse Tavern, Newport, RI	Dining	1673
2 J.E. Rhoads & Sons, Branchburg, NJ	Conveyor belts	1702
3 Wayside Inn, Sudbury, MA	Inn	1716
4 Elkridge Furnace Inn, Elkridge, MD	Inn	1744
5 Moravian Book Shop, Bethlehem, PA	Retail, books	1745
6 Pennsylvania Hospital, Philadelphia, PA	Hospital	1751
7 Philadelphia Contributorship, Philadelphia, PA	Insurance	1752
8 New Hampshire Gazette, Portsmouth, NH	Newspaper	1756
9 Hartford Courant, Hartford, CT	Newspaper	1764
10 Bachman Funeral Home, Strasburg, PA	Funeral home	1769

* Excluding mergers and transplanted companies

Source: Institute for Family Enterprise, Bryant College

Rich Lists

TOP 10 RICHEST MEN*

NAME / COUNTRY (CITIZEN/RESIDENCE, IF DIFFERENT)	SOURCE	NET WORTH ($)
1 William H. Gates III, USA	Microsoft (software)	40,000,000,000
2 Warren Edward Buffett, USA	Berkshire Hathaway (investments)	37,000,000,000
3 Carlos Slim Helu, Mexico	Communications	35,000,000,000
4 Lawrence Ellison, USA	Oracle (software)	22,500,000,000
5 Ingvar Kamprad, Sweden/Switzerland	Ikea (home furnishings)	22,000,000,000
6 Karl Albrecht, Germany	Aldi (supermarkets)	21,500,000,000
7 Mukesh Ambani, India	Reliance Industries (petrochemicals)	19,500,000,000
8 Lakshmi Mittal, India/UK	Mittal Steel	19,300,000,000
9 Theo Albrecht, Germany	Aldi (supermarkets)	18,800,000,000
10 Amancio Ortega, Spain	Zara (clothing)	18,300,000,000

* Excluding rulers and family fortunes

Source: Forbes magazine, The World's Billionaires 2009

Buffet buffeted
As a result of share price falls, Warren Buffet's fortune is $25 billion less than in 2008.

TOP 10 HIGHEST-EARNING CELEBRITIES

CELEBRITY*	PROFESSION	EARNINGS 2007–08 ($)
1 J. K. Rowling (UK)	Author	300,000,000
2 Oprah Winfrey	Talk-show host/producer	275,000,000
3 50 Cent (Curtis James Jackson III)	Rap artist	150,000,000
4 Jerry Bruckheimer	Film and TV producer	145,000,000
5 Steven Spielberg	Film producer/director	130,000,000
6 Tyler Perry	Film and TV producer/director	125,000,000
7 Tiger Woods	Golfer	115,000,000
8 Jerry Seinfeld	Actor/comedian	85,000,000
9 Jay-Z (Shawn Corey Carter)	Rap artist	82,000,000
10 = Beyoncé Knowles	Singer/actress	80,000,000
= Will Smith	Film actor	80,000,000

* Individuals, excluding groups; all from the USA unless otherwise stated

Source: Forbes magazine, The Celebrity 100 2008

TOP 10 COUNTRIES WITH THE MOST DOLLAR BILLIONAIRES

COUNTRY*	$ BILLIONAIRES*
1 USA	318
2 Germany	54
3 China (including Hong Kong)	47
4 Russia	32
5 UK	25
6 India	24
7 Canada	20
8 Japan	17
9 Saudi Arabia	14
10 Turkey	13
World total	793

* Of residence, irrespective of citizenship

Source: Forbes magazine, The World's Billionaires 2009

TOP 10 **HIGHEST-EARNING DEAD CELEBRITIES**

	CELEBRITY*	PROFESSION	DEATH	EARNINGS 2007–08 ($)
1	Elvis Presley	Rock star	Aug 16, 1977	52,000,000
2	Charles Schultz	"Peanuts" cartoonist	Feb 12, 2000	33,000,000
3	Heath Ledger (Australia)	Film actor	Jan 22, 2008	20,000,000
4	Albert Einstein (Germany/USA)	Scientist	Apr 18, 1955	18,000,000
5	Aaron Spelling	TV producer	Jun 23, 2006	15,000,000
6	Theodor "Dr. Seuss" Geisel	Author	Sep 24, 1991	12,000,000
7 =	John Lennon (UK)	Rock star	Dec 8, 1980	9,000,000
=	Andy Warhol	Artist	Feb 22, 1987	9,000,000
9	Marilyn Monroe	Actress	Aug 5, 1962	6,500,000
10	Steve McQueen	Actor	Nov 30, 1980	6,000,000

* All from the USA unless otherwise stated

Source: *Forbes* magazine, *Top-Earning Dead Celebrities 2008*

Potter philanthropy
Harry Potter *author J. K. Rowling has rocketed to pole position among celebrity earners, but has donated large sums to charities to aid children, families, and medical research.*

TOP 10 **HIGHEST-EARNING SPORTSMEN**

	SPORTSMAN / COUNTRY*	SPORT	ESTIMATED EARNINGS 2007–08
1	Tiger Woods	Golf	115,000,000
2	David Beckham (UK)	Soccer	50,000,000
3	Phil Mickelson	Golf	45,000,000
4	Kimi Raikkonen (Finland)	Motor racing	44,000,000
5	Kobe Bryant	Basketball	39,000,000
6	LeBron James	Basketball	38,000,000
7	Ronaldinho (Brazil)	Soccer	37,000,000
8	Roger Federer (Switzerland)	Tennis	35,000,000
9	Alex Rodriguez	Baseball	34,000,000
10	Fernando Alonso (Spain)	Motor racing	33,000,000

* All from the USA unless otherwise stated

Source: *Forbes* magazine, *The Celebrity 100 2008*

A league of his own
Soccer contracts and celebrity endorsements have propelled David Beckham into a wealth bracket unprecedented even in the heady world of professional soccer.

Energy

TOP 10 ENERGY-CONSUMING COUNTRIES

COUNTRY	OIL	GAS	ENERGY CONSUMPTION 2007* COAL	NUCLEAR	HEP#	TOTAL
1 USA	943.1	595.7	573.7	192.1	56.8	2,361.4
2 China†	384.9	63.3	1,318.4	14.2	109.3	1,890.1
3 Russia	125.9	394.9	94.5	36.2	40.5	692.0
4 Japan	228.9	81.2	125.3	63.1	18.9	517.4
5 India	128.5	36.2	208.0	4.0	27.7	404.4
6 Canada	102.3	84.6	30.4	21.1	83.3	321.7
7 Germany	112.5	74.5	86.0	31.8	6.2	311.0
8 France	91.3	37.7	12.0	99.7	14.4	255.1
9 South Korea	107.6	33.3	59.7	32.3	1.1	234.0
10 Brazil	96.5	19.8	13.6	2.8	84.1	216.8
World total	*3,952.8*	*2,637.7*	*3,177.5*	*622.0*	*709.2*	*11,099.2*

* Millions of tons of oil equivalent
\# Hydroelectric power
† Including Hong Kong

Source: *BP Statistical Review of World Energy 2008*

TOP 10 COUNTRIES WITH THE MOST NUCLEAR REACTORS

COUNTRY	REACTORS
1 USA	104
2 France	59
3 Japan	55
4 Russia	31
5 UK	19
6 = Canada	18
= South Korea	18
8 = China	17
= Germany	17
= India	17

Source: International Atomic Energy Agency

There are some 439 nuclear power stations in operation in a total of 30 countries around the world, with a further 41 under construction.

TOP 10 COUNTRIES WITH MOST RELIANCE ON NUCLEAR POWER

COUNTRY	NUCLEAR ELECTRICITY AS % OF TOTAL
1 France	76.9
2 Lithuania	64.4
3 Slovakia	54.3
4 Belgium	54.1
5 Ukraine	48.1
6 Sweden	46.1
7 Armenia	42.7
8 Slovenia	41.6
9 Switzerland	40.9
10 Hungary	36.8
USA	*19.4*

Source: International Atomic Energy Agency

Powering down
Prior to the planned 2009 closure of the Ignalina power station, Lithuania—one of 439 reactors in use worldwide—the country was one of the most nuclear-reliant.

TOP 10 **OIL-PRODUCING COUNTRIES**

	COUNTRY	% OF WORLD TOTAL	PRODUCTION 2007 (TONS)
1	Saudi Arabia	12.6	493,100,000
2	Russia	12.6	491,300,000
3	USA	8.0	311,500,000
4	Iran	5.4	212,100,000
5	China	4.8	186,700,000
6	Mexico	4.4	173,000,000
7	Canada	4.1	158,900,000
8	United Arab Emirates	3.5	135,900,000
9	Venezuela	3.4	133,900,000
10	Kuwait	3.3	129,600,000
	Top 10 total	62.1	2,426,000,000
	World total	100.0	3,905,900,000

Source: *BP Statistical Review of World Energy 2008*

TOP 10 **NATURAL GAS-PRODUCING COUNTRIES**

	COUNTRY	% OF WORLD TOTAL	PRODUCTION 2007 (TONS OF OIL EQUIVALENT)
1	Russia	20.6	546,700,000
2	USA	18.8	499,400,000
3	Canada	6.2	165,300,000
4	Iran	3.8	100,700,000
5	Norway	3.0	80,700,000
6	Algeria	2.8	74,700,000
7	Saudi Arabia	2.6	68,300,000
8	UK	2.5	65,200,000
9	China	2.4	62,400,000
10	Turkmenistan	2.3	60,700,000
	Top 10 total	65.0	1,724,100,000
	World total	100.0	2,654,100,000

Source: *BP Statistical Review of World Energy 2008*

TOP 10 **WIND-POWER COUNTRIES**

COUNTRY / % OF WORLD TOTAL / CAPACITY 2007 (MEGAWATTS)

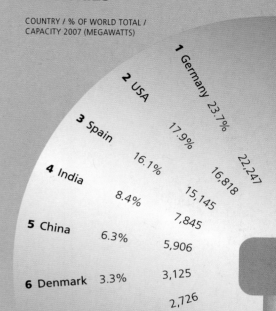

	COUNTRY	% OF WORLD TOTAL	CAPACITY 2007 (MEGAWATTS)
1	Germany	23.7%	22,247
2	USA	17.9%	16,818
3	Spain	16.1%	15,145
4	India	8.4%	7,845
5	China	6.3%	5,906
6	Denmark	3.3%	3,125
7	Italy	2.9%	2,726
8	France	2.6%	2,454
9	UK	2.5%	2,389
10	Portugal	2.3%	2,150

Source: Global Wind Energy Council, *Global Wind 2007 Report*, 2008

Wind power
The Tehachapi Pass Wind Farm, California: it has been proposed that by 2030 wind power will provide 20 percent of the USA's electricity.

Environment

TOP 10 ENVIRONMENTAL PERFORMANCE INDEX COUNTRIES

	COUNTRY	EPI SCORE*
1	Switzerland	95.5
2	=Norway	93.1
	=Sweden	93.1
4	Finland	91.4
5	Costa Rica	90.5
6	Austria	89.4
7	New Zealand	88.9
8	Latvia	88.8
9	Colombia	88.3
10	France	87.8
	USA	*81.0*

* Environmental Performance Index score out of 100

Source: Environmental Performance Index 2008

High score
Based on a range of 16 factors that include air quality, water resources, biodiversity and habitat, and sustainable energy, Switzerland tops the world Environmental Performance Index.

THE 10 WORST ENVIRONMENTAL PERFORMANCE INDEX COUNTRIES

	COUNTRY	EPI SCORE*
1	Niger	39.1
2	Angola	39.5
3	Sierra Leone	40.0
4	Mauritania	44.2
5	=Burkina Faso	44.3
	=Mali	44.3
7	Chad	45.9
8	Dem. Rep. of Congo	47.3
9	=Guinea-Bissau	49.7
	=Yemen	49.7

*Environmental Performance Index score out of 100

Source: Environmental Performance Index

THE 10 WORST OIL TANKER SPILLS

	TANKER / LOCATION	DATE	APPROX. SPILLAGE (TONS)
1	Atlantic Empress and Aegean Captain, Trinidad	Jul 19, 1979	300,930
2	Castillio de Bellver, Cape Town, South Africa	Aug 6, 1983	281,089
3	Olympic Bravery, Ushant, France	Jan 24, 1976	275,577
4	Amoco Cadiz, Finistère, France	Mar 16, 1978	245,815
5	Odyssey, Atlantic, off Canada	Nov 10, 1988	154,406
6	Haven, off Genoa, Italy	Apr 11, 1991	150,465
7	Torrey Canyon, Scilly Isles, UK	Mar 18, 1967	136,852
8	Sea Star, Gulf of Oman	Dec 19, 1972	135,777
9	Irenes Serenade, Pilos, Greece	Feb 23, 1980	131,120
10	Texaco Denmark, North Sea, off Belgium	Dec 7, 1971	112,849

Source: Environmental Technology Center, *Oil Spill Intelligence Report*

In addition to these, it is estimated that around two million tons of oil spills into the seas every year. The *Exxon Valdez* disaster in Alaska on March 24, 1989, ranks outside the 10 worst at about 35,000 tons, but resulted in major ecological damage.

On tap
India's huge population and the demands of its agricultural economy make it the world's top water consumer.

TOP 10 **FRESHWATER-CONSUMING COUNTRIES**

	COUNTRY	ANNUAL FRESHWATER WITHDRAWALS* PER CAPITA (CU FT)	TOTAL (CU MILES)
1	India	20,659	154.95
2	China	14,656	131.89
3	USA	56,503	114.44
4	Pakistan	37,857	40.64
5	Japan	24,367	21.22
6	Indonesia	13,137	19.85
7	Thailand	45,485	19.85
8	Bangladesh	19,776	19.05
9	Mexico	25,815	18.76
10	Russia	18,893	18.40

* In latest year for which data available

Source: World Resources Institute

TOP 10 **GREENEST CITIES IN THE USA**

	CITY	TOTAL
1	Portland, OR	23.1
2	San Francisco, CA	23.0
3	Boston, MA	22.7
4	Oakland, CA	22.5
5	Eugene, OR	22.4
6	=Berkeley, CA	22.2
	=Cambridge, MA	22.2
8	Seattle, WA	22.1
9	Chicago, IL	21.3
10	Austin, TX	21.0

Source: *Popular Science*

Based on 2008 rankings of cities over 100,000 population, in which they were scored out of 10 for electricity generation from renewable sources and providing incentives (such as for installing solar panels), 10 for use of public transportation and carpooling, 5 for access to green spaces, and 5 for recycling and its citizens' views on environmental issues.

TOP 10 **CARBON DIOXIDE-EMITTING COUNTRIES**

	COUNTRY	CO_2 EMISSIONS 2007 (TONS OF CARBON)
1	China	1,986,289,988
2	USA	1,748,499,980
3	Russia	476,733,712
4	India	473,554,097
5	Japan	371,879,656
6	Germany	231,071,429
7	Canada	159,546,558
8	UK	159,533,282
9	South Korea	143,379,784
10	Italy	133,469,710
	Top 10 total	*5,883,958,196*
	World total	*9,337,519,254*

Source: Carbon Dioxide Information Analysis Center (CDIAC)

Shopping Lists

-50%

TOP 10 US RETAILERS

	COMPANY	RETAIL SALES, 2007* ($)
1	Wal-Mart Stores, Inc.	374,526,000,000
2	Home Depot, Inc.	77,349,000,000
3	Kroger Co.	70,235,000,000
4	Target Corp.	63,367,000,000
5	Costco Wholesale Corp.	63,088,000,000
6	Walgreen	53,762,000,000
7	Sears Holdings	50,703,000,000
8	Lowe's Companies, Inc.	48,283,000,000
9	CVS Caremark Corp.	45,087,000,000
10	Safeway, Inc.	42,286,000,000

* Financial year

Source: Deloitte, *2009 Global Powers of Retailing*

TOP 10 NON-STORE* SHOPPING COUNTRIES

	COUNTRY	TOTAL	SPENDING $ PER CAPITA (2008)#
1	Qatar	804,900,000	940.40
2	Monaco	28,200,000	858.10
3	USA	253,643,600,000	833.10
4	Japan	102,496,000,000	802.80
5	UK	48,389,500,000	793.10
6	Germany	54,605,200,000	664.20
7	South Korea	25,149,800,000	523.60
8	Norway	2,445,100,000	520.00
9	Finland	2,732,000,000	515.70
10	Switzerland	3,546,600,000	471.00
	World	*656,311,000,000*	*97.70*

* Includes vending, home shopping, Internet retailing, and direct selling
\# Retail value excluding sales taxes

Source: Euromonitor International

TOP 10 GLOBAL RETAILERS

	COMPANY / BASE	RETAIL SALES 2007* ($)
1	Wal-Mart Stores, Inc., USA	374,526,000,000
2	Carrefour, France	112,604,000,000
3	Tesco plc, UK	94,740,000,000
4	Metro AG, Germany	87,586,000,000
5	Home Depot, Inc., USA	77,349,000,000
6	Kroger Co., USA	70,235,000,000
7	Schwarz Unternehmens Treuhand KG, Germany	69,346,000,000
8	Target Corp., USA	63,267,000,000
9	Costco Wholesale Corp., USA	63,088,000,000
10	Aldi GmbH, Germany	58,487,000,000

* Financial year

Source: Deloitte, *2009 Global Powers of Retailing*

TOP 10 OLDEST-ESTABLISHED DEPARTMENT STORES IN THE USA

	STORE / LOCATION*	FOUNDED
1	Lord & Taylor, New York, NY	1826
2	Carson Pirie Scott, Amboy, IL	1854
3	Younkers, Keokuk, IA	1856
4	Macy's, New York, NY	1858
5 =	Bloomingdale's, New York, NY	1872
=	Von Maur#, Davenport, OH	1872
7	Parisian, Birmingham, AL	1877
8	Elder-Beeman, Dayton, OH	1883
9	Loeb's, Meridian, MO	1887
10	Belk, Monroe, NC	1888

* Of original store
\# Founded as J.H.C. Petersen & Sons

TOP 10 INTERNET SHOPS IN THE USA

COMPANY / WEB SALES 2008 ($)

1	Amazon.com Inc.	14,800,000,000
2	Staples Inc.	5,600,000,000
3	Office Depot Inc.	4,900,000,000
4	Dell Inc.	4,200,000,000
5	HP Home & Home Office Store (Hewlett-Packard Co.)	3,400,000,000
6	OfficeMax Inc.	3,200,000,000
7	Apple Inc.	2,700,000,000
8	Sears Holding Corp.	2,600,000,000
9	CDW Corp.	2,400,000,000
10	Newegg.com	1,900,000,000

Source: Internet Retailer

Top of the shops
Toronto's Eaton Centre shopping mall attracts a million visitors a week, making it one of North America's foremost retail locations.

TOP 10 IN-STORE SHOPPING COUNTRIES

	COUNTRY	TOTAL	SPENDING $ PER CAPITA (2008)*
1	Norway	55,133,200,000	11,727.30
2	Qatar	9,824,900,000	11,479.20
3	Switzerland	85,519,800,000	11,357.10
4	Ireland	48,620,500,000	11,104.70
5	Denmark	53,449,900,000	9,786.60
6	Austria	77,473,900,000	9,276.30
7	Monaco	303,000,000	9,233.10
8	Belgium	97,584,100,000	9,190.10
9	Canada	303,430,100,000	9,147.90
10	Finland	47,728,400,000	9,010.10
	USA	2,317,364,800,000	7,611.10
	World	10,474,432,800,000	1,559.3

* Retail value excluding sales taxes

Source: Euromonitor International

Food Favorites

TOP 10 **VEGETABLE CONSUMERS**

COUNTRY	AVERAGE CONSUMPTION PER CAPITA (2008)		
	LB	OZ	KG
1 Greece	566	9	257.0
2 South Korea	550	11	249.8
3 Turkey	524	8	237.9
4 Jordan	475	2	215.5
5 China	468	8	212.5
6 Portugal	447	2	202.8
7 Israel	528	9	194.4
8 Romania	418	4	189.7
9 Egypt	409	6	185.7
10 United Arab Emirates	382	8	173.5
USA	*195*	*9*	*88.7*
World average	*210*	*2*	*95.3*

Source: Euromonitor International

TOP 10 **MEAT CONSUMERS**

COUNTRY	AVERAGE CONSUMPTION PER CAPITA (2008)		
	LB	OZ	KG
1 Nauru	269	6	122.2
2 Argentina	255	15	116.1
3 Australia	233	15	106.1
4 Portugal	228	3	103.5
5 New Zealand	227	8	103.2
6 Austria	224	7	101.8
7 Greece	219	9	99.6
8 Monaco	213	14	97.0
9 USA	194	11	88.3
10 Ireland	175	11	79.7
World average	*78*	*11*	*35.7*

Source: Euromonitor International

Meaty Measure

In 2008, the world devoured a total of 263,081,696 tons of beef, veal, lamb, mutton, goat, pork, poultry, and other meat.

TOP 10 **EGG CONSUMERS**

COUNTRY	TOTAL TONS	CONSUMPTION (2008) PER CAPITA		
		LB	OZ	KG
1 China	31,536,024	47	10	21.6
2 Japan	2,829,854	44	5	20.1
3 Monaco	661	41	7	18.8
4 Antigua & Barbuda	1,764	40	2	18.2
5 = Czech Republic	204,920	39	11	18.0
= Saint Kitts & Nevis	992	39	11	18.0
7 Mexico	2,153,145	39	4	17.8
8 Bulgaria	136,135	35	15	16.3
9 France	1,103,303	35	11	16.2
10 Luxembourg	8,378	35	1	15.9
USA	*5,125,637*	*33*	*12*	*15.3*
World	*68,206,504*	*20*	*8*	*9.3*

Source: Euromonitor International

TOP 10 **FISH AND SHELLFISH CONSUMERS**

COUNTRY	TOTAL TONS	CONSUMPTION (2008) PER CAPITA		
		LB	OZ	KG
1 Portugal	943,909	177	8	80.5
2 Singapore	309,198	133	6	60.5
3 Malaysia	1,679,371	121	11	55.2
4 South Korea	2,657,121	110	11	50.2
5 Brunei	18,298	92	13	42.1
6 Iceland	13,448	90	3	40.9
7 Japan	5,357,453	84	0	38.1
8 Norway	185,299	78	15	35.8
9 Myanmar	2,042,032	78	8	35.6
10 China	50,185,919	75	13	34.4
USA	*6,609,018*	*43*	*7*	*19.7*
World	*115,055,837*	*34*	*6*	*15.6*

Source: Euromonitor International

TOP 10 **POTATO CHIP AND FRENCH FRY CONSUMERS**

	COUNTRY	TOTAL TONS	CONSUMPTION (2008) PER CAPITA		
			LB	OZ	KG
1	Ireland	21,716	9	15	4.5
2	Norway	19,621	8	6	3.8
3	Nauru	55	7	15	3.6
4	Iceland	1,213	7	12	3.5
5	UK	210,87	6	13	3.1
6	= Canada	102,625	6	3	2.8
	= Netherlands	50,596	6	3	2.8
8	Spain	134,262	5	15	2.7
9	Andorra	220	5	5	2.4
10	USA	888,683	5	1	2.3
	World	*2,634,634*	*0*	*14*	*0.4*

Source: Euromonitor International

TOP 10 **FAST FOOD COUNTRIES** *

	COUNTRY	TOTAL ($)	PER CAPITA ($)
1	USA	179,410,200,000	594.6
2	Canada	18,117,200,000	551.4
3	Ireland	2,260,800,000	525.9
4	UK	26,793,800,000	441.4
5	Australia	8,632,300,000	419.5
6	New Zealand	1,259,400,000	309.0
7	Iceland	89,600,000	297.6
8	Denmark	1,359,100,000	267.2
9	Japan	33,401,800,000	261.5
10	Norway	1,146,300,000	245.4
	World total	*442,965,400,000*	*66.8*

* Ranked by per capita consumption, 2007

Source: Euromonitor International

Potato head
Fast food world leader USA is out-eaten by other countries in per capita potato chip and French fry consumption.

Beverage Report

TOP 10 FRUIT AND VEGETABLE DRINK CONSUMERS

	COUNTRY	CONSUMPTION PER CAPITA (2008) PINTS	LITERS
1	Canada	86.4	49.1
2	Netherlands	76.9	43.7
3	Poland	73.4	41.7
4	Germany	71.8	40.8
5	Slovenia	67.0	38.1
6	UK	66.9	38.0
7	Ireland	64.9	36.9
8	USA	63.4	36.0
9	Australia	63.0	35.8
10	Norway	60.7	34.5
	World average	*16.4*	*9.3*

Source: Euromonitor International (all lists)

The world drank an estimated 108,967,772,216 pints (61,922,200,000 liters) of fruit and vegetable juice in 2008.

TOP 10 WINE CONSUMERS

	COUNTRY	CONSUMPTION PER CAPITA (2008) PINTS	LITERS
1	Luxembourg	110.2	62.6
2	Italy	80.4	45.7
3	Portugal	80.1	45.5
4	France	72.0	40.9
5	Monaco	69.0	39.2
6	Switzerland	66.7	37.9
7	Slovenia	64.4	36.6
8	Austria	64.2	36.5
9	Liechtenstein	64.0	36.4
10	Greece	62.1	35.3
	USA	*15.3*	*8.7*
	World average	*7.0*	*4.0*

TOP 10 COFFEE DRINKERS

	COUNTRY	CONSUMPTION PER CAPITA (2008) LB	OZ	KG	CUPS*
1	Finland	22	1	10.0	1,500
2	Norway	18	8	8.4	1,260
3	Sweden	18	1	8.2	1,230
4	Denmark	17	7	7.9	1,185
5	Switzerland	13	0	5.9	885
6	Netherlands	12	6	5.6	840
7	Germany	11	14	5.4	810
8	Belgium	11	11	5.3	795
9	= Estonia	11	7	5.2	780
	= Iceland	11	7	5.2	780
	USA	*6*	*3*	*2.8*	*420*
	World average	*1*	*12*	*0.8*	*120*

* Based on average of 150 cups per 2 lb 3 oz.

TOP 10 **COLA DRINK CONSUMERS**

| COUNTRY | CONSUMPTION PER CAPITA (2008) | |
	PINTS	LITERS
1 Mexico	186.4	105.9

2 = Norway	175.1	99.5
= USA	175.1	99.5
4 St. Vincent and the Grenadines	154.7	87.9
5 Chile	137.6	78.2
6 Belize	134.1	76.2
7 Dominica	133.6	75.9
8 St. Lucia	131.1	74.5
9 United Arab Emirates	129.3	73.5
10 Belgium	123.0	69.9
World average	*30.6*	*17.4*

TOP 10 **TEA DRINKERS**

| COUNTRY | CONSUMPTION PER CAPITA (2008) | | | |
	LB	OZ	KG	CUPS*
1 Turkey	6	3	2.8	1,232
2 Ireland	5	12	2.6	1,144
3 Uzbekistan	5	5	2.4	1,056
4 UK	4	10	2.1	924
5 = Kazakhstan	3	12	1.7	748
= Turkmenistan	3	12	1.7	748
7 Iran	3	1	1.4	616
8 = Poland	2	14	1.3	572
= Russia	2	14	1.3	572
10 = Japan	2	7	1.1	484
= Pakistan	2	7	1.1	484
USA	*0*	*7*	*0.2*	*88*
World average	*0*	*14*	*0.4*	*176*

* Based on average 440 cups per 2 lb 3 oz

As well as a major tea consumer, Turkey is the sixth largest producer, growing over 190,000 tons a year out of a world total of 3.9 million tons. In the UK, once the quintessential bastion of the "cuppa," the consumption of traditional tea has declined as herbal and other flavors and coffee have gained ground.

TOP 10 **ALCOHOLIC DRINK CONSUMERS**

| COUNTRY | CONSUMPTION PER CAPITA (2008) | |
	PINTS	LITERS
1 Czech Republic	336.6	191.3
2 Ireland	292.5	166.2
3 Luxembourg	283.6	161.2
4 Austria	261.3	148.5
5 = Estonia	256.7	145.9
= Germany	256.7	145.9
7 Slovenia	245.8	139.7
8 Australia	230.5	131.0
9 UK	222.3	126.3
10 Slovakia	220.8	125.5
USA	*173.2*	*98.4*
World average	*61.9*	*35.2*

Prost!
Germany hosts the world's largest beer festival, the Munich Oktoberfest, its many breweries and beer halls further emphasizing the importance of alcohol in the country's culture.

Sweet Treats

TOP 10 **SUGAR AND SWEETENER CONSUMERS**

	COUNTRY	CONSUMPTION PER CAPITA (2008)	
		LB	KG
1	United Arab Emirates	156.3	70.9
2	USA	141.8	64.3
3	Hungary	140.9	63.9
4	New Zealand	135.8	61.6
5	Luxembourg	131.0	59.4
6	Sri Lanka	129.9	58.9
7	Brazil	126.5	57.4
8	Iceland	126.3	57.3
9	Belgium	125.0	56.7
10	Switzerland	123.9	56.2
	World average	*59.5*	*27.0*

Source: Euromonitor International (all lists)

TOP 10 **CHOCOLATE CONSUMERS**

COUNTRY	CONSUMPTION PER CAPITA (2008)	
	LB	KG
1 UK	25.4	11.5
2 Liechtenstein	24.0	10.9
3 Luxembourg	22.3	10.1
4 = Ireland	21.8	9.9
= Switzerland	21.8	9.9
6 Iceland	21.6	9.8
7 Germany	18.3	8.3
8 Austria	16.1	7.3
9 Norway	15.7	7.1
10 Belgium	13.2	6.0
USA	*12.8*	*5.8*
World average	*2.4*	*1.1*

TOP 10 **ICE-CREAM CONSUMERS**

COUNTRY / CONSUMPTION PER CAPITA (2008) PINTS / LITERS

1 Australia 31.7 / 18.0

2 USA 26.0 / 14.8

3 Nauru 25.3 / 14.4

4 New Zealand 23.4 / 13.3

TOP 10 JAM AND PRESERVE CONSUMERS

	COUNTRY	CONSUMPTION PER CAPITA (2008)		
		LB	OZ	KG
1	Norway	9	4	4.2
2	Sweden	7	4	3.3
3	Denmark	6	10	3.0
4	Luxembourg	6	6	2.9
5	Iceland	6	3	2.8
6	= Belgium	5	1	2.3
	= France	5	1	2.3
8	= Germany	4	3	1.9
	= Monaco	4	3	1.9
10	USA	4	0	1.8
	World average	*0*	*11*	*0.3*

TOP 10 BISCUIT CONSUMERS

	COUNTRY	CONSUMPTION PER CAPITA (2008)	
		LB	KG
1	Netherlands	23.6	10.7
2	Argentina	21.4	9.7
3	UK	19.4	8.8
4	Portugal	18.7	8.5
5	= Chile	17.6	8.0
	= New Zealand	17.6	8.0
7	= Belgium	17.2	7.8
	= USA	17.2	7.8
9	= Australia	16.3	7.4
	= Italy	16.3	7.4
	World average	*4.9*	*2.2*

TOP 10 GUM CONSUMERS

COUNTRY / TOTAL CONSUMPTION 2008 (TONS)

1 USA 218,500 **2** China 157,300 **5** Japan 52,700
3 = Brazil = Mexico 60,000 **6** UK 31,100 **7** Iran 27,600 **8** Italy 26,100
9 Russia 25,700 **10** Germany 23,100
Top 10 total 682,100 World total 1,056,900

5 Canada 22.7 / 12.9

6 Norway 22.3 / 12.7

7 Finland 20.9 / 11.9

8 Sweden 20.4 / 11.6

9 = Iceland 18.5 / 10.5
= Italy 18.5 / 10.5

World average 4.6 / 2.6

Keeping in Touch

TOP 10 **CELL PHONE CALLS**

COUNTRY / MINUTES PER CAPITA (2008)

1 Cuba 2,827.6

2 Finland 1,615.7

3 Italy 1,336.0

4 Maldives 1,332.7

5 Austria 1,160.5

6 Norway 1,129.3

Source: Euromonitor International

TOP 10 **COUNTRIES FOR INTERNATIONAL PHONE CALLS**

COUNTRY	MINUTES PER CAPITA (2008)
1 Bermuda	2,787.4
2 Andorra	989.7
3 United Arab Emirates	956.4
4 Luxembourg	916.8
5 Singapore	879.1
6 Liechtenstein	795.5
7 Barbados	692.1
8 Aruba	556.9
9 Cyprus	316.5
10 USA	308.8
World average	*32.7*

Source: Euromonitor International

7 Japan 1,067.3

8 UK 1,006.0

9 Portugal 998.8

10 Nigeria 983.3

TOP 10 **CELL PHONE COUNTRIES**

COUNTRY	% POPULATION	SUBSCRIBERS TOTAL (2008)
1 China	49.0	649,700,000
2 India	32.7	376,120,000
3 USA	85.7	260,000,000
4 Russia	121.2	172,000,000
5 Brazil	79.7	151,900,000
6 Indonesia	49.9	115,600,000
7 Japan	79.6	102,980,000
8 Germany	123.5	101,500,000
9 Pakistan	56.8	91,442,341
10 UK	116.0	70,000,000
World total	*60.6*	*4,100,000,000*

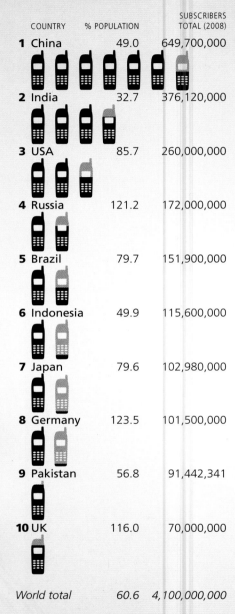

Source: CIA, *The World Factbook 2008*

Especially in countries that previously had an undeveloped landline system, the rapid increase in cell-phone usage has seen China and India take the lead. In high-uptake countries where people regularly update their phones without canceling their older contracts, the anomalous situation arises where there are more phones than people.

Japanese mail
Despite its high-tech communications, the traditional postal system remains important in Japan.

TOP 10 COUNTRIES WITH THE MOST POST OFFICES

COUNTRY	AVERAGE NO. OF PEOPLE SERVED PER OFFICE	POST OFFICES (2007)*
1 India	7,432	155,204
2 China	22,186	59,886
3 Russia	3,519	40,489
4 USA	7,471	36,721
5 Mexico	3,599	29,600
6 Japan	5,318	24,064
7 Indonesia	11,627	19,922
8 France	3,612	17,066
9 Ukraine	3,004	15,379
10 Italy	4,263	13,811

* Or latest year and in those countries for which data available

Source: Universal Postal Union

TOP 10 COUNTRIES WITH THE MOST MAILBOXES

COUNTRY	MAILBOXES (2007)*
1 India	661,887
2 USA	351,000
3 China	195,336#
4 Japan	192,300
5 France	156,000
6 Russia	153,487
7 UK	116,000
8 Germany	108,000
9 Italy	61,500
10 Poland	55,138

* Or latest year and in those countries for which data available
\# Situated on streets only

Source: Universal Postal Union

TOP 10 SOCIAL NETWORKS IN THE WORLD

NETWORK	UNIQUE VISITS*
1 Blogger	221,503,000
2 Facebook	200,189,000
3 MySpace	126,168,000
4 Wordpress	113,661,000
5 Windows Live Spaces	86,760,000
6 Yahoo Geocities	69,159,000
7 Flickr	63,866,000
8 hi5	58,069,000
9 Orkut	46,446,000
10 Six Apart	45,606,000
Total Internet audience	*996,304,000*
Total social network audience	*681,249,000*

* During November 2008

Source: comScore.com

TOP 10 SOCIAL NETWORKS IN THE USA

NETWORK	% BY INTERNET VISITS*
1 MySpace	39.37
2 Facebook	17.54
3 YouTube	10.39
4 Tagged	1.55
5 Yahoo! Answers	1.36
6 myYearbook	1.09
7 Yahoo! Groups	0.96
8 Meebo	0.64
9 Yahoo! Member Directory	0.53
10 Bebo	0.49

* During December 2008

Source: Marketingcharts.com

TOP 10 SOCIAL NETWORKS IN THE UK

NETWORK	% BY INTERNET VISITS*
1 Facebook	39.82
2 YouTube	16.57
3 Bebo	8.56
4 MySpace	4.49
5 Yahoo! Answers	1.03
6 Nasza Klasa	0.73
7 Twitter	0.66
8 Tagged	0.65
9 BBC h2g2	0.64
10 Gumtree.com	0.61

* During February 2009

World Tourism

TOP 10 TOURIST DESTINATIONS

	COUNTRY	INTERNATIONAL VISITORS (2007)
1	France	81,900,000
2	Spain	59,193,000
3	USA	55,986,000
4	China	54,720,000
5	Italy	43,654,000
6	UK	30,677,000
7	Germany	24,420,000
8	Ukraine	23,122,000
9	Turkey	22,248,000
10	Mexico	21,424,000
	Top 10 total	417,344,000
	World total	903,300,000

Source: World Tourism Organization

Le Petit Nicolas®
Textes : Goscinny - Dessins : Sempé
© Imav éditions 2006
NP 016
Imav éditions - contact@imaveditions.com
www.petitnicolas.net
Distribution : Éditions du Désastre - www.desastre.com
Printed in France

TOP 10 TOURIST EARNING COUNTRIES

	COUNTRY	INTERNATIONAL TOURISM RECEIPTS, 2007 ($)
1	USA	97,712,000,000
2	Spain	57,795,000,000
3	France	54,228,000,000
4	Italy	42,651,000,000
5	China	41,919,000,000
6	UK	37,617,000,000
7	Germany	36,029,000,000
8	Australia	22,244,000,000
9	Austria	18,887,000,000
10	Turkey	18,487,000,000
	Top 10 total	427,569,000,000
	World total	856,000,000,000

Source: World Tourism Organization

TOP 10 TOURISM SPENDING COUNTRIES

	COUNTRY	INTERNATIONAL TOURISM EXPENDITURE, 2007 ($)
1	Germany	82,900,000,000
2	USA	76,200,000,000
3	UK	72,300,000,000
4	France	36,700,000,000
5	China	29,800,000,000
6	Italy	27,300,000,000
7	Japan	26,500,000,000
8	Canada	24,800,000,000
9	Russia	22,300,000,000
10	South Korea	20,900,000,000
	Top 10 total	419,700,000,000
	World total	856,000,000,000

Source: World Tourism Organization

French leave
Along with the appeal of its food and culture, France's cities, resorts, and rural retreats have established it as the world's foremost tourist venue.

Park and ride
The former hunting park of Austrian emperors, the Vienna Prater opened as a public park on April 7, 1766.

TOP 10 **AMUSEMENT AND THEME PARKS**

PARK / LOCATION	EST. ATTENDANCE (2008)
1 The Magic Kingdom at Walt Disney World, Lake Buena Vista, Florida, USA	17,063,000
2 Disneyland, Anaheim, California, USA	14,721,000
3 Tokyo Disneyland, Tokyo, Japan	14,293,000
4 Disneyland Paris, Marne-La-Vallée, France	12,688,000
5 Tokyo Disneysea, Tokyo, Japan	12,498,000
6 Epcot at Walt Disney World, Lake Buena Vista, Florida, USA	10,935,000
7 Disney's Hollywood Studios at Walt Disney World, Lake Buena Vista, Florida, USA	9,608,000
8 Disney's Animal Kingdom at Walt Disney World, Lake Buena Vista, Florida, USA	9,540,000
9 Universal Studios Japan, Osaka, Japan	8,300,000
10 Everland, Kyonggi-Do, South Korea	7,200,000

Source: Park World

Magic kingdom
The original Disneyland opened in Anaheim, California, in 1955 and has been replicated in Florida, Japan, France, and Hong Kong.

TOP 10 **OLDEST AMUSEMENT PARKS***

PARK / LOCATION	YEAR OPENED
1 Bakken, Klampenborg, Denmark	1583
2 The Prater, Vienna, Austria	1766
3 Widam Park, Budapest, Hungary	1838
4 Blackgang Chine Cliff Top Theme Park, Ventnor, Isle of Wight, UK	1842
5 Tivoli Gardens, Copenhagen, Denmark	1843
6 Lake Compounce Amusement Park, Bristol, Connecticut, USA	1846
7 Hanayashiki, Tokyo, Japan	1853
8 Grand Pier, Teignmouth, UK	1867
9 Blackpool Central Pier, Blackpool, UK	1868
10 Cedar Point, Sandusky, Ohio, USA	1870

* In same location

Source: National Amusement Park Historical Association

TOP 10 **MOST-VISITED NATIONAL PARKS IN THE USA**

PARK / LOCATION	RECREATION VISITS (2008)
1 Great Smoky Mountains National Park, NC/TN	9,044,010
2 Grand Canyon National Park, AZ	4,425,314
3 Yosemite National Park, CA	3,431,514
4 Olympic National Park, WA	3,081,451
5 Yellowstone National Park, WY	3,066,580
6 Cuyahoga Valley National Park, near Cleveland and Akron, OH	2,828,233
7 Rocky Mountain National Park, CO	2,757,390
8 Zion National Park, UT	2,690,154
9 Grand Teton National Park, WY	2,485,987
10 Acadia National Park, ME	2,075,857

Big Wheel

One of the Vienna Prater park's most famous features, the Riesenrad Ferris wheel, opened on June 21, 1897. Invented by George Gale Ferris in 1893, this surviving example was designed by British engineer Walter Bassett, previously responsible for wheels in Blackpool and Earls Court, UK. The Riesenrad has been featured in films, most notably *The Third Man* (1949) and James Bond film *The Living Daylights* (1987).

ON THE MOVE

Road Transport

TOP 10 MOTOR-VEHICLE MANUFACTURING COUNTRIES, 2007

	COUNTRY	CARS	COMMERCIAL VEHICLES	TOTAL
1	Japan	9,944,637	1,651,690	11,596,327
2	USA	3,924,268	6,856,461	10,780,729
3	China	6,381,116	2,501,340	8,882,456
4	Germany	5,709,139	504,321	6,213,460
5	South Korea	3,723,482	362,826	4,086,308
6	France	2,550,869	464,985	3,015,854
7	Brazil	2,388,402	582,416	2,970,818
8	Spain	2,195,780	693,923	2,889,703
9	Canada	1,342,133	1,236,105	2,578,238
10	India	1,707,839	598,929	2,306,768
	World	*53,049,391*	*20,103,305*	*73,152,696*

Source: OICA Statistics Committee

TOP 10 COUNTRIES DRIVING ON THE LEFT

	COUNTRY	TOTAL VEHICLES REGISTERED (2006)
1	Japan	74,252,134
2	UK	34,974,500
3	Australia	13,410,000
4	India	12,950,000
5	Thailand	9,500,000
6	Malaysia	7,857,500
7	Indonesia	7,350,000
8	South Africa	7,180,000
9	New Zealand	2,760,000
10	Ireland	2,051,000

Source: *Ward's Motor Vehicle Facts & Figures 2008*

Some 75 countries and territories drive on the left. Where countries with different rules meet, such as China and Pakistan, drivers have to change sides as they cross the border.

TOP 10 MOTOR-VEHICLE MANUFACTURERS, 2007

COUNTRY / CARS / COMMERCIAL VEHICLES / TOTAL

General Motors (USA)
6,259,520
3,090,298
9,349,818

Toyota (Japan)
7,211,474
1,323,216
8,534,690

Volkswagen group (Germany)
5,964,004
303,887
6,267,891

Ford (USA)
3,565,626
2,681,880
6,247,506

World
56,301,121
15,877,355
72,178,476

Source: OICA Statistics Committee

Production line
Japan's motor-vehicle production leads the world.

TOP 10 **BESTSELLING CARS OF ALL TIME**

MANUFACTURER/MODEL	YEARS IN PRODUCTION	APPROX. SALES*
1 Toyota Corolla	1966–	35,000,000
2 Volkswagen Golf	1974–	25,000,000
3 Volkswagen Beetle	1937–2003#	21,529,464
4 Ford Escort/Orion	1968–2003	20,000,000
5 Ford Model T	1908–27	16,536,075
6 Honda Civic	1972–	16,500,000
7 Nissan Sunny/Sentra/Pulsar	1966–	16,000,000
8 Volkswagen Passat	1973–	15,000,000
9 Lada Riva	1980–	13,500,000
10 Chevrolet Impala/Caprice	1958–	13,000,000

* To 2008, except where otherwise indicated
\# Produced in Mexico 1978–2003

TOP 10 **MOTOR VEHICLE-OWNING COUNTRIES**

COUNTRY	CARS	VEHICLES	COMMERCIAL TOTAL (2006)
1 USA	135,046,706	108,975,048	244,021,754
2 Japan	57,521,043	16,731,091	74,252,134
3 Germany	46,569,657	3,172,042	49,741,699
4 Italy	35,297,600	4,579,600	39,877,200
5 France	30,400,000	6,261,000	36,661,000
6 China	11,000,000	24,000,000	35,000,000
7 UK	30,920,000	4,054,500	34,974,500
8 Russia	26,800,000	5,890,000	32,690,000
9 Spain	20,908,700	5,146,400	26,055,100
10 Brazil	19,446,000	4,823,200	24,269,200
World	*635,284,155*	*255,477,307*	*890,761,462*

Source: *Ward's Motor Vehicle Facts & Figures 2008*

Honda (Japan)
3,868,546
43,268
3,911,814

PSA Peugeot Citroën (France)
3,024,863
432,522
3,457,385

Nissan (Japan)
2,650,813
780,585
3,431,398

Fiat (Italy)
1,990,715
688,736
2,679,451

Renault-Dacia-Samsung (France)
2,276,044
392,996
2,669,040

Hyundai (South Korea)
2,292,075
325,650
2,617,725

Rail Transport

THE 10 FIRST UNDERGROUND RAILROAD SYSTEMS

CITY / FIRST LINE ESTABLISHED

(1) **London**, UK
Jan 10, 1863

(2) **Budapest**, Hungary
May 2, 1896

(3) **Glasgow**, UK
Dec 14, 1896

(4) **Boston**, USA
Sep 1, 1897

(5) **Paris**, France
Jul 19, 1900

(6) **Berlin**, Germany
Feb 15, 1902

TOP 10 LONGEST UNDERGROUND RAILROAD NETWORKS

CITY / OPENED / STATIONS /
TOTAL TRACK LENGTH (KM/MILES)

(1) **London**
UK 1863
268 stations
408 / 254

(2) **New York**
USA 1904
422 stations
368 / 229

(3) **Madrid**
Spain 1919
231 stations
294 / 183

(4) **Moscow**
Russia 1935
142 stations
293 / 182

(5) **Seoul**
South Korea 1974
266 stations
287 / 179

TOP 10 LONGEST RAIL NETWORKS

LOCATION / TOTAL RAIL LENGTH (KM/MILES)

(1) **USA**
226,656 / 141,367

(2) **Russia**
87,157 / 54,156

(3) **China**
75,438 / 47,051

(4) **India**
63,221 / 39,431

(5) **Germany**
48,215 / 30,072

(6) **Canada**
48,068 / 29,980

(7) **Australia**
38,550 / 24,044

(8) **Argentina**
31,902 / 19,897

(9) **France**
29,370 / 18,318

(10) **Brazil**
29,295 / 18,271

World 1,370,782 / 854,971

Source: CIA, *The World Factbook 2008*

The total length of the world rail networks today is equivalent to some 34 times round the Earth at the Equator.

TOP 10 BUSIEST UNDERGROUND RAILROAD NETWORKS

CITY	PASSENGERS PER ANNUM (2008)*
1 Tokyo, Japan	2,916,000,000
2 Moscow, Russia	2,529,000,000
3 Seoul, South Korea	2,047,000,000
4 New York, USA	1,563,000,000
5 Mexico City, Mexico	1,417,000,000
6 Paris, France	1,388,000,000
7 Hong Kong, China	1,309,000,000
8 Beijing, China	1,200,000,000
9 London, UK	1,197,000,000
10 Shanghai, China	1,122,000,000

* Or latest year for which figures available

Russian rush hour
One of the world's busiest systems, the Moscow Metro is noted for the elegance of its stations.

⑩ **Buenos Aires**, Argentina
Dec 1, 1913

⑦ **New York**, USA
Oct 27, 1904

⑧ **Philadelphia**, USA
Mar 4, 1907

⑨ **Hamburg**, Germany
Feb 15, 1912

Egypt
40,840,000,000 ⑩

⑥ **Shanghai**
China 1995
162 stations
228 / 142

⑦ **Paris**
France 1900
300 stations
214 / 133

⑧ **Tokyo**
Japan 1927
168 stations
203 / 126

⑨ **Beijing**
China 1969
123 stations
200 / 120

⑩ **Mexico City**
Mexico 1969
147 stations
177 / 110

⑨ **Italy**
46,440,000,000

⑤ **France**
78,460,000,000

⑥ **Germany**
74,730,000,000

⑦ **Ukraine**
53,230,000,000

⑧ **UK**
46,760,000,000

④ **Russia**
173,000,000,000

③ **Japan**
254,000,000,000

② **India**
696,000,000,000

① **China**
722,800,000,000

TOP 10 **BUSIEST RAIL NETWORKS**

LOCATION / PASSENGER KM PER ANNUM*

* Number of passengers multiplied by distance carried in 2008 or latest year for which figures available; totals include national and local services where applicable

Source: UIC Railisa Database

TOP 10 **FASTEST RAIL JOURNEYS**

JOURNEY*	TRAIN	DISTANCE		SPEED	
		KM	MILES	KM/H	MPH
1 Lorraine–Champagne, France	TGV 5422	167.6	104.1	279.3	173.6
2 Okayama–Hiroshima, Japan	Nozomi 1	144.9	90.0	255.7	158.9
3 Taichung–Zuoying, Taiwan	7 trains	179.5	111.5	244.7	152.0
4 Brussels, Belgium–Valence, France	Thalys Soleil	831.7	516.8	244.6	152.0
5 Frankfurt–Siegburg/Bonn, Germany	ICE 10	143.3	89.04	232.4	144.4
6 Madrid–Zaragoza, Spain	7 AVE trains	307.2	190.9	227.6	141.4
7 Shenyang–Qinhuangdao, China	D24 & D28	404.0	251.0	197.1	122.5
8 Seoul–Seodaejeon, South Korea	KTX 410 & 411	161.0	100.0	193.2	120.0
9 London–York, UK	1 IC255	303.2	188.4	173.3	107.7
10 Alvesta–Hässleholm, Sweden	X2000 543	98.0	60.9	172.9	107.4

* Fastest journey for each country; all those in the Top 10 have other equally or similarly fast services

Source: *Railway Gazette International*, 2007 World Speed Survey

Train à Grande Vitesse
The French TGV holds the record for fastest scheduled journey.

Water Transport

TOP 10 **LONGEST SHIP CANALS**

CANAL / COUNTRY
OPENED
LENGTH (MILES/KM)

1

Grand Canal, China
AD 283*
1,114 / 1,795

2

Erie Canal, USA
1825
363 / 584

3

Göta Canal, Sweden
1832
240 / 360

4

St. Lawrence Seaway,
Canada/USA
1959
180 / 290

5

Canal du Midi, France
1692
190 / 240

6

Main-Danube, Germany
1992
106 / 171

7

Suez, Egypt
1869
101 / 162

8

Albert, Belgium
1939
81 / 130

9

Moscow (formerly
Moscow-Volga, Russia
1937
80 / 129

10

Volga-Don, Russia
1952
63 / 101

* Extended from AD 605–10
and rebuilt between 1958–72

Connecting Hang Zhou in the
south to Beijing in the north,
China's Grand Canal was largely
built by manual labor alone,
long before the invention of the
mechanized digging used in the
construction of the other major
artificial waterways. The Panama
Canal, opened in 1914 (51 miles/
82 km), just fails to find a place
in the Top 10.

TOP 10 **LONGEST TRANSPORTATION CANALS IN THE USA**

CANAL / LOCATION	YEAR COMPLETED	LENGTH MILES	LENGTH KM
1 Erie Canal, New York	1918	363	584
2 Tennessee-Tombigbee Waterway, Alabama/Mississippi	1985	234	377
3 Mississippi River-Gulf Outlet Canal, Louisiana	1965	76	122
4 Champlain Canal, New York	1823	60	97
5 Chicago Sanitary and Ship Canal, Illinois	1900	28	45
6 Oswego Canal, New York	1828	24	38
7 Dismal Swamp Canal, North Carolina/ Virginia	1805	22	35
8 Cayuga-Seneca Canal, New York	1828	20	32
9 Cape Coda Canal, Massachussetts	1916	17	27
10 Chesapeake and Delaware Canal, Delaware/Maryland	1829	14	23

* Excluding defunct or abandoned canals

TOP 10 **MERCHANT SHIPPING COUNTRIES**

Grand Canal
*Suzhou's location
on both the Yangtze
river and the Grand
Canal makes it one
of China's most
important trade hubs.*

COUNTRY	SHIPS
1 Panama	6,323
2 Liberia	2,204
3 China	1,826
4 Malta	1,438
5 Singapore	1,292
6 Bahamas	1,223
7 Antigua and Barbuda	1,146
8 Hong Kong*	1,114
9 Russia	1,074
10 Marshall Islands	1,049
USA	*422*

* Special Administrative Region of China

Source: *CIA World Factbook 2008*

TOP 10 **LONGEST SAILING VESSELS***

Tall ship
The five-masted cruise ship Royal Clipper has 42 sails with a total area of 55,994 sq ft (5,202 sq m). She carries 228 passengers and a crew of 105.

	SHIP / COUNTRY BUILT	YEAR	LENGTH FT	LENGTH M
1	Wind Surf (France)	1990	617	187
2	Wind Star (France)	1986	440	134
3	Royal Clipper (Poland)	2000	439	134
4	Moshulu (UK)	1904	396	121
5	Sea Cloud II (Spain)	2001	384	117
6	Peking (Germany)	1911	378	115
7	Kruzenshtern (Germany)	1926	376	114
8 =	Juan Sebastián Elcano (Spain)	1927	370	113
=	Esmerelda (Spain)	1953	370	113
10	Dar Młodzieży (Poland)	1982	363	111

* Currently afloat

The *Preussen*
The *Preussen*, the German five-master on which the *Royal Clipper* was modeled, was the world's largest sailing ship when launched in 1902. On November 6, 1910 she was rammed by cross-channel ferry *Brighton*, beached and broke up off the coast near Dover, UK.

TOP 10 **US PORTS, 2008**

	PORT / STATE	TEUS*
1	Los Angeles, California	4,111,358
2	Long Beach, California	3,166,714
3	New York/Newark, New Jersey	2,560,007
4	Savannah, Georgia	1,071,504
5	Norfolk, Virginia	803,814
6	Oakland, California	748,971
7	Charleston, South Carolina	695,644
8	Seattle, Washington	661,184
9	Tacoma, Washington	647,325
10	Houston, Texas	529,960
	Top 10 total	14,996,480

* Twenty-foot Equivalent Unit—a standard 20-ft long shipping container

TOP 10 **BUSIEST PORTS**

	PORT / COUNTRY	CARGO 2007 (TONS)
1	Shanghai, China	618,892,686
2	Singapore, Singapore	533,095,387
3	Rotterdam, Netherlands	442,226,354
4	Ningbo, China	379,195,091
5	Guangzhou, China	378,368,357
6	Tianjin, China	341,121,258
7	Qingdao, China	292,134,544
8	Qinhuangdao , China	274,398,355
9	Hong Kong, China	270,543,572
10	Busan, South Korea	268,483,352
	Top 10 total	3,798,458,956

Source: American Association of Port Authorities

Shangai
The world's busiest port, Shanghai, handles over 26 million containers a year, a total of 1.5 million tons of goods a day.

The First to Fly

THE 10 **FIRST COUNTRIES TO HAVE BALLOON FLIGHTS***

1 France — Nov 21, 1783

The Montgolfier brothers, Joseph and Etienne, tested their first unmanned hot-air balloon in the French town of Annonay on June 5, 1783. On November 21, 1783 François Laurent, Marquis d'Arlandes and Jean-François Pilâtre de Rozier took off from the Bois de Boulogne, Paris, in a Montgolfier hot-air balloon. This first manned flight covered a distance of about 5.5 miles (9 km) in 23 minutes, landing safely near Gentilly.

2 Italy — Feb 25, 1784

Chevalier Paolo Andreani and the brothers Augustino and Carlo Giuseppe Gerli (the builders of the balloon) made the first flight outside France, at Moncucco near Milan, Italy.

3 Austria — Jul 6, 1784

Johann Georg Stuwer made the first Austrian flight from the Prater, Vienna.

4 Scotland — Aug 27, 1784

James Tytler (known as "Balloon Tytler"), a doctor and newspaper editor, took off from Comely Gardens, Edinburgh, in a hot-air balloon, achieving an altitude of 350 ft (107 m) in a 0.5-mile (0.8-km) hop in a homemade balloon.

5 England — Sep 15, 1784

Watched by a crowd of 200,000, Italian balloonist Vincenzo Lunardi ascended from the Artillery Company Ground, Moorfields, London, flying to Standon near Ware in Hertfordshire. On October 4, 1784 James Sadler flew a Montgolfier balloon at Oxford, thereby becoming the first English-born pilot.

6 Ireland — Jan 19, 1785

Although there are earlier claims, it is likely that Richard Crosbie's hydrogen-balloon flight from Ranelagh Gardens, Dublin, was the first in Ireland.

7 Holland — Jul 11, 1785

French balloon pioneer, Jean-Pierre Blanchard, took off from The Hague in a hydrogen balloon.

8 Germany — Oct 3, 1785

Blanchard made the first flight in Germany from Frankfurt.

9 Belgium — Oct 20, 1785

Blanchard flew his hydrogen balloon from Ghent.

10 Switzerland — May 5, 1788

Blanchard flew from Basel. As well as flights from other European cities, Blanchard made the first in the USA, from Philadelphia, on January 9, 1793, watched by George Washington.

* Several of the balloonists listed also made subsequent flights, but in each instance only their first flight in each country is included

THE 10 **FIRST ROCKET AND JET AIRCRAFT**

	AIRCRAFT	COUNTRY	FIRST FLIGHT
1	Heinkel He 176*	Germany	Jun 20, 1939
2	Heinkel He 178	Germany	Aug 27, 1939
3	DFS 194*	Germany	Aug 1940#
4	Caproni-Campini N-1	Italy	Aug 28, 1940
5	Heinkel He 280V-1	Germany	Apr 2, 1941
6	Gloster E.28/39	UK	May 15, 1941
7	Messerschmitt Me 163 Komet*	Germany	Aug 13, 1941
8	Messerschmitt Me 262V-3	Germany	Jul 18, 1942
9	Bell XP-59A Airacomet	USA	Oct 2, 1942
10	Gloster Meteor F Mk 1	UK	Mar 5, 1943

* Rocket-powered
# Precise date unknown

Prototypes of the rocket-powered Heinkel 176 and the turbojet Heinkel 178 first flew prior to the outbreak of World War II. The first operational jets were developed in the early years of the war, with the Messerschmitt Me 262 the first jet fighter in service. The German Arado Ar 234V-1 Blitz ("Lightning"), which first flew on June 15, 1943, was the world's first jet bomber.

Jet fighter
The Gloster Meteor was the only Allied jet fighter of World War II.

THE 10 **FIRST ROUND-THE-WORLD FLIGHTS**

PILOT(S) / AIRCRAFT	ROUTE (START/ END LOCATION)	TOTAL DISTANCE		DATES
		MILES	KM	
1 Lt. Lowell H. Smith/Lt. Leslie P. Arnold (USA), Douglas World Cruiser, Chicago	Seattle, Washington, USA	26,345	42,398	Apr 6–Sep 28, 1924
2 Lt. Erik H. Nelson/Lt. John Harding, Jr. (USA), Douglas World Cruiser, New Orleans	Seattle, Washington, USA	27,553	44,342	Apr 6–Sep 28, 1924
3 Dr. Hugo Eckener, Ernst Lehmann, and crew (Germany), Airship, Graf Zeppelin	Lakehurst, New Jersey, USA	20,373	37,787	Apr 8–29, 1929
4 Wiley Post and Harold Gatty (USA), Lockheed Vega Winne Mae York, USA	Roosevelt Field, Long Island, New	15,474	24,903	Jun 23–Jul 1, 1931
5 Wolfgang von Gronau, Ghert von Roth, Franz Hack, Fritz Albrecht (Germany), Dornier seaplane, Grönland-Wal D-2053	List, Germany	27,240	44,000	Jul 22–Nov 23, 1932
6 Wiley Post (USA), Lockheed Vega Winne Mae (first solo)	Floyd Bennett Field, New York, USA	15,596	25,093	Jul 15–22,1933
7 Howard Hughes, Lt. Thomas Thurlow, Henry P. McClean Conner, Richard Stoddart, Eddie Lund (USA), Lockheed 14, New York World's Fair 1939	Floyd Bennett Field, New York, USA	14,672	23,612	Jul 10–14, 1938
8 = Clifford Evans (USA), Piper PA-12, City of Washington	Teterboro, New, Jersey, USA	25,162	40,494	Aug 9–Dec 10, 1947
= George Truman (USA), Piper PA-12, City of the Angels	Teterboro, New, Jersey, USA	25,162	40,493	Aug 9–Dec 10, 1947
10 Capt. James Gallagher and crew of 13 (USA), Boeing B-50A, Lucky Lady II (first non-stop circumnavigation with in-flight refueling)	Fort Worth, Texas, USA	23,452	37,742	Feb 26–Mar 2, 1949

Homecoming
Circumnavigators Wiley Post and Harold Gatty are welcomed home by a New York ticker-tape parade (1931).

Air Travel

TOP 10 DOMESTIC ROUTES IN THE USA

ROUTE	PASSENGERS*
1 New York, NY to Chicago, IL	2,910,000
2 Atlanta, GA to New York, NY	2,810,000
3 Atlanta, GA to Orlando, FL	2,800,000
4 Los Angeles, CA to San Francisco, CA	2,700,000
5 Atlanta, GA to Washington, DC	2,630,000
6 Los Angeles, CA to Chicago, IL	2,540,000
7 Fort Lauderdale, FL to New York, NY	2,470,000
8 Denver, CO to Chicago, IL	2,440,000
9 New York, NY to Los Angeles, CA	2,420,000
10 Washington, DC to Chicago, IL	2,360,000

* December 2007–November 2008

Source: US Department of Transportation

TOP 10 AIRLINES WITH THE MOST AIRCRAFT

AIRLINE / COUNTRY*	MAIN FLEET SIZE#
1 American Airlines	616
2 Southwest Airlines	539
3 Delta Air Lines	457
4 United Airlines	407
5 Continental Airlines	380
6 US Airways	361
7 Lufthansa, Germany	344
8 Northwest Airlines	336
9 Air Canada, Canada	334
10 China Southern Airlines, China	299

1 symbol = 100 airplanes

* USA unless otherwise stated
# 2007 or latest available year

TOP 10 AIRLINES WITH THE MOST PASSENGERS

AIRLINE / COUNTRY / PASSENGERS CARRIED (2007)*

1 Southwest Airlines
USA
101,911,000

2 American Airlines
USA
98,162,000

3 Air France-KLM
France
94,795,000

4 Delta Air Lines
USA
72,900,000

Russian giant
Capable of carrying a load of over 250 tons, only two Antonov An-225s have been built.

TOP 10 **LONGEST AIRCRAFT**

AIRCRAFT	WEIGHT (LB)	LENGTH FT	IN	M
1 Ekranoplan KM Caspian Sea Monster	1,080,000	348	0	106.1
2 Antonov An-225 Cossack	1,322,750	275	7	84.0
3 Lockheed C-5 Galaxy	840,000	247	10	75.5
4 Airbus A340-600	807,400	246	11	75.3
5 Boeing 777-300ER	775,000	242	4	73.9
6 Lun Ekranoplan	882,000	240	0	73.2
7 Airbus A380F	1,305,000	239	3	72.9
8 Boeing 747	875,000	231	10	70.7
9 Antonov An-124 Condor	892,872	226	9	69.1
10 H-4 Hercules ("Spruce Goose"')	400,000	218	6	66.6

The 1,080,000-lb (540-ton) Ekranoplan KM Caspian Sea Monster, designed to skim above the surface of water or land, thereby evading radar detection, is as long as a soccer field.

TOP 10 **BUSIEST AIRPORTS**

AIRPORT	LOCATION	PASSENGERS (2007)
1 Atlanta Hartsfield International	Atlanta, USA	89,379,287
2 Chicago O'Hare	Chicago, USA	76,177,855
3 London Heathrow	London, UK	68,068,304
4 Tokyo International	Tokyo, Japan	66,823,414
5 Los Angeles International	Los Angeles, USA	61,896,075
6 Charles De Gaulle	Paris, France	59,922,177
7 DFW International	Dallas/Fort Worth, USA	59,786,476
8 Frankfurt	Frankfurt, Germany	54,161,856
9 Beijing	Beijing, China	53,583,664
10 Madrid	Madrid, Spain	52,122,702

Source: Airports Council International

* Total of international and domestic
Source: International Air Transport Association

5 United Airlines USA 68,400,000

6 Lufthansa Germany 62,900,000

7 China Southern Airlines China 56,900,000

8 Northwest Airlines USA 53,700,000

9 Japan Airlines International Japan 50,442,000

10 All Nippon Airways Japan 50,384,000

Transport Disasters

THE 10 WORST AIR DISASTERS

LOCATION / DATE / INCIDENT — NO. KILLED

New York, USA, Sep 11, 2001 — c. 1,622
Following a hijacking by terrorists, an American Airlines Boeing 767 was deliberately flown into the North Tower of the World Trade Center, killing all 81 passengers (including five hijackers), 11 crew on board, and an estimated 1,530.

New York, USA, Sep 11, 2001 — c. 677
As part of the coordinated attack, hijackers commandeered a second Boeing 767 and crashed it into the South Tower of the World Trade Center, killing all 56 passengers and 9 crew on board, and approximately 612 on the ground.

Tenerife, Canary Islands, Mar 27, 1977 — 583
Two Boeing 747s (PanAm and KLM, carrying 380 passengers and 16 crew, and 234 passengers and 14 crew respectively) collided and caught fire on the runway.

Mt. Ogura, Japan, Aug 12, 1985 — 520
A JAL Boeing 747 on an internal flight from Tokyo to Osaka crashed, killing all but four of the 509 passengers, and all 15 crew on board.

Charkhi Dadri, India, Nov 12, 1996 — 349
A Saudi Arabian Airlines Boeing 747 collided with a Kazakh Airlines Ilyushin IL 76 cargo aircraft and exploded, killing all 312 on the Boeing and all 37 on the Ilyushin.

Paris, France, Mar 3, 1974 — 346
Immediately after takeoff for London, a Turkish Airlines DC-10 suffered an explosive decompression when a door burst open and crashed killing all on board.

Off the Irish coast, Jun 23, 1985 — 329
An Air India Boeing 747 on a flight from Vancouver to Delhi exploded in midair, probably as a result of a terrorist bomb, killing all 307 passengers and 22 crew.

Riyadh, Saudi Arabia, Aug 19, 1980 — 301
Following an emergency landing a Saudia (Saudi Arabian) Airlines Lockheed TriStar caught fire. The crew were unable to open the doors and all on board died from smoke.

Off the Iranian coast, Jul 3, 1988 — 290
An Iran Air A300 airbus was shot down in error by a missile fired by the USS *Vincennes*, resulting in the deaths of all 274 passengers and 16 crew.

Sirach Mountain, Iran, Feb 19, 2003 — 275
An Ilyushin 76 crashed into the mountain in poor weather. It was carrying 257 Revolutionary Guards and a crew of 18, none of whom survived.

THE 10 WORST PEACETIME MARINE DISASTERS

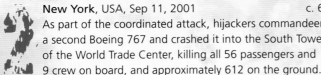

SHIP / DATE / LOCATION / INCIDENT — NO. KILLED

Doña Paz, Dec 21, 1987 — <3,000
Tabias Strait, Philippines
The ferry *Doña Paz* was struck by oil tanker MT *Vector*. Some sources claim a total of 4,341 victims.

SS Kiangya, Dec 4, 1948 — 2,750–3,920
Off Shanghai, China
The overloaded passenger steamship is believed to have struck a Japanese mine.

MV Le Joola, Sep 26, 2002 — >1,863
Off The Gambia
The overcrowded Senegalese ferry capsized in a storm.

Tek Sing, Feb 6, 1822 — 1,600
Gaspar Strait, Indonesia
The large Chinese junk laden with migrant Chinese workers ran aground and sank.

Sultana, Apr 27, 1865 — 1,547
Mississippi River, USA
A boiler on the Mississippi paddleboat *Sultana* exploded and the vessel sank.

RMS Titanic, Apr 15, 1912 — 1,517
North Atlantic
The *Titanic*, the world's largest liner, sank on her maiden voyage after striking an iceberg.

Toya Maru, Sep 26, 1954 — 1,159
Tsugaru Strait, Japan
The Japanese ferry between Hokkaido and Honshu sank in a typhoon, with an estimated 150 rescued.

General Slocum, Jun 15, 1904 — 1,021
New York, USA,
The excursion steamship caught fire in the East River, New York, with many victims burned or drowned.

MS al-Salam Boccaccio 98, Feb 3, 2006 — 1,018
Red Sea
The Egyptian car ferry sank following a fire on board.

RMS Empress of Ireland, May 29, 1914 — 1,012
Saint Lawrence River, Canada
The Royal Mail ship was struck by Norwegian collier SS *Storstad*, resulting in Canada's worst marine disaster.

THE 10 **WORST BRIDGE COLLAPSES***

BRIDGE / LOCATION / DATE / INCIDENT

NO. KILLED

Angers, France Apr 16, 1850 — 226
The bridge began to vibrate and collapsed as 478 soldiers marched across it.

Tangiwai New Zealand Dec 24, 1953 — 151
Volcanic lava engulfed the bridge over the Walouru river as a passenger train crossed; some victims were carried 30 miles (48 km) by the force of the flow.

Makahali, Nepal Nov 26, 1974 — 140
A suspension bridge over a river collapsed in the Baitadi district.

Liziyida, China Jul 9, 1981 — 130
The bridge was destroyed by a mud-flow, resulting in a train derailment.

Munnar, India Nov 8, 1984 — 125
A rope bridge collapsed over a swollen stream; the victims were mostly schoolchildren.

Hyatt Regency Skywalks,
Kansas City, USA Jul 17, 1981 — 114
The collapse of two aerial footbridges occurred during a dance at the hotel.

Mahububnagar, India Sep 2, 1956 — 112
A narrow-gauge train fell into the river when the bridge collapsed.

Colgante, Naga City, Philippines Sep 16, 1972 — 100
Many pilgrims jumped into the river as the wooden bridge collapsed.

Ashtabula, Ohio, USA Dec 29, 1876 — 92
The bridge collapsed in heavy snow, causing a train to plunge into the valley where it caught fire; at the time, this was America's worst railway disaster.

Yarmouth, Norfolk, UK May 2, 1845 — 79
As a crowd of people on the bridge watched a performer in the river below, their weight caused its suspension chains to snap.

* Those where the collapse caused the disaster; excluding those where a ship, train or other impact resulted in the collapse

THE 10 **WORST MOTOR VEHICLE AND ROAD DISASTERS**

LOCATION / DATE / INCIDENT

NO. KILLED

Afghanistan, Nov 3, 1982 — >2,000
Following a collision with a Soviet army truck, a gasoline tanker exploded in the 1.7-mile (2.7-km) Salang Tunnel. Some authorities have put the death toll from the explosion, fire and fumes as high as 3,000.

Colombia, Aug 7, 1956 — 1,200
Seven army ammunition trucks exploded at night in the centre of Cali, destroying eight city blocks, including a barracks where 500 soldiers were sleeping.

Spain, July 11, 1978 — 217
A liquid gas tanker exploded in Los Alfaques, a camping site at San Carlos de la Rapita.

Thailand, Feb 15, 1991 — 171
A dynamite truck exploded in Phang Nga.

Nigeria, Nov 5, 2000 — 150–200
A gasoline tanker collided with a line of parked cars on the Ile-Ife-Ibadan Expressway, exploding and burning many to death. Some 96 bodies were recovered, but some estimates put the final toll as high as 200.

Nepal, Nov 26, 1974 — 148
Hindu pilgrims were killed when a suspension bridge over the River Mahakali collapsed.

Egypt, Aug 9, 1973 — 127
A bus drove into an irrigation canal.

Togo, Dec 6, 1965 — >125
Two lorries collided with dancers during a festival at Sotouboua.

South Korea, Apr 28, 1995 — 110
An underground explosion destroyed vehicles and caused about 100 cars and buses to plunge into the pit it created.

The Gambia, Nov 12, 1992 — 100
After brake failure, a bus ferrying passengers to a dock plunged into a river.

SPORT & LEISURE

Olympic Countries

TOP 10 MEDAL-WINNING COUNTRIES AT THE SUMMER PARALYMPICS*

| COUNTRY | GOLD | MEDALS | | TOTAL |
		SILVER	BRONZE	
1 USA	701	604	635	1,940
2 UK	512	497	485	1,494
3 Canada	464	285	315	1,064
4 France	338	321	302	961
5 Australia	315	335	299	949
6 West Germany	303	253	242	798
7 Holland	243	210	176	629
8 Poland	209	221	180	610
9 Spain	191	187	204	582
10 Sweden	211	206	149	566

* Up to and including the 2008 Beijing Games

The first Paralympics to take place at the same venue as the Olympic Games was in Rome in 1960; they are held every four years

Paralympic power
British Paralympic champion David Weir adds a gold to his overall Olympic tally of two gold, two silver, and two bronze medals.

THE 10 LATEST CITIES TO HOST THE SUMMER OLYMPICS

CITY / COUNTRY
MOST GOLDS / COMPETING COUNTRIES
DATES

9 Montreal, Canada
USSR, 125 / 92
Jul 17–Aug 1, 1976

Munich, West Germany
USSR, 99 / 121
Aug 26–Sep 10, 1972
10

8 Moscow, USSR
USSR, 195 / 80
Jul 19–Aug 3, 1980

Beijing, China
China, 51 / 204
Aug 8–24, 2008
1

7
Los Angeles, USA
USA, 174 / 140
Jul 28–Aug 12, 1984

4
Atlanta, USA
USA, 101 / 197
Jul 20–Aug 4, 1996

5
Barcelona, Spain
Unified Team, 112 / 169
Jul 25–Aug 9, 1992

2 Athens, Greece
USA, 103 / 202
Aug 13–29, 2004

6 Seoul, South Korea
USSR, 132 / 159
Sep 17–Oct 2, 1988

All but one of the 205 IOC countries competed in the Beijing Games, Brunei being the only absentee. Three countries made their Olympic debut in 2008: the Marshall Islands, Montenegro, and Tuvalu.

Sydney, Australia
USA, 97 / 199
Sep 15–Oct 1, 2000
3

Olympic spectacle
The opening ceremony of the 2008 Beijing Summer Olympics. A total of 11,028 athletes competed in 302 events. Of the 204 competing nations, 87 of them won at least one of the 958 medals on offer.

TOP 10 MEDAL-WINNING NATIONS AT THE SUMMER OLYMPICS*

COUNTRY	MEDALS			
	GOLD	SILVER	BRONZE	TOTAL
1 USA	930	730	638	2,298
2 USSR#	395	319	296	1,010
3 Great Britain†	207	255	253	715
4 France	191	212	233	636
5 Germany§	163	163	203	529
6 Italy	190	158	174	522
7 Sweden	142	160	173	475
8 Hungary	159	140	159	458
9 Australia	131	137	164	432
10 East Germany	153	129	127	409

* Totals for all Summer Olympics, 1896–2008, excluding the 1906 Intercalated Games in Athens
# USSR totals for Summer Olympics, 1952–88; Unified Team figures for 1992 are excluded
† Great Britain totals include those won by athletes from Great Britain and Ireland, 1896–1920
§ Germany totals for 1896–1952 and 1992–2008; totals for West Germany (1968–88), East Germany (1968–88), and United Germany (1956–64) are excluded

TOP 10 MEDAL-WINNING COUNTRIES AT THE 2008 BEIJING OLYMPICS

COUNTRY	MEDALS			
	GOLD	SILVER	BRONZE	TOTAL
1 USA	36	38	36	110
2 China	51	21	28	100
3 Russia	23	21	28	72
4 Great Britain	19	13	15	47
5 Australia	14	15	17	46
6 Germany	16	10	15	41
7 France	7	16	17	40
8 South Korea	13	10	8	31
9 Italy	8	10	10	28
10 Ukraine	7	5	15	27

This list is based on medal totals. The IOC ranks countries in order of gold medals won: by this reckoning, Japan would figure at No. 8, with nine golds, six silvers, and 10 bronze medals; just outside the Top 10, Cuba—which would be in 28th place with just two golds—achieved a creditable 11 silvers and 11 bronzes, 24 medals in all, 16 of them in boxing, judo, wrestling, and Taekwondo.

Great Olympians

TOP 10 MOST GOLD MEDALS WON BY AN INDIVIDUAL MALE AT ONE SUMMER OLYMPICS*

	ATHLETE / COUNTRY	SPORT	YEAR	GOLDS
1	Michael Phelps, USA	Swimming	2008	8
2	Mark Spitz, USA	Swimming	1972	7
3 =	Vitaly Scherbo, Unified Team	Gymnastics	1992	6
=	Michael Phelps, USA	Swimming	2004	6
5 =	Anton Heida, USA	Gymnastics	1904	5
=	Willis Lee, USA	Shooting	1920	5
=	Paavo Nurmi, Finland	Track and field	1924	5
=	Matt Biondi, USA	Swimming	1988	5
9 =	Hubert Van Innis, Belgium	Archery	1920	4
=	Carl Osburn, USA	Shooting	1920	4
=	Lloyd Spooner, USA	Shooting	1920	4
=	Ville Ritola, Finland	Track and field	1924	4
=	Viktor Chukarin, USSR	Gymnastics	1956	4
=	Boris Shakhlin, USSR	Gymnastics	1960	4
=	Don Schollander, USA	Swimming	1964	4
=	Akinori Nakayama, Japan	Gymnastics	1968	4
=	Nikolay Andrianov, USSR	Gymnastics	1976	4
=	Carl Lewis, USA	Track and field	1984	4

* All Summer Olympics 1896–2008

Seven of Michael Phelps' eight gold medals in 2008 were in world-record times, and one in a new Olympic-record time.

TOP 10 MOST SUMMER OLYMPIC GOLD MEDALS*

	ATHLETE / COUNTRY	SPORT	YEARS	GOLDS
1	Michael Phelps, USA	Swimming	2004–08	14
2 =	Paavo Nurmi, Finland	Track and field	1920–28	9
=	Larissa Latynina, USSR	Gymnastics	1956–64	9
=	Mark Spitz, USA	Swimming	1968–72	9
=	Carl Lewis, USA	Track and field	1984–96	9
6 =	Sawao Kato, Japan	Gymnastics	1968–76	8
=	Birgit Fischer-Schmidt, East Germany/Germany	Canoeing	1980–2004	8
=	Matt Biondi, USA	Swimming	1984–92	8
=	Jenny Thompson, USA	Swimming	1992–2004	8
10 =	Aladár Gerevich, Hungary	Fencing	1932–60	7
=	Viktor Chukarin, USSR	Gymnastics	1952–56	7
=	Boris Shakhlin, USSR	Gymnastics	1956–64	7
=	Vera Caslavska, Czechoslovakia	Gymnastics	1960–68	7
=	Nikolay Andrianov, USSR	Gymnastics	1972–80	7

* All Summer Olympics 1896–2008

THE 10 FIRST ATHLETES TO WIN MEDALS AT FIVE OR MORE SUMMER OLYMPICS

	ATHLETE / COUNTRY	SPORT	YEARS
1	Heikki Ilmari Savolainen, Finland	Gymnastics	1928–52
2	Aladár Gerevich, Hungary	Fencing	1932–60
3 =	Pál Kovács, Hungary	Fencing	1936–60
=	Edoardo Mangiarotti, Italy	Fencing	1936–60
5	Gustav Fischer, Switzerland	Dressage	1952–68
6	Hans Günther Winkler, United Germany/West Germany	Show-jumping	1956–76
7	Ildikó Ságiné–Rejtö née Uljaki-Rejtö, Hungary	Fencing	1960–76
8	John Michael Plumb, USA	Three-Day Event	1964–84
9	Reiner Klimke, United Germany/West Germany	Dressage	1964–88
10 =	Birgit Fischer-Schmidt, East Germany/Germany	Canoeing	1980–2004
=	Teresa Edwards, USA	Basketball	1984–2000
=	Stephen Redgrave, Great Britain	Rowing	1984–2000

Michael Phelps
Phelps beat Mark Spitz's 36-year Olympic record with eight golds in 2008.

TOP 10 **MOST MEDALS IN A SUMMER OLYMPICS CAREER (MEN)***

	ATHLETE / COUNTRY / SPORT	YEARS	GOLD	SILVER	BRONZE	TOTAL
1	Michael Phelps, USA Swimming	2004–08	14	0	2	16
2	Nikolai Andrianov, USSR Gymnastics	1972–80	7	5	3	15
3	= Edoardo Mangiarotti, Italy Fencing	1936–60	6	5	2	13
	= Takashi Ono, Japan Gymnastics	1952–64	5	4	4	13
	= Boris Shakhlin, USSR Gymnastics	1956–64	7	4	2	13
6	= Paavo Nurmi, Finland Track and Field	1920–28	9	3	0	12
	= Sawao Kato, Japan Gymnastics	1968–76	8	3	1	12
	= Alexei Nemov, Russia Gymnastics	1996–2000	4	2	6	12
9	= Carl Osburn, USA Shooting	1912–24	5	4	2	11
	= Viktor Chukarin, USSR Gymnastics	1952–56	7	3	1	11
	= Mark Spitz, USA Swimming	1968–72	9	1	1	11
	= Matt Biondi, USA Swimming	1984–92	8	2	1	11

* All Summer Olympics 1896–2008

TOP 10 **MOST MEDALS IN A SUMMER OLYMPICS CAREER (WOMEN)***

	ATHLETE / COUNTRY / SPORT	YEARS	GOLD	SILVER	BRONZE	TOTAL
1	Larissa Latynina, USSR Gymnastics	1956–64	9	5	4	18
2	= Birgit Fischer-Schmidt, East Germany/Germany Canoeing	1980–2004	8	4	0	12
	= Dara Torres, USA Swimming	1984–2008	4	4	4	12
	= Jenny Thompson, USA Swimming	1992–2000	8	3	1	12
5	= Vera Cáslavská, Czechoslovakia Gymnastics	1960–68	7	4	0	11
	= Natalie Coughlin, USA Swimming	2004–08	3	4	4	11
7	= Agnes Keleti, Hungary Gymnastics	1952–56	5	3	2	10
	= Polina Astakhova, USSR Gymnastics	1956–64	5	2	3	10
9	= Lyudmila Tourischeva, USSR Gymnastics	1968–76	4	3	2	9
	= Nadia Comaneci, Romania Gymnastics	1976–80	5	3	1	9

* All Summer Olympics 1896–2008

Athletics

TOP 10 MEDAL-WINNING COUNTRIES IN TRACK AND FIELD EVENTS AT THE 2008 BEIJING OLYMPICS

	COUNTRY	GOLD	SILVER	BRONZE	TOTAL
1	USA	7	9	7	23
2	Russia	6	5	7	18
3	Kenya	5	5	4	14
4	Jamaica	6	3	2	11
5	=Belarus	1	3	3	7
	=Ethiopia	4	1	2	7
7	=Cuba	1	2	2	5
	=Ukraine	1	1	3	5
9	=Australia	1	2	1	4
	=Great Britain	1	2	1	4

100-m Records

When Usain Bolt set a new world record in the 2008 100-m final at the Beijing Olympics, he broke his own world record of 9.72 seconds, which he had set at New York on May 31, 2008. The women's 100-m world record is 10.49 seconds, set by Florence Griffith-Joyner (USA) at Indianapolis on July 16, 1988.

TOP 10 FASTEST MEN OVER 100 METERS*

	ATHLETE / COUNTRY / VENUE	DATE	TIME (SECS)
1	**Usain Bolt**, Jamaica Beijing, China	Aug 16, 2008	9.69
2	**Asafa Powell**, Jamaica Rieti, Italy	Sep 9, 2007	9.74
3	**Tyson Gay**, USA Eugene, Oregon, USA	Jun 28, 2008	9.77
4	**Maurice Greene**, USA Athens, Greece	Jun 16, 1999	9.79
5	=**Donovan Bailey**, Canada Atlanta, Georgia, USA	Jul 27, 1996	9.84
	=**Bruny Surin**, Canada Seville, Spain	Aug 22, 1999	9.84
7	=**Leroy Burrell**, USA Lausanne, Switzerland	Jul 6, 1994	9.85
	=**Justin Gatlin**, USA Athens, Greece	Aug 22, 2004	9.85
	=**Olusoji A. Fasuba**, Nigeria Doha, Qatar	May 12, 2006	9.85
10	=**Carl Lewis**, USA Tokyo, Japan	Aug 25, 1991	9.86
	=**Frank Fredericks**, Namibia Lausanne, Switzerland	Jul 3, 1996	9.86
	=**Ato Boldon**, Trinidad Walnut, California, USA	Apr 19, 1998	9.86
	=**Francis Obikwelu**, Portugal Athens, Greece	Aug 22, 2004	9.86

* Based on the fastest time ever achieved by each

Source: IAAF

Lightning Bolt
Jamaican athlete Usain Bolt won three gold medals at the 2008 Olympics, setting a new world record for the 100 m.

TOP 10 FASTEST MARATHONS*

ATHLETE / COUNTRY / VENUE / DATE / TIME (HR:MIN:SECS)

10 Paul Tergat,
Kenya
London, Apr 14, 2002
2:05:48

9 Khalid Khannouchi,
USA
Chicago, Oct 24, 1999
2:05:42

8 Khalid Khannouchi,
USA
London, Apr 14, 2002
2:05:38

7 Abderrahim Goumri,
Morocco
London, Apr 13, 2008
2:05:30

6 Samuel Kamau Wanjiru,
Kenya
London, Apr 13, 2008
2:05:24

* As at January 1, 2009

Source: IAAF

TOP 10 **LONGEST LONG JUMPS** *

	ATHLETE#	VENUE	DATE	DISTANCE (M)
1	Mike Powell	Tokyo, Japan	Aug 30, 1991	8.95
2	Bob Beamon	Mexico City	Oct 18, 1968	8.90
3	Carl Lewis	Tokyo, Japan	Aug 30, 1991	8.87
4	Robert Emmiyan, Russia	Tsakhkadzor, Armenia	May 22, 1987	8.86
5	Carl Lewis	Indianapolis, USA	Jun 19, 1983	8.79
6	= Carl Lewis	Indianapolis, USA	Jul 24, 1982	8.76
	= Carl Lewis	Indianapolis, USA	Jul 18, 1988	8.76
8	Carl Lewis	Indianapolis, USA	Aug 16, 1987	8.75
9	= Larry Myricks	Indianapolis, USA	Jul 18, 1988	8.74
	= Erick Walder	El Paso, USA	Apr 2, 1994	8.74

* As at January 1, 2009
# All USA unless otherwise stated

Source: IAAF

The longest jump in the twenty-first century is 8.73 meters by Irving Saladino (Panama) at Hengelo, the Netherlands, on May 24, 2008. He equaled that mark in winning the gold medal at the Beijing Olympics. The women's world record is 7.52 meters, set by Galina Chistyakova (Russia) at Leningrad on June 11, 1988.

The fastest women's marathon is 2 hours 15 minutes 25 seconds by Paula Radcliffe (GB) in winning the London Marathon on April 13, 2003.

3 Paul Tergat,
Kenya
Berlin, Sep 28, 2003
2:04:55

1 Haile Gebrselassie,
Ethiopia
Berlin, Sep 30, 2007
2:04:26

5 Martin Lel,
Kenya
London, Apr 13, 2008
2:05:15

4 Sammy Korir,
Kenya
Berlin, Sep 28, 2003
2:04:56

2 Haile Gebrselassie,
Ethiopia
Dubai, Sep 28, 2003
2:04:53

Baseball

Barry Bonds
Bonds leads the home-runs table with 762 in his 21-year career with the Pittsburgh Pirates and San Francisco Giants.

TOP 10 **MOST HOME RUNS IN A CAREER***

	PLAYER	YEARS	HOME RUNS
1	Barry Bonds	1986–2007	762
2	Hank Aaron	1954–76	755
3	Babe Ruth	1914–36	714
4	Willie Mays	1951–73	660
5	Ken Griffey, Jr.	1989–2008	611
6	Sammy Sosa	1989–2007	609
7	Frank Robinson	1956–76	586
8	Mark McGwire	1986–2001	583
9	Harmon Killebrew	1954–75	573
10	Rafael Palmeiro	1986–2005	569

* Up to and including the 2008 season

TOP 10 **MOST HOME RUNS IN A SINGLE SEASON**

	PLAYER	TEAM	YEAR	HOME RUNS
1	Barry Bonds	San Francisco Giants	2001	73
2	Mark McGwire	St. Louis Cardinals	1998	70
3	Sammy Sosa	Chicago Cubs	1998	66
4	Mark McGwire	St. Louis Cardinals	1999	65
5	Sammy Sosa	Chicago Cubs	2001	64
6	Sammy Sosa	Chicago Cubs	1999	63
7	Roger Maris	New York Yankees	1961	61
8	Babe Ruth	New York Yankees	1927	60
9	Babe Ruth	New York Yankees	1921	59
10 =	Jimmie Foxx	Philadelphia Athletics	1932	58
=	Hank Greenberg	Detroit Tigers	1938	58
=	Mark McGwire	Oakland Athletics/ St. Louis Cardinals	1997	58
=	Ryan Howard	Philadelphia Phillies	2006	58

* Up to and including the 2008 season

TOP 10 MOST STRIKEOUTS IN A SINGLE WORLD SERIES*

	PLAYER	TEAM / OPPONENTS	YEAR	STRIKEOUTS
1	Bob Gibson*	St. Louis Cardinals v. Detroit Tigers	1968	35
2	Bob Gibson	St. Louis Cardinals v. New York Yankees	1964	31
3	Sandy Koufax	Los Angeles Dodgers v. Minnesota Twins	1965	29
4	Bill Dinneen	Boston Red Sox v Pittsburgh Pirates	1903	28
5	=Bob Gibson	St. Louis Cardinals v. Boston Red Sox	1967	26
	=Curt Schilling	Arizona Diamondbacks v. New York Yankees	2001	26
7	Sandy Koufax	Los Angeles Dodgers v. New York Yankees	1963	23
8	=Deacon Phillippe#	Pittsburgh Pirates v. Boston Red Sox	1903	22
	=Hal Newhouser	Detroit Tigers v. Chicago Cubs	1945	22
10	=Joe Wood	Boston Red Sox v. New York Giants	1912	21
	=Mickey Lolich	Detroit Tigers v. St. Louis Cardinals	1968	21

* Up to and including the 2008 World Series
# Pitcher played on the losing side

TOP 10 PITCHERS WITH THE MOST CAREER WINS*

	PLAYER	YEARS	WINS
1	Cy Young	1890–1911	511
2	Walter Johnson	1907–27	417
3	=Grover Alexander	1911–30	373
	=Christy Mathewson	1900–16	373
5	Pud Galvin	1879–92	364
6	Warren Spahn	1942–65	363
7	Kid Nichols	1890–1906	361
8	Greg Maddux	1986–2008	355
9	Roger Clemens	1984–2007	354
10	Tim Keefe	1880–93	342

* Up to and including the 2008 season

TOP 10 MOST WORLD SERIES WINS*

	TEAM	FIRST	WINS LAST	TOTAL
1	New York Yankees	1923	2000	26
2	St. Louis Cardinals	1926	2006	10
3	Oakland Athletics (5 titles as Philadelphia Athletics)	1910	1989	9
4	Boston Red Sox	1903	2007	7
5	Los Angeles Dodgers (1 title as Brooklyn Dodgers)	1955	1988	6
6	=Pittsburgh Pirates	1909	1979	5
	=Cincinatti Reds	1919	1990	5
	=San Francisco Giants (all titles as New York Giants)	1905	1954	5
9	Detroit Tigers	1935	1984	4
10	=Chicago White Sox	1906	2005	3
	=Atlanta Braves (1 title as Boston Braves, 1 as Milwaukee Braves	1914	1995	3
	=Minnesota Twins (1 title as Washington Senators)	1924	1991	3
	=Baltimore Orioles	1966	1983	3

* Up to and including the 2008 World Series

The Braves are the only team to win the World Series with three different franchises.

TOP 10 MOST APPEARANCES IN MAJOR LEAGUE BASEBALL*

	PLAYER	TEAMS	YEARS	APPEARANCES
1	Pete Rose	Cincinnati Reds, Philadelphia Phillies, Montreal Expos	1962–86	3,562
2	Carl Yastrzemski	Boston Red Sox	1961–83	3,308
3	Hank Aaron	Milwaukee/Atlanta Braves, Milwaukee Brewers	1954–76	3,298
4	Rickey Henderson	Oakland Athletics, New York Yankees, Toronto Blue Jays, Anaheim Angels, San Diego Padres, New York Mets, Seattle Mariners, Boston Red Sox, Los Angeles Dodgers	1979–2003	3,081
5	Ty Cobb	Detroit Tigers, Philadelphia Athletics	1905–28	3,035
6	=Stan Musial	St. Louis Cardinals	1941–63	3,026
	=Eddie Murray	Baltimore Orioles, New York Mets, Los Angeles Dodgers, Cleveland Indians, Anaheim Angels	1977–97	3,026
8	Cal Ripken	Baltimore Orioles	1981–2001	3,001
9	Willie Mays	New York/San Francisco Giants, New York Mets	1951–73	2,992
10	Barry Bonds	Pittsburgh Pirates, San Francisco Giants	1986–2007	2,986

* Regular season only, up to and including 2008

Ball Games

TOP 10 **MOST ALL-IRELAND GAELIC FOOTBALL TITLES***

	TEAM	WINS		
		FIRST	LAST	TOTAL
1	Kerry	1903	2007	35
2	Dublin	1891	1995	22
3	Galway	1925	2001	9
4	Meath	1949	1999	7
5	Cork	1890	1990	6
6	=Down	1960	1994	5
	=Cavan	1933	1952	5
	=Wexford	1893	1918	5
9	=Kildare	1905	1928	4
	=Tipperary	1889	1920	4

* All-Ireland Senior Football Championship 1887–2008

The senior final is played at Croke Park, Dublin, on either the third or fourth Sunday each September. The winners receive the Sam Maguire trophy.

Above: Hurling
Cork vs. Waterford in the 2007 Championship. Between them they have 32 hurling titles.

Right: Norm Duke
Norm Duke became the first professional bowler to win three consecutive major tournaments.

TOP 10 **MOST ALL-IRELAND HURLING TITLES***

	TEAM	TITLES		
		FIRST	LAST	TOTAL
1	Kilkenny	1904	2008	31
2	Cork	1890	2005	30
3	Tipperary	1887	2001	25
4	Limerick	1897	1973	7
5	=Dublin	1889	1938	6
	=Wexford	1910	1996	6
7	=Galway	1923	1988	4
	=Offaly	1981	1998	4
9	Clare	1914	1997	3
10	Waterford	1948	1959	2

* The All-Ireland Senior Hurling Championship from 1887–2008

The senior final is played at Dublin's Croke Park on the first or second Sunday each September. The winning team receives the Liam McCarthy Cup.

TOP 10 **MOST PROFESSIONAL BOWLERS ASSOCIATION (PBA) TITLES**

	BOWLER* / TOTAL WINS#
1	Walter Ray Williams Jr 45
2	Earl Anthony 43
3	=Mark Roth 34
	=Pete Weber 34
5	Parker Bohn III 32
6	=Norm Duke 30
	=Dick Weber 30
8	Mike Aulby 29
9	Don Johnson 26
10	Brian Voss 24

* All bowlers from the USA
# As at January 1, 2009

TOP 10 **MOST WOMEN'S MAJOR FAST-PITCH SOFTBALL TITLES***

	TEAM / LOCATION	TITLES FIRST	LAST	TOTAL
1	Raybestos/Stratford Brakettes, Stratford, Connecticut	1958	2007	26
2	Orange Lionettes, California	1950	1970	9
3	Jax Maids, New Orleans, Louisiana	1942	1947	5
4	California Commotion, Woodland Hills, California	1996	1999	4
5	=Arizona Ramblers, Phoenix, Arizona	1940	1949	3
	=Redding Rebels, California	1993	1995	3
7	=National Screw & Manufacturing, Cleveland, Ohio	1936	1937	2
	=J. J. Krieg's, Alameda, California	1938	1939	2
	=Hi-Ho Brakettes, Stratford, Connecticut	1985	1988	2
	=Phoenix Storm, Phoenix, Arizona	2000	2001	2
	=Southern California Hurricanes, Lake Forest, California	2005	2008	2

* Amateur Softball Association of America (ASA) titles 1933–2008

TOP 10 **MOST WORLD SNOOKER RANKING EVENT TITLES***

	PLAYER / COUNTRY	TITLES FIRST	LAST	TOTAL
1	Stephen Hendry, Scotland	1987	2005	36
2	Steve Davis, England	1981	1995	28
3	Ronnie O'Sullivan, England	1993	2008	21
4	John Higgins, Scotland	1994	2008	19
5	Mark Williams, Wales	1996	2006	16
6	Jimmy White, England	1986	2004	10
7	John Parrott, England	1989	1996	9
8	Peter Ebdon, England	1993	2006	7
9	Ken Doherty, Ireland	1993	2006	6
10	Ray Reardon, Wales	1974	1982	5

* As at January 1, 2009

The World Professional Billiards and Snooker Association (WPBSA) introduced its ranking system in 1976, but positions were based solely on performances in the World Championship. Following the 1982 World Championship, two more events—the Jameson International and Professional Players Tournament—were designated as ranking tournaments. In the 2008–09 season, eight tournaments were classed as ranking events.

Ronnie O'Sullivan
Ronnie O'Sullivan capturing his third World Professional title against Ali Carter in 2008. On the way to the final, both men compiled maximum 147 breaks.

Basketball

TOP 10 **MOST POINTS IN AN NBA CAREER**

PLAYER	YEARS	POINTS
1 Kareem Abdul-Jabbar	1969–89	38,387
2 Karl Malone	1985–2004	36,928
3 Michael Jordan	1984–2003	32,292
4 Wilt Chamberlain	1959–73	31,419
5 Moses Malone	1976–95	27,409
6 Elvin Hayes	1968–84	27,313
7 Hakeem Olajuwon	1984–2002	26,946
8 Oscar Robertson	1960–74	26,710
9 Dominique Wilkins	1982–99	26,668
10 John Havlicek	1962–78	26,395

Source: NBA

If figures from the American Basketball Association (ABA), which existed from 1967–76, were included then Julius Erving (30,026 points) and Dan Issel (27,482 points) would be added to the list; the total for Moses Malone would also increase to 29,580 points.

TOP 10 **MOST CAREER POINTS IN NBA PLAYOFF GAMES**

PLAYER	YEARS	POINTS
1 Michael Jordan	1985–98	5,987
2 Kareem Abdul-Jabbar	1970–89	5,762
3 Shaquille O'Neal	1994–2008	5,121
4 Karl Malone	1986–2004	4,761
5 Jerry West	1961–74	4,457
6 Larry Bird	1980–92	3,897
7 John Havlicek	1963–77	3,776
8 Hakeem Olajuwon	1985–2002	3,755
9 Magic Johnson	1980–96	3,701
10 Kobe Bryant	1997–2008	3,686

Source: NBA

If his ABA (American Basketball Association) career playoff points were also included, Julius Erving would be on the list at No. 5 with 4,580 points.

TOP 10 **MOST POINTS IN A SINGLE NBA GAME***

PLAYER / TEAM	OPPONENTS	DATE	POINTS
1 Wilt Chamberlain, Philadelphia Warriors	New York Knicks	Mar 2, 1962	100
2 Kobe Bryant, Los Angeles Lakers	Toronto Raptors	Jan 22, 2006	81
3 Wilt Chamberlain, Philadelphia Warriors	Los Angeles Lakers	Dec 8, 1961#	78
4 =Wilt Chamberlain, Philadelphia Warriors	Chicago Packers	Jan 13, 1962	73
=Wilt Chamberlain, San Francisco Warriors	New York Knicks	Nov 16, 1962	73
=David Thompson, Denver Nuggets	Detroit Pistons	Apr 9, 1978	73
7 Wilt Chamberlain, San Francisco Warriors	Los Angeles Lakers	Nov 3, 1962	72
8 =Elgin Baylor, Los Angeles Lakers	New York Knicks	Nov 15, 1960	71
=David Robinson, San Antonio Spurs	Los Angeles Clippers	Apr 24, 1994	71
10 Wilt Chamberlain, San Francisco Warriors	Syracuse Nationals	Mar 10, 1963	70

* As at the end of the 2007–08 season
# Including three periods of overtime

The Birth of Basketball

The Aztecs' game of ollamalitzli, and similar ball and hoop games among other South American peoples, may have influenced the modern game of basketball, which was invented in December 1891 by Canadian physical education teacher Dr. James A. Naismith at the International YMCA College at Springfield, Massachusetts. He set out to devise a game that could be played indoors during the winter. Peach baskets were originally used (players had to climb a ladder to retrieve the ball, until someone hit on the idea of removing the bottom!), but these were soon replaced by metal rings with netting.

TOP 10 **MOST THREE-POINT FIELD GOALS MADE IN AN NBA CAREER***

	PLAYER	YEARS	3-POINTERS MADE
1	Reggie Miller	1987–2005	2,560
2	Ray Allen	1996–2008	2,100
3	Dale Ellis	1983–2000	1,719
4	Glen Rice	1988–2004	1,559
5	Eddie Jones	1994–2008	1,546
6	Tim Hardaway	1989–2003	1,542
7	Nick Van Exel	1993–2006	1,528
8	Peja Stojakovic	1998–2008	1,426
9	Antoine Walker	1996–2008	1,386
10	Dan Majerle	1988–2002	1,360

* As at end of 2007–08 regular season

The three-point field goal had been tried many times since first tested in 1933, but it was not officially adopted by the NBA until the 1979–80 season.

THE 10 **MOST APPEARANCES IN THE NBA CHAMPIONSHIP FINALS***

	TEAM	TITLES	FINALS
1	Los Angeles Lakers/Minneapolis Lakers	15	29
2	Boston Celtics	16	20
3	Philadelphia 76ers/Syracuse Nationals	3	9
4	New York Knicks	2	8
5	Detroit Pistons	3	7
6	= Chicago Bulls	6	6
	= Philadelphia Warriors/Golden State Warriors San Francisco Warriors	3	6
8	= Baltimore Bullets/Washington Bullets	1	4
	= Houston Rockets	2	4
	= San Antonio Spurs	4	4
	= St Louis Hawks	1	4

* Up to and including the 2008 Championship

Miller thriller
Reggie Miller's 18-year career with the Indiana Pacers saw him achieve a total of 25,279 points, including 2,560 three-pointers and 4,141 assists. He was in the gold-medal winning US basketball team at the 1996 Olympics.

Combat Sports

TOP 10 OLYMPIC SHOOTING COUNTRIES*

COUNTRY# / MEDALS GOLD/SILVER/BRONZE/TOTAL

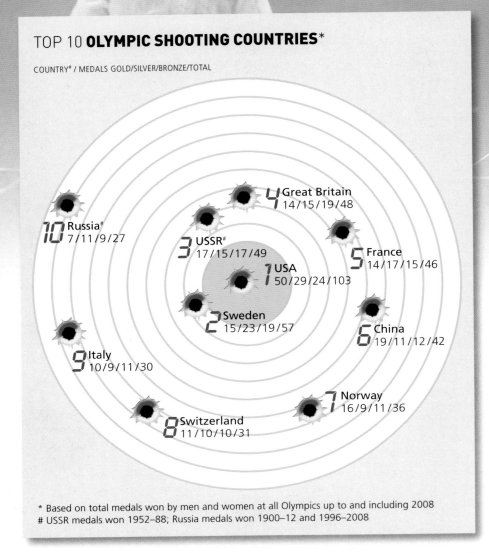

10 Russia# 7/11/9/27

4 Great Britain 14/15/19/48

3 USSR# 17/15/17/49

5 France 14/17/15/46

1 USA 50/29/24/103

2 Sweden 15/23/19/57

6 China 19/11/12/42

9 Italy 10/9/11/30

7 Norway 16/9/11/36

8 Switzerland 11/10/10/31

* Based on total medals won by men and women at all Olympics up to and including 2008
# USSR medals won 1952–88; Russia medals won 1900–12 and 1996–2008

TOP 10 OLYMPIC FENCING COUNTRIES*

	COUNTRY#	MEDALS			
		GOLD	SILVER	BRONZE	TOTAL
1	France	44	41	35	120
2	Italy	45	39	32	116
3	Hungary	34	22	27	83
4	USSR	18	15	16	49
5	USA	3	9	14	26
6	Germany	7	8	8	23
7	Poland	4	9	9	22
8 =	Russia	9	2	5	16
=	West Germany	7	8	1	16
10	Romania	3	4	7	14

* Based on total medals won by men and women at all Olympics up to and including 2008
# USSR medals won 1952–88; Russia medals won 1900–1912 and 1996–2008; Germany medals won 1896–1952 and 1992–2008; West Germany medals won 1968–88

TOP 10 OLYMPIC JUDO COUNTRIES*

	COUNTRY#	MEDALS			
		GOLD	SILVER	BRONZE	TOTAL
1	Japan	35	15	15	65
2 =	France	10	8	19	37
=	South Korea	9	14	14	37
4	Cuba	5	11	16	32
5	USSR	5	5	13	23
6	The Netherlands	4	2	14	20
7	China	8	2	8	18
8	Great Britain	0	7	9	16
9	Brazil	2	3	10	15
10	Germany	3	0	10	13

* Based on total medals won by men and women at all Olympics up to and including 2008
# USSR medals won 1964–88; Germany medals won 1992–2008

Martial arts masters
Satoshi Ishii, one of Japan's judo gold medallists at Beijing 2008. The first of Japan's judo gold medallists was Takehide Nakatani in 1964.

THE 10 **LAST UNDISPUTED WORLD HEAVYWEIGHT BOXING CHAMPIONS**

	BOXER*	REIGN FROM	REIGN ENDED
1	Mike Tyson	Aug 1, 1987	May 6, 1989
2	Leon Spinks	Feb 15, 1978	Mar 18, 1978#
3	Muhammad Ali	Oct 30, 1974	Feb 15, 1978
4	George Foreman	Jan 22, 1973	Oct 30, 1974
5	Joe Frazier	Feb 16, 1970	Jan 22, 1973
6	Muhammad Ali	Feb 6, 1967	Apr 29, 1967†
7	Cassius Clay (later Muhammad Ali)	Feb 25, 1964	Jun 29, 1964§
8	Sonny Liston	Sep 22, 1962	Feb 25, 1964
9	Floyd Patterson	Jun 20, 1960	Sep 25, 1962
10	Ingemar Johansson (Sweden)	Jun 26, 1959	Jun 20, 1960

* As at January 1, 2009; all from the USA unless otherwise stated
# Spinks was stripped of his title by the WBC for refusing to fight the No. 1 contender, Ken Norton
† Ali was stripped of his title by the WBA and then WBC for failing to be drafted into the US Army
§ The WBA withdrew recognition of Ali after his refusal to participate in a re-match with Sonny Liston

Mike Tyson held the WBC, WBA, and IBF titles from August 1, 1987 to February 11, 1990, and was generally acknowledged as the universal champion, despite the fact that a new body, the IBO, came into being in 1988 and had its first heavyweight champion (Francesco Damiani of Italy) in May 1989.

TOP 10 **LONGEST REIGNS AS WWE (WORLD WRESTLING ENTERTAINMENT) WORLD HEAVYWEIGHT CHAMPION***

	WRESTLER	REIGN FROM	REIGN ENDED	DAYS
1	Batista	Apr 3, 2005	Jan 10, 2006	282
2	Triple H	Dec 15, 2002	Sep 21, 2003	280
3	Chris Benoit	Mar 14, 2004	Aug 15, 2004	154
4 =	King Booker	Jul 23, 2006	Nov 16, 2006	126
=	Batista	Nov 26, 2006	Apr 1, 2007	126
6	Rey Mysterio	Apr 2, 2006	Jul 23, 2006	112
7	Edge	Dec 16, 2007	Mar 30, 2008	105
8 =	Triple H	Dec 14, 2003	Mar 4, 2004	91
=	Batista	Sep 16, 2007	Dec 16, 2007	91
10	Triple H	Sep 12, 2004	Dec 6, 2004	85

* As at January 1, 2009

Paul Michael Levesque, better known as Triple H (formerly Hunter Hearst Helmsley), has held the title for a record 616 days over a total of five reigns. The World Heavyweight Championship on the Raw brand of the WWE was launched in 2002, with Triple H winning the first title.

Have an Edge
Edge knocked down Chris Benoit at Wrestlemania 21 before getting hold of the Money in the Bank briefcase to win the match.

On Two Wheels

A close-run thing
The 23 seconds that separated winner Contador (left) and Evans (right) in the 2007 Tour de France was the closest of the twenty-first century.

THE 10 CLOSEST TOURS DE FRANCE*

	WINNER / COUNTRY	RUNNER-UP / COUNTRY	YEAR	WINNING MARGIN MIN	SEC
1	Greg LeMond, USA	Laurent Fignon, France	1989	0	8
2	Alberto Contador, Spain	Cadel Evans, Australia	2007	0	23
3	Oscar Pereiro, Spain	Andreas Klöden, Germany	2006	0	32
4	Jan Janssen, Netherlands	Herman Van Springel, Belgium	1968	0	38
5	Tony Roche, Ireland	Pedro Delgado, Spain	1987	0	40
6	Bernard Thévenet, France	Hennie Kuiper, Netherlands	1977	0	48
7	Jacques Anquetil, France	Raymond Poulidor, France	1964	0	55
8	Carlos Sastre, Spain	Cadel Evans, Australia	2008	0	58
9	Lance Armstrong, USA	Jan Ullrich, Germany	2003	1	1
10	Lucien Almar, France	Jan Janssen, Netherlands	1966	1	7

* Based on difference between the winner's time and that of the runner-up; up to and including the 2008 race

TOP 10 COUNTRIES WITH THE MOST WINNERS OF THE UCI WORLD ROAD RACE CHAMPIONSHIPS

	COUNTRY	MEN	WOMEN	TOTAL*
1	Belgium	25	6	31
2	Italy	19	2	21
3	France	8	9	17
4	Netherlands	7	7	14
5 =	Great Britain	1	4	5
=	Spain	5	0	5
=	Switzerland	3	2	5
=	USA	3	2	5
9	West Germany	2	2	4
10 =	Germany	1	2	3
=	Lithuania	0	3	3
=	Soviet Union	0	3	3

* Up to and including 2008

TOP 10 MOTORCYCLE MANUFACTURERS WITH THE MOST WORLD TITLES*

	MANUFACTURER / COUNTRY	MOTOGP	500CC	350CC	250CC	125CC	80CC	50CC	TOTAL
1	Honda, Japan	4	13	6	19	15	0	2	59
2	MV Agusta, Italy	0	16	9	5	7	0	0	37
3	Yamaha, Japan	2	9	5	14	4	0	0	34
4	Aprilia, Italy	0	0	0	8	8	0	0	16
5	Suzuki, Japan	0	7	0	0	3	0	5	15
6	Kawasaki, Japan	0	0	4	4	1	0	0	9
7 =	Derbi, Spain	0	0	0	0	3	3	2	8
=	Kreidler, Germany	0	0	0	0	0	0	8	8
9	Moto Guzzi, Italy	0	0	4	3	0	0	0	7
10	Gilera, Italy	0	5	1	0	0	0	0	6

* Solo classes only up to and including 2008

TOP 10 COUNTRIES PROVIDING THE MOST WORLD MOTORCYCLE CHAMPIONS*

	COUNTRY	500CC/ MOTOGP	350CC	250CC	125CC	50/80CC	TOTAL
1	Italy	19	8	21	23	2	73
2	UK	17	13	9	4	1	44
3	Spain	1	0	6	12	12	31
4	USA	15	0	2	0	0	17
5	West Germany	0	2	7	2	4	15
6	Australia	7	1	1	3	0	12
7 =	Rhodesia	1	5	2	0	0	8
=	Switzerland	0	0	0	4	4	8
9	Japan	0	1	2	4	0	7
10 =	France	0	0	3	2	0	5
=	South Africa	0	3	2	0	0	5

* Solo classes only up to and including 2008

Marco makes a mark
Marco Simoncelli's victory in the 2008 World 250cc Championship further increased his and Italy's commanding lead in the league table.

TOP 10 RIDERS WITH THE MOST MOTOGP RACE WINS*

	RIDER / COUNTRY / YEARS	WINS
1	Valentino Rossi, Italy, 2000–08	71
2	Giacomo Agostini, Italy, 1965–76	68
3	Mick Doohan, Australia, 1990–98	54
4	Mike Hailwood, UK, 1961–67	37
5	Eddie Lawson, USA, 1984–92	31
6	Kevin Schwantz, USA, 1988–94	25
7	Wayne Rainey, USA, 1988–93	24
8 =	Geoff Duke, UK, 1950–59	22
=	John Surtees, UK, 1956–60	22
=	Kenny Roberts, USA, 1978–83	22

* 500cc 1949–2001; MotoGP 2002–08

Hockey

THE 10 PLAYERS WINNING THE MOST ART ROSS TROPHIES*

	PLAYER	TEAM(S)	YEARS WON	WINS
1	Wayne Gretzky	Edmonton Oilers Los Angeles Kings	1981–87 1990–91, 1994	10
2 =	Gordie Howe	Detroit Red Wings	1951–54, 1957, 1963	6
=	Mario Lemieux	Pittsburgh Penguins	1988–89, 1992–93, 1996–97	6
4 =	Phil Esposito	Boston Bruins	1969, 1971–74	5
=	Jaromir Jagr	Pittsburgh Penguins	1995, 1998–2001	5
6	Stan Mikita	Chicago Black Hawks	1964–65, 1967–68	4
7 =	Bobby Hull	Chicago Black Hawks	1960, 1962, 1966	3
=	Guy Lafleur	Montreal Canadiens	1976–78	3
9 =	Bernie Geoffrion	Montreal Canadiens	1955, 1961	2
=	Dickie Moore	Montreal Canadiens	1958–59	2
=	Bobby Orr	Boston Bruins	1970, 1975	2

* To the end of the 2007–08 season

The Art Ross Trophy is awarded to the top points-scorer in the NHL each season, and was first won by Elmer Lach of Montreal Canadiens who scored 61 points in the 1947–48 season.
The trophy is named after Art Ross, the former general manager and head coach of the Boston Bruins, who presented the trophy to the NHL.

TOP 10 NHL TEAMS*

	TEAM	YEARS PLAYED	GAMES PLAYED	WINS
1	Montreal Canadiens	1918–2008	5,792	2,980
2	Boston Bruins	1925–2008	5,632	2,669
3	Toronto Maple Leafs Toronto St Patricks Toronto Arenas	1918–2008	5,792	2,535
4	Detroit Red Wings Detroit Cougars Detroit Falcons	1927–2008	5,566	2,521
5	New York Rangers	1927–2008	5,566	2,359
6	Chicago Blackhawks Chicago Black Hawks	1927–2008	5,566	2,273
7	Philadelphia Flyers	1968–2008	3,178	1,577
8	Buffalo Sabres	1971–2008	2,952	1,401
9	St. Louis Blues	1968–2008	3,178	1,376
10	Dallas Stars Minnesota North Stars	1968–2008	3,178	1,353

* Based on most regular season wins in the NHL to the end of the 2007–08 season; previous franchises in italics

As well as topping this list, Montreal Canadiens have the best win percentage (0.591). The fewest wins by any current team is 206 from 574 games by Columbus Blue Jackets.

TOP 10 POINTS-SCORERS IN STANLEY CUP PLAYOFF MATCHES*

	PLAYER	YEARS	PLAYED	POINTS
1	Wayne Gretzky	1980–97	208	382
2	Mark Messier	1980–97	236	295
3	Jari Kurri	1981–98	200	233
4	Glenn Anderson	1981–96	225	214
5	Paul Coffey	1981–99	194	196
6	Brett Hull	1986–2004	202	190
7 =	Joe Sakic	1993–2008	172	188
=	Doug Gilmour	1984–2002	182	188
9	Steve Yzerman	1984–2006	196	185
10	Bryan Trottier	1976–94	221	184

* To the end of the 2007–08 playoffs

TOP 10 GOALTENDERS IN AN NHL CAREER*

	PLAYER	YEARS	GAMES	WINS
1	Patrick Roy	1984–2003	1,029	551
2	Martin Brodeur	1991–2008	968	538
3	Ed Belfour	1988–2007	963	484
4	Curtis Joseph	1989–2008	922	449
5	Terry Sawchuk	1949–70	971	447
6	Jacques Plante	1952–73	837	437
7	Tony Esposito	1968–84	886	423
8	Glenn Hall	1952–71	906	407
9	Grant Fuhr	1981–2000	868	403
10	Dominik Hasek	1990–2008	735	389

* Based on career wins, as at the end of the 2007–08 season

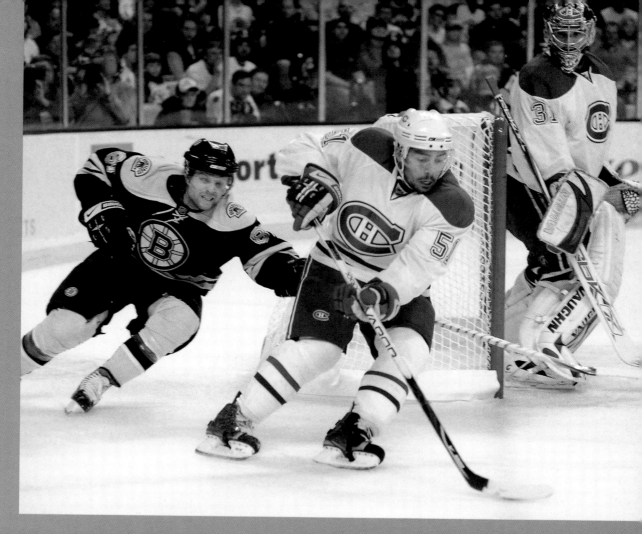

Canadiens vs. Bruins
The top two teams fight it out in 2008. The Canadiens still have a significant lead in the table totals.

TOP 10 **POINTS-SCORERS IN AN NHL CAREER***

	PLAYER	YEARS	GAMES	POINTS
1	Wayne Gretzky	1970–99	1,487	2,857
2	Mark Messier	1979–2004	1,756	1,887
3	Gordie Howe	1946–80	1,767	1,850
4	Ron Francis	1981–2004	1,731	1,798
5	Marcel Dionne	1971–89	1,348	1,771
6	Steve Yzerman	1983–2006	1,514	1,755
7	Mario Lemieux	1984–2006	915	1,723
8	Joe Sakic	1988–2008	1,363	1,629
9	Jaromir Jagr	1990-2008	1,273	1,599
10	Phil Esposito	1963–81	1,282	1,590

* Regular season; as at end of the 2007-08 season

Gordie Howe became the first player to achieve 1,000 points when he scored for Detroit in their 2–0 win over Toronto on November 27, 1960. When Wayne Gretzky achieved the same feat on December 19, 1984, he became the 18th to pass the milestone, and remains the only player to exceed 2,000 points.

TOP 10 **MOST STANLEY CUP WINS***

	TEAM	FIRST WIN	LAST WIN	TOTAL WINS
1	Montreal Canadiens	1916	1993	24
2	Toronto Maple Leafs	1918	1967	13
3	Detroit Red Wings	1936	2008	11
4	= Boston Bruins	1929	1972	5
	= Edmonton Oilers	1984	1990	5
6	= Ottawa Senators	1920	1927	4
	= New York Rangers	1928	1994	4
	= New York Islanders	1980	1983	4
9	= Chicago Blackhawks	1934	1961	3
	= New Jersey Devils	1995	2003	3

* Since the abolition of the challenge match format in 1915, up to and including the 2008 Stanley Cup

Source: NHL

Golf

TOP 10 MOST MEN'S MAJORS IN A CAREER*

	GOLFER	YEARS	US MASTERS	US OPEN	BRITISH OPEN	US PGA	TOTAL
(1)	Jack Nicklaus	1962–86	6	4	3	5	18
(2)	Tiger Woods	1997–2008	4	3	3	4	14
(3)	Walter Hagen	1914–29	0	2	4	5	11
(4)	=Ben Hogan	1946–53	2	4	1	2	9
	=Gary Player, South Africa	1959–78	3	1	3	2	9
(6)	Tom Watson	1975–83	2	1	5	0	8
(7)	=Harry Vardon, England	1896–1914	0	1	6	0	7
	=Gene Sarazen	1922–35	1	2	1	3	7
	=Bobby Jones	1923–30	0	4	3	0	7
	=Sam Snead	1942–54	3	0	1	3	7
	=Arnold Palmer	1958–64	4	1	2	0	7

* Professional Majors only, up to and including 2008; all golfers from the USA unless otherwise stated

In 1930, Bobby Jones achieved an unprecedented Grand Slam when he won the US and British Open titles, as well as the Amateur titles of both countries. Nicklaus, Woods, Hogan, Player, and Sarazen are the only golfers to have won all four Majors at least once.

Tiger Woods
Despite being in pain, Tiger Woods won the 2008 US Open. Shortly afterward he had surgery on his troubled knee, which kept him out of the game for eight months.

TOP 10 MOST CAREER WINS ON THE US LPGA TOUR*

	GOLFER	YEARS	WINS
(1)	Kathy Whitworth	1962–85	88
(2)	Mickey Wright	1956–73	82
(3)	Annika Sörenstam	1995–2008	72
(4)	Patty Berg	1937–62	60
(5)	Louise Suggs	1946–62	58
(6)	Betsy Rawls	1951–72	55
(7)	Nancy Lopez	1978–97	48
(8)	JoAnne Carner	1969–85	43
(9)	Sandra Haynie	1962–82	42
(10)	Babe Zaharias	1940–55	41

* Up to and including the 2008 season; all golfers from the USA except Sörenstam (Sweden)

TOP 10 MOST CAREER WINS ON THE US PGA TOUR*

	GOLFER	YEARS	WINS
(1)	Sam Snead	1936–65	82
(2)	Jack Nicklaus	1962–86	73
(3)	Tiger Woods	1996–2008	65
(4)	Ben Hogan	1938–59	64
(5)	Arnold Palmer	1955–73	62
(6)	Byron Nelson	1935–51	52
(7)	Billy Casper	1956–75	51
(8)	Walter Hagen	1916–36	44
(9)	Cary Middlecoff	1945–61	40
(10)	=Gene Sarazen	1922–41	39
	=Tom Watson	1974–98	39

* Up to and including 2008; all golfers from the USA

Nick Faldo
After playing in 46 Ryder Cup matches, Nick Faldo eventually received the honor of captaining the European team in 2008.

TOP 10 MOST WOMEN'S MAJORS IN A CAREER*

	GOLFER	YEARS	A	B	C	D	E	F	G	TOTAL
1	Patty Berg	1937–58	–	–	1	–	–	7	7	15
2	Mickey Wright	1958–66	–	4	4	–	–	2	3	13
3	= Babe Zaharias	1940–54	–	–	3	–	–	3	4	10
	= Louise Suggs	1946–59	–	1	1	–	–	4	4	10
	= Annika Sörenstam, Sweden	1995–2006	3	3	3	1	–	–	–	10
6	Betsy Rawls	1951–69	–	2	4	–	–	–	2	8
7	= Juli Inkster	1984–2002	2	2	2	–	1	–	–	7
	= Karrie Webb, Australia	1999–2006	2	1	2	1	1	–	–	7
9	= Kathy Whitworth	1965–75	–	3	–	–	–	2	1	6
	= Pat Bradley	1980–86	1	1	1	–	3	–	–	6
	= Patty Sheehan	1983–96	1	3	2	–	–	–	–	6
	= Betsy King	1987–97	3	1	2	–	–	–	–	6

* As recognized by the Ladies Professional Golf Association (LPGA) up to and including 2008; all from the USA unless otherwise stated
A Kraft Nabisco Championship (previously Nabisco Dinah Shore, Nabisco Championship) 1983–2008
B LPGA Championship 1955–2008
C US Women's Open 1946–2008
D Women's British Open 2001–08
E du Maurier Classic 1979–2000
F Titleholders Championship 1937–42, 1946–66, 1972
G Western Open 1930–67

Karrie Webb
Australia's Karrie Webb, the last back-to-back winner of the US Women's Open, in 2000 and 2001.

TOP 10 MOST MATCHES IN THE RYDER CUP*

	GOLFER / COUNTRY	TEAM(S)	YEARS	MATCHES
1	Nick Faldo, England	GB & I/Europe	1977–97	46
2	Bernhard Langer, Germany	Europe	1981–2002	42
3	Neil Coles, England	GB/GB & I	1961–77	40
4	= Billy Casper, USA	USA	1961–75	37
	= Seve Ballesteros, Spain	Europe	1979–95	37
6	= Christy O'Connor, Snr., Ireland	GB/GB & I	1955–73	36
	= Colin Montgomerie, Scotland	Europe	1991–2006	36
8	Tony Jacklin, England	GB/GB & I/E	1967–79	35
9	Lanny Wadkins, USA	USA	1977–93	34
10	Arnold Palmer, USA	USA	1961–73	32

* Up to and including 2008

Great Britain (GB): 1921 to 1971; Great Britain & Ireland (GB & I): 1973 to 1977; Europe (E): 1979 to 2008

Horse Sports

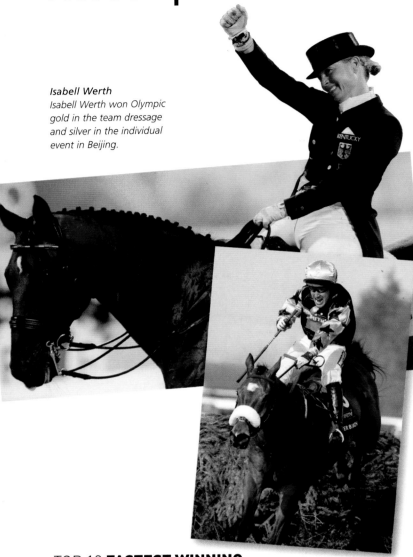

Isabell Werth
Isabell Werth won Olympic gold in the team dressage and silver in the individual event in Beijing.

TOP 10 OLYMPIC EQUESTRIAN MEDALLISTS*

	RIDER / COUNTRY	YEARS	GOLD	SILVER	BRONZE	TOTAL
1	Reiner Klimke, West Germany	1964–88	7	0	2	9
2 =	Isabell Werth, Germany	1992–2008	5	3	0	8
=	Anky van Grunsven, Netherlands	1992–2008	3	5	0	8
4	Hans-Günther Winkler, West Germany	1956–76	5	1	1	7
5 =	Piero d'Inzeo, Italy	1956–72	0	2	4	6
=	Raimondo d'Inzeo, Italy	1956–72	1	2	3	6
=	Josef Neckermann, West Germany	1960–72	2	2	2	6
=	Michael Plumb, USA	1964–84	2	4	0	6
9 =	Earl Thomson, USA	1932–48	2	3	0	5
=	André Jousseaumé, France	1932–52	2	2	1	5
=	Henri Chammartin, Switzerland	1952–68	1	2	2	5
=	Gustav Fischer, Switzerland	1952–68	0	3	2	5
=	Liselott Linsenhoff, West Germany	1956–72	2	2	1	5
=	Christine Stückelberger, Switzerland	1976–88	1	3	1	5
=	Mark Todd, New Zealand	1984–2000	2	1	2	5

* Up to and including the 2008 Beijing Olympics

The Olympic equestrian events are divided into three separate disciplines: Dressage, Three-Day Eventing and Show Jumping. Both men and women compete together and medals are awarded separately for individual and team performances in each of the three disciplines.

TOP 10 FASTEST WINNING TIMES OF THE KENTUCKY DERBY*

HORSE / YEAR / TIME (MINS:SECS)

10 **Funny Cide**
2003
2:01.19

9 **War Emblem**
2002
2:01.13

8 **Fusaichi Pegasus**
2000
2:01.00

7 **Grindstone**
1996
2:01.00

6 **Proud Clarion**
1967
2:00.60

* Up to and including 2008
The times of the substitute races held at Gatwick in the years 1916–18 are not included.

TOP 10 **JOCKEYS IN THE BREEDERS' CUP**

	JOCKEY	YEARS	WINS*
1	Jerry Bailey	1991–2005	15
2	Pat Day	1984–2001	12
3	Mike Smith	1992–2008	12
4	Chris McCarron	1985–2001	9
5	= Gary Stevens	1990–2000	8
	= Frankie Dettori	1994–2008	8
	= Garrett Gomez	2005–08	8
8	= Eddie Delahoussaye	1984–93	7
	= Laffit Pincay Jr.	1985–93	7
	= Jose Santos	1986–2002	7
	= Pat Valenzuela	1986–2003	7
	= Corey Nakatani	1996–2006	7
	= John Velazquez	1998–2006	7

* Up to and including 2008

Source: The Breeders' Cup

The 14 Breeders' Cup races in 2008 were worth $25.5 million in prize money, with the Breeders' Cup Classic offering $5 million.

Frankie Dettori takes the lead
Frankie Dettori rode the 2008 Breeders' Cup Classic winner and is the most successful European jockey in the Breeders' Cup.

TOP 10 **MOST TIMES HEADING THE ANNUAL MONEY-LEADING JOCKEYS TABLE IN THE USA**

	JOCKEY	FIRST	TITLES LAST	TOTAL
1	Bill Shoemaker	1951	1964	10
2	Laffit Pincay Jr.	1970	1985	7
3	= Eddie Arcaro	1940	1955	6
	= Jerry Bailey	1995	2003	6
5	Braulio Baeza	1965	1975	5
6	= Chris McCarron	1980	1991	4
	= Jose Santos	1986	1989	4
8	= Angel Cordero Jr.	1976	1983	3
	= Earl Sande	1921	1927	3
	= Garrett Gomez	2006	2008	3

5 Decidedly
1962
2:00.40

4 Spend A Buck
1985
2:00.20

3 Northern Dancer
1964
2:00.00

2 Monarchos
2001
1:59.97

1 Secretariat
1973
1:59.40

Motor Sport

TOP 10 **FASTEST WINNING SPEEDS OF THE INDIANAPOLIS 500***

	DRIVER	CAR	YEAR	SPEED MPH	SPEED KM/H
1	Arie Luyendyk, Netherlands	Lola-Chevrolet	1990	185.981	299.307
2	Rick Mears	Chevrolet-Lumina	1991	176.457	283.980
3	Bobby Rahal	March-Cosworth	1986	170.722	274.750
4	Juan Montoya, Colombia	G Force-Aurora	2000	167.607	269.730
5	Emerson Fittipaldi, Brazil	Penske-Chevrolet	1989	167.581	269.695
6	Helio Castroneves, Brazil	Dallara-Chevrolet	2002	166.499	267.954
7	Rick Mears	March-Cosworth	1984	163.612	263.308
8	Mark Donohue	McLaren-Offenhauser	1972	162.962	262.619
9	Al Unser	March-Cosworth	1987	162.175	260.995
10	Tom Sneva	March-Cosworth	1983	162.117	260.902

* Up to and including the 2008 race; all drivers from USA unless otherwise stated

TOP 10 **MOST NASCAR SPRINT CUP SERIES RACE WINS***

	DRIVER	WINS FIRST	WINS LAST	TOTAL
1	Richard Petty	1960	1984	200
2	David Pearson	1961	1980	105
3	= Bobby Allison	1966	1988	84
	= Darrell Waltrip	1975	1992	84
5	Cale Yarborough	1965	1985	83
6	Jeff Gordon#	1994	2007	81
7	Dale Earnhardt	1979	2000	76
8	Rusty Wallace	1986	2004	55
9	Lee Petty	1949	1961	54
10	= Ned Jarrett	1955	1965	50
	= Junior Johnson	1955	1965	50

* Up to and including 2008
# Active in 2008

THE 10 **NEWEST GRANDS PRIX TO BE ADDED TO THE FORMULA ONE CALENDAR**

	RACE	FIRST HELD
1	Singapore GP*	Sep 28, 2008
2	Turkish GP*	Aug 21, 2005
3	Chinese GP*	Sep 26, 2004
4	Bahrain GP*	Apr 4, 2004
5	Malaysian GP*	Oct 17, 1999
6	Luxembourg GP	Sep 28, 1997
7	Pacific GP	Apr 17, 1994
8	Hungarian GP*	Aug 10, 1986
9	Australian GP*	Nov 3, 1985
10	European GP*	Sep 25, 1983

* Still part of Formula One schedule in 2009

The Luxembourg Grand Prix was discontinued in 1998 and the Pacific Grand Prix in 1995.

Below: Jeff Gordon
Jeff Gordon (No. 24) in action in his DuPont Chevrolet during the 2008 NASCAR Sprint Cup Series. He ended the season finishing seventh in the Series and amassing winnings of $4,650,649.

TOP 10 **MOST RACE WINS BY A DRIVER IN A FORMULA ONE CAREER***

	DRIVER / COUNTRY	YEARS	WINS
1	Michael Schumacher, Germany	1992–2006	91
2	Alain Prost, France	1981–93	51
3	Ayrton Senna, Brazil	1985–93	41
4	Nigel Mansell, UK	1985–94	31
5	Jackie Stewart, UK	1965–73	27
6	= Jim Clark, UK	1962–68	25
	= Niki Lauda, Austria	1974–85	25
8	Juan-Manuel Fangio, Argentina	1950–57	24
9	Nelson Piquet, Brazil	1980–91	23
10	Damon Hill, UK	1993–98	22

* Up to and including the 2008 season

TOP 10 **MOST FORMULA ONE GRAND PRIX RACE WINS BY A DRIVER IN A SEASON***

	DRIVER / COUNTRY	SEASON	WINS
1	Michael Schumacher, Germany	2004	13
2	Michael Schumacher	2002	11
3	= Nigel Mansell, UK	1992	9
	= Michael Schumacher	1995	9
	= Michael Schumacher	2000	9
	= Michael Schumacher	2001	9
7	= Ayrton Senna, Brazil	1988	8
	= Michael Schumacher	1994	8
	= Damon Hill, UK	1996	8
	= Mika Häkkinen, Finland	1998	8

* To the end of the 2008 season

Top: Singapore circuit
Spaniard Fernando Alonso won the first Formula One Singapore Grand Prix in September 2008.

Above: Michael Schumacher
Michael Schumacher winning the 2006 European GP, one of seven wins in his final season.

Football

TOP 10 MOST POINTS IN A SEASON*

PLAYER / TEAM	SEASON	TD	PAT	FG	POINTS
1 LaDainian Tomlinson, San Diego Chargers	2006	31	0	0	186
2 Paul Hornung, Green Bay Packers	1960	15	41	15	176
3 Shaun Alexander, Seattle Seahawks	2005	28	0	0	168
4 Gary Anderson, Minnesota Vikings	1998	0	59	35	164
5 Jeff Wilkins, St. Louis Rams	2003	0	46	39	163
6 Priest Holmes, Kansas City Chiefs	2003	27	0	0	162
7 Mark Moseley, Washington Redskins	1983	0	62	33	161
8 Marshall Faulk, St. Louis Rams	2000	26	4	0	160
9 Mike Vanderjagt, Indianapolis Colts	2003	0	46	37	157
10 Gino Cappelletti, Boston Patriots	1964	7	38	25	155

* To end of 2008 regular season

TD=Touchdown (6 pts), PAT=Point After Touchdown (1 pt), FG=Field Goal (3 pts)

TOP 10 BIGGEST WINNING MARGINS IN THE SUPER BOWL*

	WINNERS	RUNNERS-UP	YEAR	SCORE	MARGIN
1	San Francisco 49ers	Denver Broncos	1990	55–10	45
2	Chicago Bears	New England Patriots	1986	46–10	36
3	Dallas Cowboys	Buffalo Bills	1993	52–17	35
4	Washington Redskins	Denver Broncos	1988	42–10	32
5	Los Angeles Raiders	Washington Redskins	1984	38–9	29
6	= Baltimore Ravens	New York Giants	2001	34-7	27
	= Tampa Bay Buccaneers	Oakland Raiders	2003	48–21	27
8	Green Bay Packers	Kansas City Chiefs	1967	35–10	25
9	San Francisco 49ers	San Diego Chargers	1995	49-26	23
10	San Francisco 49ers	Miami Dolphins	1985	38–16	22

* Up to and including Super Bowl XLIII (2009)

New York giant
John Carney of the New York Giants – one of the highest points-scoring footballers in an NFL career.

TOP 10 **MOST TOUCHDOWNS IN A CAREER***

	PLAYER / YEARS	TOUCHDOWNS
1	Jerry Rice, 1984–2004	207
2	Emmitt Smith, 1990–2004	175
3	Marcus Allen, 1982–97	144
4 =	Terrell Owens, 1996–2008	141
=	LaDainian Tomlinson, 2001–08	141
6 =	Marshall Faulk, 1994–2006	136
=	Randy Moss, 1998–2008	135
8	Cris Carter, 1987–2002	130
9	Marvin Harrison, 1996–2008	128
10	Jim Brown, 1957–65	126

* To end of 2008 regular season

Wide receiver
Terrell Owens of the Dallas Cowboys runs a touchdown pass reception past Leon Hall of the Cincinnati Bengals, October 2008.

TOP 10 **MOST TOUCHDOWNS IN A SEASON**

	PLAYER / TEAM	SEASON	TOUCHDOWNS
1	LaDainian Tomlinson, San Diego Chargers	2006	31
2	Shaun Alexander, Seattle Seahawks	2005	28
3	Priest Holmes, Kansas City Chiefs	2003	27
4	Marshall Faulk, St. Louis Rams	2000	26
5	Emmitt Smith, Dallas Cowboys	1995	25
6 =	John Riggins, Washington Redskins	1983	24
=	Priest Holmes, Kansas City Chiefs	2002	24
8 =	O.J. Simpson, Buffalo Bills	1975	23
=	Jerry Rice, San Francisco 49ers	1987	23
=	Terrell Davis, Denver Broncos	1998	23
=	Randy Moss, New England Patriots	2007	23

* To end of 2008 regular season

TOP 10 **MOST POINTS IN AN NFL CAREER***

	PLAYER	YEARS	POINTS
1	Morten Andersen	1982–2007	2,544
2	Gary Anderson	1982–2004	2,434
3	George Blanda	1949-75	2,002
4	John Carney	1988–2008	1,955
5	Matt Stover	1991–2008	1,944
6	Jason Elam	1993–2008	1,915
7	Jason Hanson	1992–2008	1,747
8	Norm Johnson	1982–99	1,736
9	Nick Lowery	1980–96	1,711
10	Jan Stenerud	1967–85	1,699

* To end of 2008 regular season

As well as topping this list, LaDainian Tomlinson set a new NFL record for the most points in a season in 2006 when his tally of 186 beat the old record of 176 set by Paul Hornung (Green Bay Packers) in 1960.

Lawn Tennis

TOP 10 MOST WINS IN THE MASTERS SERIES*

	PLAYER / COUNTRY	YEARS	WINS
①	Andre Agassi, USA	1990–2004	17
②	Roger Federer, Switzerland	2002–07	14
③	Rafael Nadal, Spain	2005–08	12
④	Pete Sampras, USA	1992–2000	11
⑤	Thomas Muster, Austria	1990–97	8
⑥	Michael Chang, USA	1990–97	7
⑦	=Boris Becker, Germany	1990–96	5
	=Jim Courier, USA	1991–93	5
	=Gustavo Kuerten, Brazil	1999–2001	5
	=Marcelo Rios, Chile	1997–99	5
	=Marat Safin, Russia	2000–04	5

* As at the end of the 2008 Masters Series

The Association of Tennis Professionals (ATP) Masters Series was launched in 1990, its nine (eight in 2009) tournaments regarded as the most prestigious after the four Grand Slam events. In 2009, the series became known as the Masters 1000, because the winner of each tournament will receive 1000 ranking points.

TOP 10 MOST WEEKS SPENT AT THE TOP OF THE ATP RANKINGS*

	PLAYER / COUNTRY	FIRST YEAR AT NO. 1	LAST YEAR AT NO. 1	WEEKS
①	Pete Sampras, USA	1993	1999	286
②	Ivan Lendl, Czechoslovakia	1983	1990	270
③	Jimmy Connors, USA	1974	1983	268
④	Roger Federer, Switzerland	2004	2008	237
⑤	John McEnroe, USA	1980	1985	170
⑥	Björn Borg, Sweden	1977	1981	109
⑦	Andre Agassi, USA	1995	2003	101
⑧	Lleyton Hewitt, Australia	2001	2003	80
⑨	Stefan Edberg, Sweden	1990	1992	72
⑩	Jim Courier, USA	1992	1993	58

* As at January 1, 2009

Source: ATP (Association of Tennis Professionals)

Federer's total were consecutive weeks and is the record for the most consecutive weeks at No. 1, beating the previous 160 of Jimmy Connors.

Mallorcan master
Rafael Nadal is one of two players from Mallorca to top the ATP rankings—Carlos Moya is the other.

TOP 10 **MOST CAREER TITLES (WOMEN)***

	PLAYER / COUNTRY	YEARS	TITLES
(1)	Martina Navratilova, Czechoslovakia/USA	1974–94	167
(2)	Chris Evert, USA	1971–88	154
(3)	Steffi Graf, Germany	1986–99	107
(4)	Margaret Court (née Smith), Australia	1968–76	92
(5)	Evonne Cawley (née Goolagong), Australia	1970–80	68
(6)	Billie Jean King, USA	1968–83	67
(7)	= Lindsay Davenport, USA	1993–2008	55
	= Virginia Wade, UK	1968–78	55
(9)	Monica Seles, Yugoslavia/USA	1989–2002	53
(10)	Martina Hingis, Switzerland	1996–2007	43

* In the Open era 1968–2008 as recognized by the WTA (women);
as at January 1, 2009

TOP 10 **MOST CAREER TITLES (MEN)***

	PLAYER / COUNTRY	YEARS	TITLES
(1)	Jimmy Connors, USA	1972–89	109
(2)	Ivan Lendl, Czechoslovakia/USA	1980–93	94
(3)	John McEnroe, USA	1978–91	77
(4)	Pete Sampras, USA	1990–2002	64
(5)	Björn Borg, Sweden	1974–81	63
(6)	Guillermo Vilas, Argentina	1973–83	62
(7)	Andre Agassi, USA	1987–2005	60
(8)	= Ilie Nastase, Romania	1969–78	57
	= Roger Federer, Switzerland	2001–08	57
(10)	Boris Becker, Germany	1985–96	49

* In the Open era 1968-2008 as recognized by the ATP (men);
as at January 1, 2009

TOP 10 **MOST WEEKS SPENT AT THE TOP OF THE WTA RANKINGS**

	PLAYER / COUNTRY	YEARS AT NO. 1		WEEKS
		FIRST	LAST	
(1)	Steffi Graf, Germany	1987	1997	377
(2)	Martina Navratilova, Czechoslovakia/USA	1978	1987	331
(3)	Chris Evert, USA	1975	1985	260
(4)	Martina Hingis, Switzerland	1997	2001	209
(5)	Monica Seles, Yugoslavia/USA	1991	1996	178
(6)	Justine Henin, Belgium	2003	2008	117
(7)	Lindsay Davenport, USA	1998	2006	98
(8)	Serena Williams, USA	2002	2008	61
(9)	Amélie Mauresmo, France	2004	2006	39
(10)	Tracy Austin, USA	1980 (Apr)	1980 (Nov)	22

* As at January 1, 2009

Source: WTA (Women's Tennis Association)

The most consecutive weeks at No. 1 is 186 by Steffi Graf between August 1987 and March 1991.

Justine Henin
Justine Henin first claimed the No. 1 spot in October 2003, displacing her fellow Belgian Kim Clijsters.

Titanic Victory

Swiss-born Richard Norris Williams (1891–1968) is the only survivor of the *Titanic* disaster to win an Olympic gold medal, as part of the US mixed doubles in Paris in 1924. Williams also won five US titles and one Wimbledon title.

Water Sports

TOP 10 OLDEST CURRENT SWIMMING WORLD RECORDS*

	EVENT	SWIMMER / COUNTRY	TIME MINS:SECS	DATE SET
1	Women's 100 m Butterfly	Inge de Bruijn, Netherlands	56.61	Sep 17, 2000
2	Men's 1500 m Freestyle	Grant Hackett, Australia	14:34.56	Jul 29, 2001
3	Men's 400 m Freestyle	Ian Thorpe, Australia	3:40.08	Jul 30, 2002
4	Men's 50 m Breaststroke	Oleg Lisogor, Ukraine	27.18	Aug 2, 2002
5	Men's 50 m Backstroke	Thomas Rupprath, Germany	24.80	Jul 27, 2003
6	Men's 50 m Butterfly	Roland Schoeman, South Africa	22.96	Jul 25, 2005
7	Men's 800 m Freestyle	Grant Hackett, Australia	7:38.65	Jul 27, 2005
8	Men's 100 m Butterfly	Ian Crocker, USA	50.40	Jul 30, 2005
9	Women's 50 m Breaststroke	Jade Edmistone, Australia	30.31	Jan 30, 2006
10	Women's 100 m Breaststroke	Leisel Jones, Australia	1:05.09	Mar 20, 2006

* Long course swimming, as at January 1, 2009

TOP 10 MEDAL-WINNING SWIMMING COUNTRIES AT THE COMMONWEALTH GAMES*

	COUNTRY	GOLD	MEDALS SILVER	BRONZE	TOTAL
1	Australia	225	151	132	508
2	Canada	94	113	105	312
3	England	77	101	108	286
4	New Zealand	10	24	29	63
5	South Africa	14	23	15	52
6	Scotland	13	17	18	48
7	Wales	3	6	7	16
8	Jamaica	0	1	2	3
9	Malaysia	0	1	1	2
10 =	British Guiana	0	1	0	1
=	Papua New Guinea	1	0	0	1
=	Zimbabwe	1	0	0	1

* 1930–2006

Phelps' Records

Seven of Michael Phelps' record eight gold medals at the 2008 Beijing Olympics were set in new world record times. The eighth, the 100 metres butterfly, established a new Olympic record.

Swimming to victory
The United States is the leading nation in Olympic swimming events with 489 medals— 321 more than second-placed Australia.

TOP 10 **MEDAL-WINNING NATIONS IN AQUATIC EVENTS*** **AT THE 2008 BEIJING OLYMPICS**

	COUNTRY	GOLD	MEDALS SILVER	BRONZE	TOTAL
1	USA	12	11	10	33
2	Australia	7	7	9	23
3	China	8	4	6	18
4	Russia	3	4	4	11
5	= France	1	2	3	6
	= Japan	2	0	4	6
	= UK	2	2	2	6
8	Germany	2	1	2	5
9	= Hungary	1	3	0	4
	= Zimbabwe	1	3	0	4

* Swimming, synchronized swimming, diving and water polo

All but two of the USA's 33 medals were won in swimming events. The other two were both silver medals, and both in the water polo competition. Hungary beat the US 14–10 in the men's final and Netherlands won 9–8 in the women's final.

Alinghi
When Alinghi won the America's Cup for Switzerland in 2003, it was the first time a landlocked country had won the trophy.

THE 10 **LATEST WINNERS OF THE AMERICA'S CUP**

YEAR	VENUE	WINNER / COUNTRY	SKIPPER(S)
2007	Valencia, Spain	**Alinghi**, Switzerland	Brad Butterworth
2003	Auckland, New Zealand	**Alinghi**, Switzerland	Russell Coutts
2000	Auckland, New Zealand	**Team New Zealand,** New Zealand	Russell Coutts/ Dan Barker
1995	San Diego, USA	**Black Magic**, New Zealand	Russell Coutts
1992	San Diego, USA	**America3**, USA	Bill Koch/Buddy Melges
1988	San Diego, USA	**Stars & Stripes**, USA	Dennis Conner
1987	Fremantle, Australia	**Stars & Stripes**, USA	Dennis Conner
1983	Newport, USA	**Australia II**, Australia	John Bertrand
1980	Newport, USA	**Freedom**, USA	Dennis Conner
1977	Newport, USA	**Courageous**, USA	Ted Turner

There is uncertainty as to when the next America's Cup will be held. A court case in July 2008 ruled that it could take place sometime in 2009, but legal disputes have continued with no indication as to when they would be resolved.

Winter Sports

Canadian gold
Hayley Wickenheiser of Canada challenges Nanna Jansson of Sweden for the puck at the 2006 Turin Olympic Winter Games.

TOP 10 HOCKEY COUNTRIES AT THE OLYMPIC GAMES*

	COUNTRY	MEDALS GOLD	SILVER	BRONZE	TOTAL
1	Canada	9	5	2	16
2	USA	3	8	2	13
3	Sweden	2	3	5	10
4	USSR#	7	1	1	9
5	Czechoslovakia†	0	4	4	8
6	Finland	0	2	3	5
7 =	Czech Republic†	1	0	1	2
=	Great Britain	1	0	1	2
=	Russia#	0	1	1	2
=	Switzerland	0	0	2	2

* Up to and including the 2006 Turin Olympics
\# Competed as the USSR 1956–88; Russia 1994–2006
† Competed as Czechoslovakia 1920–92; Czech Republic 1996–2006

Hockey was first contested at the Summer Olympics in 1920 and has featured at the Winter Olympics since 1924 for men and since 1998 for women.

TOP 10 FIS NORDIC COMBINED WORLD CUP TITLES*

	SKIER / COUNTRY	YEARS	TITLES
1	Hannu Manninen, Finland	2004–07	4
2 =	Kenji Ogiwara, Japan	1993–95	3
=	Ronny Ackermann, Germany	2002–03, 2008	3
4 =	Klaus Sulzenbacher, Austria	1988, 1990	2
=	Samppa Lajunen, Finland	1997, 2000	2
=	Bjarte Engen Vik, Norway	1998–99	2
7 =	Tom Sandberg, Norway	1984	1
=	Geir Andersen, Norway	1985	1
=	Hermann Weinbuch, West Germany	1986	1
=	Torbjørn Løkken, Norway	1987	1
=	Trond-Arne Bredesen, Norway	1989	1
=	Fred Børre Lundberg, Norway	1991	1
=	Fabrice Guy, France	1992	1
=	Knut Tore Apeland, Norway	1996	1
=	Felix Gottwald, Austria	2001	1

* As at the end of the 2008–09 season

The FIS Nordic Combined World Cup was first held in the 1983–84 season, when it was won by Tom Sandberg of Norway.

TOP 10 MEDAL-WINNING COUNTRIES AT THE WINTER OLYMPICS*

	COUNTRY	MEDALS GOLD	SILVER	BRONZE	TOTAL
1	Norway	98	98	84	280
2	USA	78	80	58	216
3	USSR#	78	57	59	194
4	Austria	51	64	70	185
5	Germany†	60	59	41	160
6	Finland	41	57	52	150
7	Canada	38	38	43	119
8	Sweden	43	31	44	118
9	Switzerland	37	37	43	117
10	East Germany	39	36	35	110

* Up to and including the 2006 Turin Games, including medals won at figure skating and ice hockey included in the Summer Olympics prior to the inauguration of the Winter Games in 1924
\# 1956–88
† 1928–32, 1952, and 1992–2006

TOP 10 MOST OVERALL ALPINE SKIING WORLD CUP TITLES (WOMEN)

	SKIER / COUNTRY	YEARS	TITLES
1	Annemarie Moser-Pröll, Austria	1971–75, 1979	6
2	= Vreni Schneider, Switzerland	1989, 1994–95	3
	= Petra Kronberger, Austria	1990–92	3
	= Janica Kostelic, Croatia	2001, 2003, 2006	3
5	= Nancy Greene, Canada	1967–68	2
	= Hanni Wenzel, Liechtenstein	1978, 1980	2
	= Erika Hess, Switzerland	1982, 1984	2
	= Michela Figini, Switzerland	1985, 1988	2
	= Maria Walliser, Switzerland	1986–87	2
	= Katja Seizinger, Germany	1996, 1998	2
	= Anja Pärson, Sweden	2004–05	2
	= Lindsey Vonn, USA	2008–09	2

* As at the end of the 2008–09 season

TOP 10 MOST OVERALL ALPINE SKIING WORLD CUP TITLES (MEN)

	SKIER / COUNTRY	YEARS	TITLES
1	Marc Girardelli, Luxembourg	1985–86, 1989, 1991, 1993	5
2	= Gustav Thöni, Italy	1971–73, 1975	4
	= Pirmin Zurbriggen, Switzerland	1984, 1987–88, 1990	4
	= Hermann Maier, Austria	1998, 2000–01, 2004	4
5	= Ingemar Stenmark, Sweden	1976–78	3
	= Phil Mahre, USA	1981–83	3
7	= Jean-Claude Killy, France	1967–68	2
	= Karl Schranz, Austria	1969–70	2
	= Lasse Kjus, Norway	1996, 1999	2
	= Stephan Eberharter, Austria	2002–03	2
	= Bode Miller, USA	2006, 2008	2
	= Aksel Lund Svindal, Norway	2007–09	2

* As at the end of the 2008–09 season

Alpine racer
In addition to his World Cup titles, Austrian champion Hermann Maier has won Olympic golds in the Super G and Giant slalom events, and three World Championship golds.

Extreme Sports

TOP 10 **GOLD MEDALLISTS AT THE SUMMER X GAMES**

	ATHLETE* / COUNTRY	SPORT	YEARS	GOLDS
1	Dave Mirra, USA	BMX	1996–2005	13
2	Tony Hawk, USA	Skateboarding	1995–2003	9
3	=Andy Macdonald, USA	Skateboarding	1996–2002	8
	=Travis Pastrana, USA	Moto X/Rally car racing	1999–2008	8
5	Fabiola da Silva*, Brazil	In-line skating	1996–2007	7
6	Bucky Lasek, USA	Skateboarding	1999–2006	6
7	=Biker Sherlock, USA	Street luge	1996–98	5
	=Bob Burnquist, Brazil	Skateboarding	2001–08	5
9	=Jamie Bestwick, England	BMX	2000–07	4
	=Ryan Nyquist, USA	BMX	2000–03	4
	=Pierre-Luc Gagnon, Canada	Skateboarding	2002-08	4
	=Dallas Friday*, USA	Water sports	2001–05	4
	=Danny Harf, USA	Water sports	2001–05	4
	=Elissa Steamer*, USA	Skateboarding	2004-08	4

* Female competitors; all others male

The first ESPN Extreme Games (now X Games) for "alternative" sports were held in June–July 1995. The Games are held every year and since 1997 there has also been an annual Winter X Games. The current Summer X sports are: Freestyle BMX, MotoX (stunt motorcycling), Skateboarding, and Rallying. Andy Macdonald holds the record with 15 X Games medals.

Pastrama (left)
All-round performer Travis Pastrana was also the 2000 AMA 125 cc National Motocross champion.

Pudzianowski (below)
Shortly after winning his record fifth Strongest Man title in 2008, Mariusz Pudzianowski announced his retirement.

THE 10 **LATEST WINNERS OF THE WORLD'S STRONGEST MAN CONTEST**

YEAR	STRONGMAN / COUNTRY
2008	Mariusz Pudzianowski, Poland
2007	Mariusz Pudzianowski, Poland
2006	Phil Pfister, USA
2005	Mariusz Pudzianowski, Poland
2004	Vasyl Virastyuk, Ukraine
2003	Mariusz Pudzianowski, Poland
2002	Mariusz Pudzianowski, Poland
2001	Svend Karlsen, Norway
2000	Janne Virtanen, Finland
1999	Jouko Ahola, Finland

The World's Strongest Man title has been contested since 1977. After the 2008 contest, staged in Charleston, West Virginia, USA, five-time winner Mariusz Pudzianowski announced his retirement.

Chivas vs. Ghurkas
Chivas Regal (in yellow), four-time winners of the World Championship, in
action against the Ghurkas in the 26th annual competition—which they won.

TOP 10 **MOST ELEPHANT POLO WORLD TITLES**

	TEAM / COUNTRY	FIRST	WINS LAST	TOTAL
1	**Tiger Tops Tuskers**, Nepal	1983	2003	8
2	**National Parks**, Nepal	1986	1999	6
3	**Chivas Regal**, Scotland	2001	2005	4
4	=**James Manclark Team**, Scotland	1982	1982	1
	=**Oberoi**, India	1989	1989	1
	=**Grindlays Maharajahs**, Nepal	1990	1990	1
	=**J&B Rare**, International Team	1993	1993	1
	=**International Distillers**, Philippines	1995	1995	1
	=**Tiger Mountain**, India	1997	1997	1
	=**Angus Estates**, Scotland	2006	2006	1
	=**Chopard**, Hong Kong/China	2007	2007	1
	=**Air Tusker**, England	2008	2008	1

The first Elephant Polo World Championship was in 1982. The
Championship is now held at Meghauly near the Chitwan National
Park in Nepal each year.

TOP 10 **FASTEST WINNING TIMES FOR THE HAWAII IRONMAN**

	WINNER / COUNTRY	YEAR	TIME HRS:MINS:SECS
1	**Luc Van Lierde**, Belgium	1996	8:04:08
2	**Mark Allen**, USA	1993	8:07:45
3	**Mark Allen**	1992	8:09:08
4	**Mark Allen**	1989	8:09:15
5	**Norman Stadler**, Germany	2006	8:11:56
6	**Faris Al-Sultan**, Germany	2005	8:14:17
7	**Chris McCormack**, Australia	2007	8:15:34
8	**Luc Van Lierde**	1999	8:17:17
9	**Chris Alexander**, Australia	2008	8:17:45
10	**Mark Allen**	1991	8:18:32

Considered one of the most grueling of all sporting contests,
competitors engage in a 2.4-mile (3.86-km) swim, a 112-mile
(180-km) cycle race, and full marathon (26 miles 385 yards/
42.195 km). The first Hawaii Ironman was held at Waikiki Beach
in 1978, but since 1981 the event's home has been at Kailua-Kona.

Leisure Pursuits

TOP 10 **COUNTRIES SPENDING THE MOST ON VIDEO GAMES**

COUNTRY / SPEND PER CAPITA, 2008 ($)

1 UK	**2** Australia	**3** France	**4** Sweden	**5** USA
67.00	61.10	50.40	42.90	41.60

6 Netherlands	**7** Spain	**8** Canada	**9** Belgium	**10** Germany
34.00	30.70	30.30	26.30	18.40

World average *3.90*   Source: Euromonitor International

Interactive
Wii Music designer Shigeru Miyamoto demonstrates his creation. Over 50 million Nintendo Wii consoles have been sold.

TOP 10 **LEISURE ACTIVITIES IN THE USA**

	ACTIVITY	NO.*
1	Dining out	107,4563,000
2	Entertaining friends or relatives at home	90,197,000
3	Reading books	86,715,000
4	Barbecuing	77,941,000
5	Going to the beach	52,463,000
6	Playing cards	50,325,000
7	Baking	47,647,000
8	Cooking for fun	44,912,000
9	PC/computer games	44,287,000
10	Going to bars/ night clubs	40,762,000

* Participated during previous 12 months, from sample interviewed in 2007

Source: *Statistical Abstract of the United States 2009*/Mediamark Research, Inc.

TOP 10 **COUNTRIES SPENDING THE MOST ON TOYS AND GAMES**

COUNTRY / SPEND PER CAPITA, 2008 ($)

UK	Australia	USA	France	Netherlands	Sweden
184.90	177.80	151.40	147.30	130.70	120.60

Belgium	Canada	Spain	Italy
113.70	105.80	93.40	85.70

World average *15.20*

Source: Euromonitor International

TOP 10 MEDALS AT THE FLYING DISC WORLD CHAMPIONSHIPS*

	THROWER / COUNTRY	MALE/ FEMALE	GOLD	SILVER	BRONZE	TOTAL
1	Harvey Brandt, USA	M	1	5	1	7
2 =	Amy Bekken, USA	F	3	0	1	4
=	Christian Sandström, Sweden	M	3	0	1	4
=	Sune Wentzel, Norway	M	3	1	0	4
5	Conrad Damon, USA	M	0	2	1	3
6 =	Tomas Burvall, Sweden	M	1	0	1	2
=	Amanda Carreiro, USA	F	2	0	0	2
=	Jennifer Griffin, USA	F	1	1	0	2
=	Mary Jorgenson, USA	F	0	2	0	2
=	Yukari Komatsu, Japan	F	1	1	0	2
=	Rick LeBeau, USA	M	0	1	1	2
=	Regina Olnils, Sweden	F	1	1	0	2
=	Snapper Pierson, USA	M	2	0	0	2
=	Judy Robbins, USA	F	1	0	1	2
=	Yumiko Tauchi, Japan	F	0	1	1	2

* In the overall competition, men and women, up to and including 2008.

TOP 10 PARTICIPATION ACTIVITIES IN THE USA

	ACTIVITY	NO. PARTICIPATING*
1	Exercise walking	89,800,000
2	Exercising with equipment	52,800,000
3	Swimming	52,300,000
4	Camping (vacation/overnight)	47,500,000
5	Bowling	43,500,000
6	Bicycle riding	37,400,000
7	Fishing	35,300,000
8	Workout at a club	33,800,000
9	Weightlifting	33,200,000
10	Boating (motor/power)	31,900,000

* Seven years of age and older, participated more than once during 2007

Source: National Sporting Goods Association

THE 10 LATEST WINNERS OF THE SPORTS ILLUSTRATED SPORTSMAN/SPORTSWOMAN OF THE YEAR AWARD

YEAR	WINNER	SPORT
2008	Michael Phelps	Swimming
2007	Brett Favre	Football
2006	Dwyane Wade	Football
2005	Tom Brady	Football
2004	Boston Red Sox	Baseball
2003	Tim Duncan and David Robinson	Basketball
2002	Lance Armstrong	Cycling
2001	Curt Schilling and Randy Johnson	Baseball
2000	Tiger Woods	Golf
1999	US Women's World Cup Squad	Soccer

Further Information

THE UNIVERSE & THE EARTH

Astronautics
www.astronautix.com
Spaceflight news and reference

Caves
www.caverbob.com
Lists of long and deep caves

Disasters
www.emdat.be
Emergency Events Database covering major
disasters since 1900

Islands
islands.unep.ch
Information on the world's islands

Mountains
peaklist.org
Lists of the world's tallest mountains

NASA
www.nasa.gov
The main website for the US space program

Oceans
www.oceansatlas.org
The UN's resource on oceanographic issues

Planets
www.nineplanets.org
A multimedia tour of the Solar System

Rivers
www.rev.net/~aloe/river
The River Systems of the World website

Space exploration
www.spacefacts.de
Manned spaceflight data

LIFE ON EARTH

American Forests
www.americanforests.org
A website covering all aspects of forests and
trees in the USA

Animals
animaldiversity.ummz.umich.edu
A wealth of animal data

Birds
www.bsc-eoc.org/avibase
A database on the world's birds

Conservation
iucn.org
The leading nature conservation site

Endangered
www.cites.org
Lists of endangered species of flora and fauna

Environment
www.unep.ch
Links to the UN's Earthwatch and other
programs

Fish
www.fishbase.org
Global information on fish

Food and Agriculture Organization
www.fao.org
Statistics from the UN's FAO website

Insects
ufbir.ifas.ufl.edu
The University of Florida Book of Insect Records

Sharks
www.flmnh.ufl.edu/fish/sharks
The Florida Museum of Natural History's shark
data files

THE HUMAN WORLD

Death penalty
www.deathpenaltyinfo.org
Facts and statistics from the Death Penalty
Information Center

Bureau of Justice
ojp.usdoj.gov/bjs
US Crime statistics

FBI
www.fbi.gov
Information and links on crime in the USA

Health
www.cdc.gov/nchs
Information and links on health for US citizens

Leaders
www.terra.es/personal2/monolith/00index.htm
Facts about world leaders since 1945

Names
www.ssa.gov/OACT/babynames
Most common names since 1879 from the
Social Security Administration

Prisons
www.bop.gov
Public information on the US prison system

Religions
www.worldchristiandatabase.org
World religion data

Rulers
rulers.org
A database of the world's rulers and political
leaders

US Presidents
www.whitehouse.gov/history/presidents
Biographies, facts, and figures from the White
House

TOWN & COUNTRY

Bridges and tunnels
en.structurae.de
Facts and figures on the world's buildings,
tunnels, and other structures

Buildings
www.emporis.com/en
The Emporis database of buildings

Countries
www.theodora.com/wfb
Country data, rankings, etc.

Country and city populations
www.citypopulation.de
A searchable guide to the world's countries
and major cities

Country data
www.cia.gov/library/publications/the-world-
factbook
The CIA World Factbook

Country populations
www.un.org/esa/population/unpop
The UN's worldwide data on population issues

Development
www.worldbank.org
Global development and other statistics

Population
www.census.gov/ipc/www
International population statistics

Skyscrapers
skyscraperpage.com
Data and images of the world's skyscrapers

Tunnels
home.no.net/lotsberg
A database of the longest rail, road, and canal
tunnels

CULTURE & LEARNING

Books
www.publishersweekly.com
Publishers Weekly, the trade journal of
American publishers

Education
nces.ed.gov
The home of federal education data

Languages of the world
www.ethnologue.com
Online reference work on the world's 6,912
living languages

Libraries
www.ala.org
US library information and book awards from
the American Library Association

The Library of Congress
www.loc.gov
The gateway to one of the world's greatest
collections of words and pictures

Newspapers
www.wan-press.org
The World Association of Newspapers' website

The New York Public Library
www.nypl.org
One of the country's foremost libraries

The Pulitzer Prizes
www.pulitzer.org
A searchable guide to the US literary prize

Translations
databases.unesco.org/xtrans/stat/xTransList.a
UNESCO's lists of the most translated books
and authors

UNESCO
portal.unesco.org
Comparative international statistics on
education and culture

MUSIC

All Music Guide
www.allmusic.com
A comprehensive guide to all genres of music

**American Society of Composers, Authors,
and Publishers**
www.ascap.com
ASCAP songwriter and other awards

Billboard
www.billboard.com
US music news and charts data

Classical music
classicalusa.com
An online guide to classical music in the USA

Country Music Hall of Fame
www.countrymusichalloffame.com
The history of and information about Country music

Grammy Awards
www.naras.org
The official site for the famous US music awards

MTV
www.mtv.com
The online site for the TV music channel

Recording Industry Association of America
www.riaa.org
Searchable data on gold and platinum disk award winners

Rock and Roll Hall of Fame
www.rockhall.com
The museum of the history of rock

Rolling Stone magazine
www.rollingstone.com
Features on popular music since 1967

ENTERTAINMENT

Academy Awards
www.oscars.org
The official "Oscars" website

Emmy Awards
www.emmyonline.org
Emmy TV awards from the National Television Academy site

Golden Globe Awards
www.goldenglobes.org
Hollywood Foreign Press Association's Golden Globes site

Hollywood
www.hollywood.com
A US movie theater site with details on all the new releases

Internet Movie Database
www.imdb.com
The best of the publicly accessible film websites; IMDbPro is available to subscribers

Internet Broadway Database
www.ibdb.com
Broadway theater information

Internet Theatre Database
www.theatredb.com
A Broadway-focused searchable stage site

Tony Awards
www.tonyawards.com
Official website of the American Theatre Wing's Tonys

Variety
www.variety.com
Extensive entertainment information (extra features available to subscribers)

Yahoo! Movies
movies.yahoo.com
Charts plus features and links to the latest movie releases

THE COMMERCIAL WORLD

The Economist
www.economist.com
Global economic and political news

Energy
www.eia.doe.gov
Official US energy statistics

Mail
www.upu.int
World mail statistics from the Universal Postal Union

Organization for Economic Co-operation and Development
www.oecd.org
World economic and social statistics

Rich lists
www.forbes.com
Forbes magazine's celebrated lists of the world's wealthiest people

Telecommunications
www.itu.int
Worldwide telecommunications statistics

Travel industry
www.tia.org
Stats on travel to and within the USA

The World Bank
www.worldbank.org
World development, trade, and labor statistics

World Tourism Organization
www.world-tourism.org
The world's principal travel and tourism organization

United Nations Development Program
www.undp.org
Country GDPs and other development data

ON THE MOVE

Air disasters
www.airdisaster.com
Reports on aviation disasters

Airports
www.airports.org
Airports Council International statistics on the world's airports

Air safety
aviation-safety.net
Data on air safety and accidents

Air speed records
www.fai.org/records
The website of the official air speed record governing body

Aviation
www.aerofiles.com
Information on a century of American aviation

Car manufacture
www.oica.net
The International Organization of Motor Vehicle Manufacturers' website

Ports
www.aapa-ports.org
US and world port stats from the American Association of Port Authorities

Rail
www.uic.org
World rail statistics

Railroads
www.railwaygazette.com
The world's railway business in depth from *Railway Gazette International*

Shipwrecks
www.shipwreckregistry.com
A huge database of the world's wrecked and lost ships

SPORT & LEISURE

Baseball
mlb.mlb.com
The official website of Major League Baseball

Basketball
www.nba.com
The official website of the NBA

Cycling
www.uci.ch
The Union Cycliste Internationale, the competitive cycling governing body

Football
www.nfl.com
The official website of the NFL

Golf
www.pgatour.com
The Professional Golfers' Association (PGA) Tour

Hockey
www.nhl.com
The official website of the NHL

Olympics
www.olympic.org
The official website of the International Olympic Committee

Skiing
www.fis-ski.com
Fédèration Internationale de Ski, the world governing body of skiing and snowboarding

Sports Illustrated
sportsillustrated.cnn.com
Sports Illustrated's comprehensive coverage of all major sports

Tennis
www.iaaf.org
The world governing body of athletics

Index

Acknowledgments

Special research: Ian Morrison (sport); Dafydd Rees (music)

Academy of Motion Picture Arts and Sciences – Oscar statuette is the registered trademark and copyrighted property of the Academy of Motion Picture Arts and Sciences
African Elephant Status Report 2007 (IUCN)
Airports Council International
Alexa
American Association of Port Authorities
American Film Institute
American Forests
American Library Association
American Music Awards
American Society of Composers, Authors, and Publishers
Amnesty International
Arbitron, *American Radio Listening Trends, 2007*
Artnet
The Art Newspaper
Association of Tennis Professionals
Audit Bureau of Circulations Ltd
Avibase
Roland Bert
Billboard
BitTorrent
Peter Bond
Box Office Mojo
BP Statistical Review of World Energy 2008
Richard Braddish
Breeders' Cup
Thomas Brinkhoff
British Film Institute
British Library
British National Corpus
Carbon Dioxide Information Analysis Center
Central Intelligence Agency, *The World Factbook 2008*
Christie's
Classic FM
Classical Music magazine
Commonwealth War Graves Commission
Computer Industry Almanac
ComScore.com
Corruption Perceptions Index (Transparency International)
The Cremation Society of Great Britain
Death Penalty Information Center
DVD Release Report
Earth Impact Database, Planetary and Space Science Center, University of New Brunswick
EarthTrends
The Economist
Philip Eden
EM-DAT, CRED, University of Louvain
Emporis
Environmental Performance Index
Environmental Technology Center
Ethnologue
Euromonitor International
Federal Bureau of Investigation
Fédération Internationale de Motorcyclisme
Fédération Internationale de Ski
Film Database
Financial Times
Food and Agriculture Organization of the United Nations

Christopher Forbes
Forbes magazine
Formula One
Fortune
Freedom House
Global Education Digest 2008 (UNESCO)
Global Forest Resources Assessment 2005 (FAO)
Global Powers of Retailing 2009 (Deloitte)
Global Wind Energy Council
Russell E. Gough
Robert Grant
Bob Gulden
Human Development Report (United Nations)
Imperial War Museum, London
Index Translationum 1979–2008 (UNESCO)
Indianapolis Motor Speedway
Institute for Family Enterprise, Bryant College
International Air Transport Association
International Association of Athletics Federations
International Atomic Energy Agency
International Commission on Large Dams
International Federation of Audit Bureaux of Circulations
International Hydrographic Organization
The International Institute for Strategic Studies, *The Military Balance 2009*
International Labour Organization
International Obesity Task Force
International Olympic Committee
International Organization of Motor Vehicle Manufacturers
International Shark Attack File, Florida Museum of Natural History
International Telecommunication Union
International Union for Conservation of Nature and Natural Resources
Internet Movie Database
Internet Retailer
Internet World Stats
Inter-Parliamentary Union
Ladies Professional Golf Association
John Steven Lasher
Major League Baseball
Man Booker Prize
Marketingcharts.com
Chris Mead
Mediamark Research, Inc.
Ministry of Public Security (China)
Mininova
Music Information Database
National Academy of Recording Arts and Sciences (Grammy Awards)
National Aeronautics and Space Administration
National Amusement Park Historical Association
National Basketball Association
National Center for Education Statistics
National Football League
National Hockey League
National Sporting Goods Association
Natural History Museum, London
AC Nielsen
Nielsen Media Research
Nielsen SoundScan
Nobel Foundation
NSS GEO2 Committee on Long and

Deep Caves
Online Computer Library Center
Organisation for Economic Co-operation and Development
Organisation Internationale des Constructeurs d'Automobiles
Roberto Ortiz de Zarate
Popular Science
Population Reference Bureau
Professional Bowlers Association
Professional Golfers' Association
The Pulitzer Prizes
Railway Gazette International
Recording Industry Association of America
River Systems of the World
Rolling Stone magazine
Royal Aeronautical Society
Royal Astronomical Society
Screen Digest
Screen International
Robert Senior
Social Security Administration
Softball Association of America
Sotheby's
Sports Illustrated
Statistical Abstract of the United States
Statistics Denmark
Stockholm International Peace Research Institute
Stores
Torrentfreak.com
Transparency International
UIC Railisa Database
United Nations
United Nations Educational, Scientific and Cultural Organization
United Nations Environment Programme
United Nations Population Division
United Nations Statistics Division
Universal Postal Union
US Census Bureau
US Census Bureau International Data Base
US Department of Justice
US Department of Transportation
Lucy T. Verma
Ward's Motor Vehicle Facts & Figures 2008
Women's Tennis Association
World Association of Newspapers
World Atlas of Coral Reefs (UNEP)
World Bank
World Christian Database
World Conservation Monitoring Centre
World Development Indicators (World Bank)
World Health Organization
World Nuclear Association
World Population Data Sheet 2008 (Population Reference Bureau)
World Register of Large Dams
World Resources Institute
World Tennis Association
World Tourism Organization
The World's Mangroves 1980–2005 (FAO)
Jarosław Maciej Zawadzki, *1000 Najpopularniejszych Nazwisk w Polsce* (2002)

Picture Credits

Corbis: 4b, 141 Juan Medina/Reuters; 5tl, 62-63 Kevin Dodge; 5tr, 108b Chen Wei/EyePress/epa; 5b, 199 G. Bowater; 12t, 95tl Roger Ressmeyer; 13tl Gianni Dagli Orti; 13bl Michael Jenner; 25 Francesc Muntada; 26 Michel Gounot/Godong; 27t, 91l Fridmar Damm/zefa; 29tr Winfried Wisniewski/zefa; 29tr (inset) Tim Davis; 30-31 Kimimasa Mayama/Reuters; 36l Tim Davis; 36r Martin B. Withers/Frank Lane Picture Agency; 38br Patrick Bennett; 40-41b Paul Souders; 45t Joe McDonald; 46bl Esther Beaton; 49tl Steven Vidler/Eurasia Press; 49tr Mak Remissa/epa; 55 Stringer/India/Reuters; 56l, 73b, 110, 124b, 136t, 140l, 148tr, 203b Bettmann; 56r Jose Mendez/epa; 57b Dani Cardona/Reuters; 59t Finbarr O'Reilly/Reuters; 68 Noah K. Murray/Star Ledger; 71b Lucas Dolega/epa; 74b, 75b Corbis; 76bl Pool/Reuters; 76br Altaf Qadri/epa; 79br Badri Media/epa; 80-81 Christian Schmidt/zefa; 83tl Amit Bhargava; 83tr Gavin Hellier/Robert Harding World Imagery; 86b Valdrin Xhemaj/epa; 88tl Qin Huai/Xinhua Press; 88tr The Francis Frith Collection; 91r Bruno Domingos/Reuters; 93t Arctic-Images; 94tl PoodlesRock; 94tc Chip East/Reuters; 94tr Jim Zuckerman; 95tr Ludovic Maisant/Hemis; 96l Ramin Talaie; 97r OMA/epa; 98 Chan Shu Kai; 98-99 Michael S. Lewis; 99tl Richard Cummins; 100tr, 105t, 181b, 216 Reuters; 101b Philippe Caron/Sygma; 107t Pallava Bagla; 109b Jason Hawkes; 111, 192-193 Blaine Harrington III; 113t Anders Wiklund/epa; 117br, 193b Atlantide Phototravel; 119b Andy Rain/epa; 121, 128 Mario Anzuoni/Reuters; 122 Michael Ochs Archives; 123 Rune Hellestad; 124tl Kalaene Jens/dpa; 125tr Neal Preston; 129l Stephane Cardinale/People Avenue; 129r Karoly Arvai/Reuters; 130tr Tobias Hase/epa; 130b Tobias Hase/dpa; 131b Jacek Bednarczyk/epa; 132 Kieran Doherty/Reuters; 133t Rick Nederstigt/epa; 133b Chip Somodevilla/Pool; 135t David Farrell/Lebrecht Music & Arts; 136b Underwood & Underwood; 136-137, 139b Hulton-Deutsch Collection; 137b Royal Mail/Handout/Reuters; 138 Joel Brodsky; 139t Steve Pope/epa; 145t, 149b Robbie Jack; 167 Ryan Pyle; 172 Keren Su; 175bl Ming Ming/Reuters; 177tl Matthew Cavanaugh/epa; 177bl Alessia Pierdomenico/Reuters; 177br CSPA/NewSport; 178bl ELTA/Reuters; 179b Lester Lefkowitz; 180tl Jose Fuste Raga; 181t Liba Taylor; 183b Michele Falzone/JAI; 185r Jean Michel Foujols/zefa; 187br Murat Taner/zefa; 189cr Jon Feingersh/zefa; 191t Peter M. Wilson; 193t Yuriko Nakao/Reuters; 197t Everett Kennedy Brown/epa; 201t Ludovic Maisant; 201b Shanghai Sanya/Redlink; 205t Thomas Frey/dpa; 209r, 214-215t Gero Breloer/epa; 210tr Liu Dawei/Xinhua Press; 211 Jiao Weiping/Xinhua Press; 213 Fei Maohua/Xinhua Press; 224t Eric Lalmand/epa; 227t CJ Gunther/epa; 228l Chris Williams/Icon SMI; 229c Leo Mason; 229b STR/epa; 230t Jochen Luebke/epa; 231t Andrew Gompert/epa; 232-233 George Tiedemann/GT Images; 233t How Hwee Young/epa; 233b Schlegelmilch; 236 Christophe Karaba/epa; 237 Rhona Wise/epa; 238 Tom Fox/Dallas Morning News; 239 Pascal Lauener/Reuters; 242b Bartomiej Zborowski/PAP; 244t Fred Prouser/Reuters.

Fotolia: 5cl, 182 pressmaster; 5cr, 228r, 229t sebastiankiek; 16t Kwest; 16b NatUlrich; 22-23b Sean Gladwell; 24 moodboard; 24tr Andy Mac; 27b Earl Robbins; 28t wildman; 28c Suto Norbert; 28b Gildas Douessin; 29b imageteam; 30l sparky; 30c Sebastian Kaulitzki; 30r Gudellaphoto; 31r grivelphoto; 33 Monty Chandler; 34-35b Eric Gevaert; 36-37b Nici Heuke; 37r, 42tr, 42-43b, 44t, 48cl, 48cr Eric Isselée; 38t kristian sekulic; 38cl Makhnach; 38cr Papo; 42tl Perrush; 43tl Johanna Goodyear; 44b Cynthia Warner-Dobrowski; 45b Mirko Milutinovic; 46tl Patricia Elfreth; 47tr Jamie Wilson; 47br, 49b vnlit; 48t Alison Cornford-Matheson; 48c 'c'; 48b klikk; 50t Olga Lyubkina; 50cl momanuma; 50cr ann triling; 51t & cbr eyewave; 51ctl SergioPh; 51cbl Maciej Mamro; 51cbc arnowssr; 51cr Werg; 51-52b Kudryashka; 52t Alex; 52c zentilia; 58t Jose Manuel Gelpi; 58-59b (background) nra; 60tl Nikola Bilic; 60bl Tomislav Forgo; 60r angelo.gi; 61t, 150b Gino Santa Maria; 61b Hallgerd; 64 tl, second tl, ctl & second bl, 65ctr, cbr & br moonrun; 64bl KeepCoolBaby; 64cbl saschi79; 64-65 Antonio Nunes; 65tr chrisharvey; 66t Michael Drager; 66b, 155tl TimurD; 69b, 142b, 143b James Steidl; 70b ckalt; 70-71b Kasia Biel; 72bl, 189bcr Elena Elisseeva; 72br, 73tr, 75tr Victoria Martensson; 75tl Leo; 75tr Piter Pkruger; 76tl, 77tr sabri deniz kizil; 76tr Elnur; 77tl Cmon; 78bl Vladimir Mucibabic; 78br Pavlo Perets; 78-79t Jose Alves; 81tr objectsforall; 82t Anobis; 82b AlienCat; 83b bornholm; 85 iofoto; 90t Miqul; 90b broker; 92-93c RTimages; 94-95b iofoto; 103, 116-117 (insets) JChMedinger; 104l, 112r Andrzej Tokarski; 104tr RTimages; 104br janaka Dharmasena; 105b, 186tl ZTS; 106r Daniel Burch; 108t Volodymyr Kyrylyuk; 110-111 Renato Francia; 112-113 milosluz; 114l Palabra; 116tl, 117tl Michael Flippo; 116tr, 117tr Aleksey Bakaleev; 116b ZDM; 118t & b Igor Nikolayev; 118c clearviewstock; 118c (inset) ktsdesign; 119b Stephen Coburn; 124-125t foxygrl; 126-127t Julydfg; 130tl, 142tr DWP; 131t Yuri Arcurs; 134t waltart; 144t Laura Lévy; 144b sumnersgraphicsinc; 144-145b Sherri Camp; 145b Carolina K Smith MD; 148-149t Irochka; 152-153t Julian Addington-Barker; 152-153 Olga Mishyna; 154tr ville ahonen; 154br Dušan Zidar; 154-155 Vladimir Wrangel; 155bl Alexander Glagolev; 155bc marc hericher; 155br Victoria Short; 160-161t Tommroch; 162b Pavel Losevsky; 164t G.Light; 165b, 168t Michelle Robek; 168bl Freehand; 168br Ilja Mašík; 171 Franz Pfluegl; 176l Robert Ainsworth; 176r Vladyslav Danilin; 178 Nikos; 178tr Farouk Laboudi; 179tl Eray Haciosmanoglu; 179tr Anton Bryksin; 180tr Marko Plevnjak; 180b Artyshot; 184tl Denis Pepin; 184tr, 185tl & bl Harris Shiffman; 184bl Liv Friis-larsen; 186c Luminis; 186br davidjmorgan; 187l SWT; 187tr Matthew Bowden; 188tl Paul Binet; 188tr Fotolia VI; 188cl picamaniac; 188bl & bcr Maria.P.; 188bcl Markus Mohr; 188br Greg; 189tl broker; 189tr gunnar3000; 189bl & bc robynmac; 189br Graça Victoria; 190 Monika Adamczyk; 191b Okea; 192 Gabriel-Ciscardi; 196t Krom; 196cr awx; 196-197b Alvin Teo; 196-197b (background) Simon Pow; 202-203t mite; 204t enrique ayuso; 204c xiver; 204bl rimglow; 204bcl Jose Vazquez; 204bcr Yong Hian Lim; 204br Philophoto; 205bl Dmitry Rukhlenko; 205bcl & br steamroller; 205bc Olga Shelego; 205bcr, 245br Andres Rodriguez; 206-207 surpasspro; 209l, 220r Albo; 210 TFphotos; 210b Ramin Khojasteh; 212r Dariusz Kopestynski; 214-215b Accent ; 217 vivalapenler; 218 Peter Baxter; 218br Jean-Luc Cochonneau; 219t Nessquick; 219c Stacy Barnett; 220l Ana Vasileva; 222t Howard; 222c Christos Georghiou; 223t Sportlibrary; 224b sharply_done; 226l sumnersgraphicsinc; 226r Dusty Cline; 227b Nicholas Piccillo; 230-231b TMAX; 234 Michael Drager; 240cl & cr, 241t davorr; 240b kathy libby; 240-241 Torsten Wenzler; 244b picsfive; 245tl 2windspa; 247 Aramanda.

Getty Images: 4t, 46-47b Colin Keates/Dorling Kindersley; 43tr Tim Flach; 46-47t Frank Greenaway; 57t Theo Westenberger; 67 Bhutan Government DIT; 69t Sven Creutzmann/Mambo Photo; 70tl University Of Pennsylvania; 77b Scott Nelson; 78-79b VCL/Chris Ryan; 112l Mark Mainz; 114tr Manpreet Romana/AFP; 115t Khin Maung Win/AFP; 126tr Keystone; 127b, 137t Michael Ochs Archives; 134b Ethan Miller; 135b Serge Thomann/WireImage; 140r Maria R. Bastone/AFP; 148bl Gjon Mili/Time Life Pictures; 173t Tang Chhin Sothy/AFP; 173b Mitchell Kanashkevich; 174bl Robyn Beck/AFP; 174-175tc Philippe Huguen/AFP; 198 Melanie Stetson Freeman/The Christian Science Monitor; 218bl Craig Hacker; 219b Bryn Lennon; 221 Ron Hoskins/NBAE; 222bl Toshifumi Kitamura/AFP; 223b John Shearer/WireImage for BWR Public Relations; 225b Andreas Solaro/AFP; 230c Andrew Yates/AFP; 234 Elsa; 235 Ronald Martinez; 240tl Brian Bahr; 241b Agence Zoom; 242t Phillip Ellsworth/WireImage; 243 Prakash Mathema/AFP.

iStockphoto: 6-7b Oleg Prikhodko; 20t linearcurves; 22tl, 31l jtgray; 58-59b Jill Fromer; 65bl blackred; 78-79c iStockphoto.com; 86-87 Valerie Loiseleux; 87r Albert Campbell; 88b Evgeniy Ivanov; 89b Mike Bentley; 92t Lachlan Currie; 92-93b Hugo Lacasse; 106l & 107bl Jonathan Werve; 106-107 Yasinguneysu; 108-109 Stock photo; 114-115 Don Bayley; 126bl Julie de Leseleuc; 126br Lise Gagne; 154tl Stephen Shockley; 166 Sergei Ivlev; 183t Andres Peiro Palmer; 184br juicybits; 189bcl Malcolm Romaine; 195 Stephen Strathdee; 225t Björn Kindler.

The Kobal Collection: 4cr, 156, 163, 169 Dreamworks; 142tl, 158t Warner Bros.; 143t Universal/Playtone; 147, 159l Walt Disney; 150t Warner Bros/DC Comics; 151 Danjaq/EON/UA; 152bl, 154bl, 165t MGM; 153br New Line Cinema/Vinet, Pierre; 155tr Columbia; 157 20th Century Fox; 158b Lucasfilm/Paramount Pictures; 159r Warner Bros./Bailey, Alex; 160b Walt Disney Pictures/Walden Media/Bray, Phil; 161t Dreamworks/Warner Bros./Morton, Merrick; 161b 20th Century Fox/Pera, Diyah; 162t 20th Century Fox/Wetcher, Barry.

NASA: 3, 13tr Jet Propulsion Laboratory; 4cl, 14-15 NASA; 9, 11 Space Telescope Science Institute; 12 Jet Propulsion Laboratory-Caltech; 14t, 15t Johnson Space Center; 4cl, 14-15 NASA; 31c Image courtesy of MODIS Rapid Response Project at NASA/GSFC.

PA Photos: 218t Niall Carson/PA Archive/PA Photos.

Peter Bull Art Studio: 27br (artwork).

Photolibrary: 17 J-C & D. Pratt; 18 Steve Vidier; 19, 107br Photolibrary; 20-21 Michael Snell; 22-23t Chad Ehlers; 35r David Paynter; 39 David B Fleetham; 41l Mark Jones; 41r Mike Hill; 52b Vladimir Medvedev; 53l Roberto Rinaldi; 53r Walter Chorozewski; 97l JTB Photo; 100-101t Yann Guichaoua; 109t Angelo Tondini; 115b Daniel Thierry; 200 Ken Gillham.

Rex Features: 5tc, 96r Sipa Press.

Science Photo Library: 34t Roger Harris.

TopFoto: 14b RIA Novosti; 73cr ullsteinbild; 149c Clive Barda/ArenaPAL; 202b Topfoto.

Publisher's Acknowledgments
Cover design by Grade Design Consultants
www.gradedesign.com

Packager's Acknowledgments
Palazzo Editions would like to thank Richard Constable and James Hollywell for their design contributions.